ASP.NET Core 1.0
High Performance

Create fast, scalable, and high performance applications
with C#, ASP.NET Core 1.0, and MVC 6

James Singleton

BIRMINGHAM - MUMBAI

ASP.NET Core 1.0 High Performance

First published: June 2016

Production reference: 1170616

Published by Packt Publishing Ltd.
Livery Place
35 Livery Street
Birmingham
B3 2PB, UK.
ISBN 978-1-78588-189-3

www.packtpub.com

Credits

Author

James Singleton

Reviewer

Jason De Oliveira

Commissioning Editor

Edward Gordon

Acquisition Editor

Chaitanya Nair

Content Development Editor

Merint Thomas Mathew

Technical Editor

Kunal Chaudhari

Copy Editor

Priyanka Ravi

Project Coordinator

Suzanne Coutinho

Proofreader

Safis Editing

Indexer

Mariammal Chettiyar

Graphics

Kirk D'Penha

Production Coordinator

Melwyn Dsa

Foreword

"The most amazing achievement of the computer software industry is its continuing cancellation of the steady and staggering gains made by the computer hardware industry."

– Henry Petroski

We live in the age of distributed systems. Computers have shrunk from room-sized industrial mainframes to embedded devices that are smaller than a thumbnail. However, at the same time, the software applications that we build, maintain, and use every day have grown beyond measure. We create distributed applications that run on clusters of virtual machines scattered all over the world, and billions of people rely on these systems, such as e-mail, chat, social networks, productivity applications, and banking, every day. We're online 24 hours a day, seven days a week, and we're hooked on instant gratification. A generation ago, we'd happily wait until after the weekend for a cheque to clear, or allow 28 days for delivery. Today, we expect instant feedback, and why shouldn't we? The modern web is real-time, immediate, on-demand, built on packets of data flashing around the world at the speed of light, and when it isn't, we notice. We've all had that sinking feeling... you know, when you've just put your credit card number into a page to buy some expensive concert tickets, and the site takes *just a little* too long to respond. Performance and responsiveness are a fundamental part of delivering great user experience in the distributed age. However, for a working developer trying to ship your next feature on time, performance is often one of the most challenging requirements. How do you find the bottlenecks in your application performance? How do you measure the impact of those problems? How do you analyze them, design and test solutions and workarounds, and monitor them in production so that you can be confident that they won't happen again?

This book has the answers. Inside, James Singleton presents a pragmatic, in-depth, and balanced discussion of modern performance optimization techniques, and how to apply them to your .NET and web applications. Starting from the premise that we should treat performance as a core feature of our systems, James shows how you can use profiling tools such as Glimpse, MiniProfiler, Fiddler, and Wireshark to track down the bottlenecks and bugs that cause your performance problems. He addresses the scientific principles behind effective performance tuning, monitoring, instrumentation, and the importance of using accurate and repeatable measurements when you make changes to a running system to try and improve performance.

This book goes on to discuss almost every aspect of modern application development: database tuning, hardware optimisations, compression algorithms, network protocols, and object-relational mappers. For each topic, James describes the symptoms of common performance problems, identifies the underlying causes of those symptoms, and then describes the patterns and tools that you can use to measure and fix these underlying causes in your own applications. There's in-depth discussion of high-performance software patterns such as asynchronous methods and message queues, accompanied by real-world examples showing you how to implement these patterns in the latest versions of the .NET framework. Finally, James shows how you can not only load test your applications as a part of your release pipeline, but you can continuously monitor and measure your systems in production, letting you find and fix potential problems long before they start upsetting your end users.

When I worked with James here at Spotlight, he consistently demonstrated a remarkable breadth of knowledge, from ASP.NET to Arduinos, from Resharper to resistors. One day, he'd build reactive frontend interfaces in ASP.NET and JavaScript, the next he'd create build monitors by wiring microcontrollers into Star Wars toys, or working out how to connect the bathroom door lock to the intranet so that our bicycling employees could see from their desks when the office shower was free. After James moved on from Spotlight, I've been following his work with Cleanweb and Computing 4 Kids Education. He's one of those rare developers who really understands the social and environmental implications of technology—that whether it's delivering great user interactions or just saving electricity, improving your systems' performance is a great way to delight your users. With this book, James has distilled years of hands-on lessons and experience into a truly excellent all-round reference for .NET developers who want to understand how to build responsive and scalable applications. It's a great resource for new developers who want to develop a holistic understanding of application performance, but the coverage of cutting-edge techniques and patterns means it's also ideal for more experienced developers who want to make sure they're not getting left behind. Buy it, read it, share it with your team, and let's make the web a better place.

Dylan Beattie

Systems architect

REST evangelist, technical speaker

Co-organizer of the London .NET User Group

About the Author

James Singleton is a British software developer, engineer, and entrepreneur, who has been writing code since the days of the BBC Micro. His formal training is in electrical and electronic engineering, yet he has worked professionally in .NET software development for nearly a decade.

He is active in the London start-up community and helps organize Cleanweb London events for environmentally conscious technologists. He runs Cleanweb Jobs, which aims to help get developers, engineers, managers, and data scientists into roles that can help tackle climate change and other environmental problems. He also does public speaking, and he has presented talks at many local user groups, including at the Hacker News London meet up.

James holds a first class degree (with honors) in electronic engineering with computing, and he has designed and built his own basic microprocessor on an FPGA along with a custom instruction set to run on it. He is also a Science, Technology, Engineering, and Mathematics (STEM) ambassador, who encourages young people to study these fields.

James contributes to and is influenced by many open source projects, and regularly uses alternative technologies, such as Python, Ruby, and Linux. He is enthusiastic about the direction that Microsoft is taking .NET in and their embracing of open source practices.

He is particularly interested in hardware, environmental, and digital rights projects and is keen on security, compression, and algorithms. When not hacking on code, or writing for books and magazines, he enjoys walking, skiing, rock climbing, traveling, brewing, and craft beer.

James has gained varied skills from working in many diverse industries and roles, from high performance stock exchanges to video encoding systems. He has worked as a business analyst, consultant, tester, developer, and technical architect. He has a wide range of knowledge, gained from big corporates to startups, and a lot of places in between. He has first-hand experience of the best and worst ways of building high performance software.

You can read his blog at unop.uk.

Acknowledgments

I would like to thank all of my friends and family for being so supportive while I've been working on this book. I would especially like to thank my dad for getting me into technology at a young age, and Lou for her limitless enthusiasm and positivity. I would also like to thank Dylan for writing the foreword to this book.

Writing a book is much harder work than most people probably imagine, and I couldn't have done it without the constant encouragement. Many sacrifices needed to be made and I thank everyone for their understanding. Sorry for all the events that I've had to miss and to anyone who I've forgotten to thank here.

I would also like to acknowledge Radio Paradise for keeping me sane from the noise of the inconsiderate constructors next door. Finally, I apologize in advance to my British (or Aussie, Kiwi, Canadian, and so on) readers for any of the less-correctly spelled words used in this book.

About the Reviewer

Jason De Oliveira works as CTO for MEGA International (http://www.mega.com), a Software Company in Paris (France) that provides Modeling Tools for Enterprise Architecture, Enterprise Governance Risk, and Compliance Management. He is an experienced Manager and Senior Solutions Architect with high skills in Software Architecture and Enterprise Architecture.

He loves sharing his knowledge and experience via his blog, by speaking at conferences, writing technical books, writing articles in the technical press, giving software courses as MCT, and coaching co-workers in his company. He frequently collaborates with Microsoft, and you can find him quite often at the Microsoft Technology Center (MTC) in Paris.

Microsoft awarded him in 2011 with the Microsoft® Most Valuable Professional (MVP C#) Award for his numerous contributions to the Microsoft community. Microsoft seeks to recognize the best and brightest from technology communities around the world with the MVP Award. These exceptional and highly-respected individuals come from more than 90 countries, serve their local online and offline communities, and have an impact worldwide. Jason is very proud to be one of them.

Please feel free to contact him via his blog if you need any technical assistance or want to discuss technical subjects (http://www.jasondeoliveira.com).

Jason has worked on the following books:

- *.NET 4.5 Expert Programming Cookbook* (English)
- *WCF 4.5 Multi-tier Services Development with LINQ to Entities* (English)
- *.NET 4.5 Parallel Extensions Cookbook* (English)
- *WCF 4.5 Multi-layer Services Development with Entity Framework Third Edition* (English)
- *Visual Studio 2013: Concevoir, développer et gérer des projets Web, les gérer avec TFS 2013* (French)

I would like to thank my lovely wife, Orianne, and my beautiful daughters, Julia and Léonie, for supporting me in my work and for accepting long days and short nights during the week and sometimes even during the weekend. My life would not be the same without them!

www.PacktPub.com

eBooks, discount offers, and more

Did you know that Packt offers eBook versions of every book published, with PDF and ePub files available? You can upgrade to the eBook version at www.PacktPub.com and as a print book customer, you are entitled to a discount on the eBook copy. Get in touch with us at customercare@packtpub.com for more details.

At www.PacktPub.com, you can also read a collection of free technical articles, sign up for a range of free newsletters and receive exclusive discounts and offers on Packt books and eBooks.

https://www2.packtpub.com/books/subscription/packtlib

Do you need instant solutions to your IT questions? PacktLib is Packt's online digital book library. Here, you can search, access, and read Packt's entire library of books.

Why subscribe?

- Fully searchable across every book published by Packt
- Copy and paste, print, and bookmark content
- On demand and accessible via a web browser

Table of Contents

Preface

Microsoft has released a new open source and cross-platform web application framework, called ASP.NET Core. It runs on top of .NET Core, which is also open source, and is primarily used with the C# programming language. You are no longer tied to using Windows with ASP.NET, and you can now develop on a Mac and deploy to Linux. This new platform also offers much higher performance.

In today's world, a web application that only performs well on a developer's workstation and fails to deliver high-performance in production, is unacceptable. The way that web applications are now deployed at scale has changed, and development practices must adapt to take advantage of this. By reading this book, you'll learn about the modern way of making high-performance web applications, and how to do this with ASP.NET Core.

This book addresses web application performance-improvement techniques from both a general standpoint (HTTP, HTTPS, HTTP/2, TCP/IP, database access, compression, I/O, asset optimization, caching, message queuing, and other concerns) and from a C#, ASP.NET Core, and .NET Core perspective. This includes delving into the details of the latest frameworks and demonstrating software design patterns that improve performance.

We will highlight common performance pitfalls, which can often occur unnoticed on developer workstations, along with strategies to detect and resolve these issues early. By understanding and addressing challenges upfront, you can avoid nasty surprises when it comes to deployment time.

We will introduce performance improvements along with the trade-offs that they entail. We will strike a balance between premature optimization and inefficient code by taking a scientific and evidence-based approach, focusing on the big problems and avoiding changes that have little impact.

We assume that you understand the importance of performance for web applications, but we will recap why it's crucial. However, you may not have had any specific or actionable advice, or have much experience of performance problems occurring in the wild.

By reading this book, you'll understand what problems can occur when web applications are deployed at scale to distributed infrastructure, and know how to avoid or mitigate these issues. You will gain experience of how to write high-performance applications without having to learn about issues the hard way, possibly late at night.

You'll see what's new in ASP.NET Core, why it's been rebuilt from the ground up, and what this means for performance. You will understand the future of .NET Core and how you can now develop on and deploy to Windows, Mac OS X, and Linux. You'll appreciate the performance of new features in ASP.NET Core, including updates to the Razor view engine, and you will be aware of cross platform tools, such as Visual Studio Code.

What this book covers

Let's take a look at what topics we'll be covering throughout the book.

Chapter 1, *Why Performance Is a Feature*, discusses the basic premise of this book and shows you why you need to care about the performance of your software. Responsive applications are vital, and it's not simply enough to have functionality work, it also needs to be quick.

Think of the last time you heard someone complaining about an app or website, and it's likely they were unhappy with the performance. Poor performance doesn't only make users unhappy, it also affects your bottom-line. There's good data to suggest that fast performance increases engagement and improves conversion rates, which is why it's rewarded by search engines.

Chapter 2, *Measuring Performance Bottlenecks*, tells you that the only way you can solve performance problems is to carefully measure your application. Without knowing where a problem lies, your chance of solving it is extremely slim, and you won't even know whether you've improved matters or made things worse.

We will highlight a few ways of manually monitoring performance and some helpful tools that you can use to measure statistics. You'll see how to gain insights into the database, application, HTTP, and network levels of your software so that you know what is going on internally. We'll also show you how to build your own basic timing code and cover the importance of taking a scientific approach to the results.

Chapter 3, *Fixing Common Performance Problems*, looks at some of the most frequent performance mistakes. We'll show you how to fix simple issues across a range of different application areas, for example, how to optimize media with image resizing or encoding, Select N+1 problems, and asynchronous background operations.

We will also talk a little about using hardware to improve performance once you know where the bottlenecks lie. This approach buys you some time and allows you to fix things properly at a reasonable pace.

Chapter 4, *Addressing Network Performance*, digs into the networking layer that underpins all web applications. We'll show you how remote resources can slow down your app and demonstrate what you can do about measuring and addressing these problems.

We will look at internet protocols, including TCP/IP, HTTP, HTTP/2, and WebSockets, along with a primer on encryption and how all of these can alter performance. We'll cover compression of textual and image-based assets, including some exotic image formats. Finally, we will introduce caching at the browser, server, proxy, and Content Delivery Network (CDN) levels, showing you some of the basics.

Chapter 5, *Optimizing I/O Performance*, focuses on input/output and how this can negatively affect performance. We will look at disks, databases, and remote APIs, many of which use the network, particularly if virtualized. We'll cover batching your requests and optimizing database usage with aggregates or sampling, aiming to reduce the data and time required.

Due to networking's ubiquity in cloud environments, we'll spend considerable time on network diagnostics, including pinging, route tracing, and looking up records in the domain name system. You'll learn how latency can be driven by physical distance, or geography, and how this can cause problems for your application. We'll also demonstrate how to build your own networking information gathering tools using .NET.

Chapter 6, *Understanding Code Execution and Asynchronous Operations*, jumps into the intricacies of C# code and looks at how its execution can alter performance. We'll look at the various open source projects that make up ASP.NET Core and .NET Core, including Kestrel—a high-performance web server.

We will examine the importance of choosing the correct data structures and look at various examples of different options, such as lists and dictionaries. We'll also look at hashing, serialization, and perform some simple benchmarking.

You will learn some techniques that can speed up your processing by parallelizing it, such as Single Instruction Multiple Data (SIMD) and parallel extensions programming with the Task Parallel Library (TPL) and Parallel LINQ (PLINQ). You'll also see some practices that are best avoided, due to their performance penalties, such as reflection and regular expressions.

Chapter 7, *Learning Caching and Message Queuing*, initially looks at caching, which is widely regarded as difficult. You'll see how caching works from a HTTP perspective in browsers, web servers, proxies, and CDNs. You will learn about cache busting (or breaking) to force your changes and using the new JavaScript service workers in modern browsers to gain finer control over caching.

Additionally, we'll examine caching at the application and database levels in your infrastructure. We will see the benefits of in-memory caches, such as Redis, and how these can reduce the load on your database, lower latency, and increase the performance of your application.

We will investigate message queuing as a way to build a distributed and reliable system. We'll use analogies to explain how asynchronous message passing systems work and show you some common styles of message queuing, including unicast and pub/sub.

We will also show you how message queuing can be useful to an internal caching layer by broadcasting cache invalidation data. You'll learn about message brokers, such as RabbitMQ, and various libraries to interact with them from .NET.

Chapter 8, *The Downsides of Performance-Enhancing Tools*, concentrates on the negatives of the techniques that we will have covered because nothing comes for free. We'll discuss the virtues of various methods to reduce complexity, use frameworks, and design distributed architecture. We will also cover project culture and see how high-performance is not simply about code but about people too.

We'll look into possible solutions to tackle the problem of distributed debugging and see some available technologies to centrally manage application logging. We'll have a brief introduction to statistics so that you can make sense of your performance metrics, and we will touch upon managing caches.

Chapter 9, *Monitoring Performance Regressions*, again takes a look at at measuring performance, but in this case, from an automation and Continuous Integration (CI) perspective. We'll reiterate the importance of monitoring and show how you can build this into your development workflow to make it routine and almost transparent. You will see how it is possible to automate almost any type of testing, from simple unit testing to integration testing, and even complex browser User Interface (UI) testing.

We'll show you how you can make your tests more realistic and useful using techniques, such as blue-green deployment and feature switching. You will discover how to perform A/B testing of two versions of a webpage with some very basic feature switching and a few options for fun hardware to keep people engaged in test results. We'll also cover DevOps practices and cloud hosting, both of which make CI easier to implement and complement it nicely.

Chapter 10, *The Way Ahead*, briefly sums up the lessons of the book and then has a look at some advanced topics that you may like to read more about. We will also try to predict the future for the .NET Core platforms and give you some ideas to take further.

What you need for this book

You will need a development environment to follow the code examples in this book, either Visual Studio Community 2015 or Visual Studio Code if you're not on Windows. You can also use your text editor of choice and the `dotnet` command line tool. If you use Visual Studio, then you should also install the .NET Core SDK and tooling and the latest NuGet extension.

For some of the chapters, you will also need SQL Server 2014 Express. You can use 2016 too, particularly if you are on Linux. However, you can also use Azure and run against a cloud database.

There are other tools that we will cover, but we will introduce these as they are used. The detailed software/hardware list is uploaded along with the code files.

Who this book is for

This book is mainly aimed at ASP.NET and C# developers, but developers used to other open source platforms may also be interested in .NET Core. You should have experience with the MVC framework for web-application development and be looking to deploy applications that will perform well on live-production environments. These can be virtual machines or hosted by a cloud-service provider, such as AWS or Azure.

Conventions

In this book, you will find a number of text styles that distinguish between different kinds of information. Here are some examples of these styles and an explanation of their meaning.

Code words in text, database table names, folder names, filenames, file extensions, pathnames, dummy URLs, user input, and Twitter handles are shown as follows: "The `fetch` function is the modern version of an `XMLHttpRequest`."

A block of code is set as follows:

```
var client = new SmtpClient();
HostingEnvironment.QueueBackgroundWorkItem(ct =>
    client.SendMailAsync(message));
```

Any command-line input or output is written as follows:

```
tracert ec2.ap-southeast-2.amazonaws.com
```

New terms and **important words** are shown in bold. Words that you see on the screen, for example, in menus or dialog boxes, appear in the text like this: "If you select **Cache Storage**, you will see the contents of the cache."

Warnings or important notes appear in a box like this.

Tips and tricks appear like this.

Reader feedback

Feedback from our readers is always welcome. Let us know what you think about this book-what you liked or disliked. Reader feedback is important for us as it helps us develop titles that you will really get the most out of. To send us general feedback, simply e-mail feedback@packtpub.com, and mention the book's title in the subject of your message. If there is a topic that you have expertise in and you are interested in either writing or contributing to a book, see our author guide at www.packtpub.com/authors.

Customer support

Now that you are the proud owner of a Packt book, we have a number of things to help you to get the most from your purchase.

Downloading the example code

You can download the example code files for this book from your account at http://www.packtpub.com. If you purchased this book elsewhere, you can visit http://www.packtpub.com/support and register to have the files e-mailed directly to you.

You can download the code files by following these steps:

1. Log in or register to our website using your e-mail address and password.
2. Hover the mouse pointer on the **SUPPORT** tab at the top.
3. Click on **Code Downloads & Errata**.

4. Enter the name of the book in the **Search** box.
5. Select the book for which you're looking to download the code files.
6. Choose from the drop-down menu where you purchased this book from.
7. Click on **Code Download**.

You can also download the code files by clicking on the **Code Files** button on the book's webpage at the Packt Publishing website. This page can be accessed by entering the book's name in the **Search** box. Please note that you need to be logged in to your Packt account.

Once the file is downloaded, please make sure that you unzip or extract the folder using the latest version of:

- WinRAR / 7-Zip for Windows
- Zipeg / iZip / UnRarX for Mac
- 7-Zip / PeaZip for Linux

The code bundle for the book is also hosted on GitHub at `https://github.com/PacktPublishing/ASP.NET-Core-1.0-High-Performance` We also have other code bundles from our rich catalog of books and videos available at `https://github.com/PacktPublishing/`. Check them out!

Errata

Although we have taken every care to ensure the accuracy of our content, mistakes do happen. If you find a mistake in one of our books-maybe a mistake in the text or the code-we would be grateful if you could report this to us. By doing so, you can save other readers from frustration and help us improve subsequent versions of this book. If you find any errata, please report them by visiting `http://www.packtpub.com/submit-errata`, selecting your book, clicking on the **Errata Submission Form** link, and entering the details of your errata. Once your errata are verified, your submission will be accepted and the errata will be uploaded to our website or added to any list of existing errata under the Errata section of that title.

To view the previously submitted errata, go to `https://www.packtpub.com/books/content/support` and enter the name of the book in the search field. The required information will appear under the **Errata** section.

Piracy

Piracy of copyrighted material on the Internet is an ongoing problem across all media. At Packt, we take the protection of our copyright and licenses very seriously. If you come across any illegal copies of our works in any form on the Internet, please provide us with the location address or website name immediately so that we can pursue a remedy.

Please contact us at `copyright@packtpub.com` with a link to the suspected pirated material.

We appreciate your help in protecting our authors and our ability to bring you valuable content.

Questions

If you have a problem with any aspect of this book, you can contact us at `questions@packtpub.com`, and we will do our best to address the problem.

1
Why Performance Is a Feature

This is an exciting time to be a **C#** developer. Microsoft is in the middle of one of the biggest changes in its history, and it is embracing open source software. The ASP.NET and .NET frameworks are being rebuilt from the ground up to be componentized, cross-platform, and open source.

ASP.NET Core 1.0 and **.NET Core 1.0** (previously called **ASP.NET 5** and **.NET Core 5**) embrace many ideas from popular open source projects, such as **Go**'s ability to produce a statically-linked, standalone binary. You can now compile a single native executable that is free of any external dependencies and run it on a system without **.NET** installed.

The ASP.NET **Model View Controller** (**MVC**) web application framework, which is now part of ASP.NET Core 1.0, borrows heavily from **Ruby on Rails** and Microsoft is keen in promoting tools, such as **Node.js**, **Grunt**, **gulp**, and **Yeoman**. There is also **TypeScript**, which is a statically-typed version of JavaScript that was developed at Microsoft.

By reading this book, you will learn how to write high-performance software using these new .NET Core technologies. You'll be able to make your web applications responsive to input and scalable to demand.

We'll focus on the latest Core versions of .NET. Yet, many of these techniques also apply to previous versions, and they will be useful for web application development in general (in any language or framework).

Understanding how all of these new frameworks and libraries fit together can be a bit confusing. We'll present the various available options while still using the newest technology, guiding you down the path to high-speed success, and avoiding performance pitfalls.

After finishing this book, you will understand what problems can occur when web applications are deployed at scale (to distributed infrastructure) and know how to avoid or mitigate these issues. You will gain the experience of how to write high-performance applications without learning about issues the hard way.

In this chapter, we will cover the following topics.

- Performance as a feature
- The common classes of performance issues
- Basic hardware knowledge
- Microsoft tools and alternatives
- New .NET naming and compatibility

Performance as a feature

You may have previously heard about the practice of treating performance as a first-class feature. Traditionally, performance (along with things such as security, availability and uptime) was only considered a **Non-Functional Requirement** (**NFR**) and usually had some arbitrary made-up metrics that needed to be fulfilled. You may have heard the term "performant" before. This is the quality of performing well and, often, is captured in requirements without quantification, providing very little value. It is better to avoid this sort of corporate jargon when corresponding with clients or users.

Using the outdated waterfall method of development, these NFRs were inevitably left until the end, and dropped from an over-budget and late project in order to get the functional requirements completed. This resulted in a substandard product that was unreliable, slow, and often insecure (as reliability and security are also often neglected NFRs). Think about how many times you're frustrated at software that lags behind in responding to your input. Perhaps, you used a ticket-vending machine or a self-service checkout that is unresponsive to the point of being unusable.

There is a better way. By treating performance as a feature and considering it at every stage of your **agile** development process, you can get users and customers to love your product. When software responds quicker than a user can perceive, it is a delight to use, and this doesn't slow them down. When there is noticeable lag, then users need to adjust their behavior to wait for the machine instead of working at their own pace.

Computers have incredible amounts of processing power today, and they now possess many more resources than they did even just a few years ago. So, why do we still have software that is noticeably slow at responding, when computers are so fast and can calculate much quicker than people can? The answer to this is poorly written software that does not consider performance. Why does this happen? The reason is that often the signs of poor performance are not visible in development, and they only appear when deployed. However, if you know what to look for, then you can avoid these problems before releasing your software to the production environment.

This book will show you how to write software that is a joy to use and never keeps the user waiting or uninformed. You will learn how to make products that users will love instead of products that frustrate them all the time.

Common classes of performance problems

Let's take a look at some common areas of performance problems and see whether they matter or not. We will also learn why we often miss these issues during development.

Language considerations

People often focus on the speed of the programming language that is used. However, this often misses the point. This is a very simplistic view that glosses over the nuances of technology choices. It is easy to write slow software in any language.

With the huge amounts of processing speed that is available today, relatively "slow" interpreted languages can often be fast enough, and the increase in development speed is worth it. It is important to understand the arguments and the trade-offs involved even if by reading this book you have already decided to use C# and .NET.

The way to write the fastest software is to get down to the metal and write in assembler (or even machine code). This is extremely time consuming, requires expert knowledge, and ties you to a particular processor architecture and instruction set; therefore, we rarely do this these days. If this happens, then it's only done for very niche applications (such as virtual reality games, scientific data crunching, and sometimes embedded devices) and usually only for a tiny part of the software.

The next level of abstraction up is writing in a language, such as Go, C, or C++, and compiling the code to run on the machine. This is still popular for games and other performance-sensitive applications, but you often have to manage your own memory (which can cause memory leaks or security issues, such as buffer overflows).

A level above is software that compiles to an intermediate language or byte code and runs on a virtual machine. Examples of this are **Java, Scala, Clojure**, and, of course, C#. Memory management is normally taken care of, and there is usually a **Garbage Collector** (**GC**) to tidy up unused references (Go also has a GC). These applications can run on multiple platforms, and they are safer. However, you can still get near to native performance in terms of execution speed.

Above these are interpreted languages, such as **Ruby**, **Python**, and JavaScript. These languages are not usually compiled, and they are run line-by-line by an interpreter. They usually run slower than a compiled language, but this is often not a problem. A more serious concern is catching bugs when using dynamic typing. You won't be able to see an error until you encounter it, whereas many errors can be caught at compile time when using statically-typed languages.

It is best to avoid generic advice. You may hear an argument against using Ruby on Rails, citing the example of Twitter having to migrate to Java for performance reasons. This may well not be a problem for your application, and indeed having the popularity of Twitter would be a nice problem to have. A bigger concern when running Rails may be the large memory footprint, making it expensive to run on cloud instances.

This section is only to give you a taste, and the main lesson is that normally, language doesn't matter. It is not usually the language that makes a program slow, it's poor design choices. C# offers a nice balance between speed and flexibility that makes it suitable for a wide range of applications, especially server-side web applications.

Types of performance problems

There are many types of performance problems, and most of them are independent of the programming language that is used. A lot of these result from how the code runs on the computer, and we will cover the impact of this later on in the chapter.

We will briefly introduce common performance problems here and will cover them in more detail in later chapters of this book. Issues that you may encounter will usually fall into a few simple categories, including the following:

- Latency:
    - Memory latency
    - Network latency
    - Disk and I/O latency
    - Chattiness / handshakes

- Bandwidth:
    - Excessive payloads
    - Unoptimized data
    - Compression
- Computation:
    - Working on too much data
    - Calculating unnecessary results
    - Brute forcing algorithms
- Doing work in the wrong place:
    - Synchronous operations that could be done offline
    - Caching and coping with stale data

When writing software for a platform, you are usually constrained by two resources. These are the computation processing speed and accessing remote (to the processor) resources.

Processing speed is rarely a limiting factor these days, and this could be traded for other resources, for example, compressing some data to reduce the network transfer time.

Accessing remote resources, such as main memory, disk, and the network will have various time costs. It is important to understand that speed is not a single value, and it has multiple parameters. The most important of these are bandwidth and, crucially, **latency**.

Latency is the lag in time before the operation starts, whereas bandwidth is the rate at which data is transferred once the operation starts. Posting a hard drive has a very high bandwidth, but it also has very high latency. This would make it very slow to send lots of text files back and forth, but perhaps, this is a good choice to send a large batch of 3D videos (depending on the Weissman score). A mobile phone data connection may be better for the text files.

Although this is a contrived example, the same concerns are applicable to every layer of the computing stack often with similar orders of magnitude in time difference. The problem is that the differences are too quick to perceive, and we need to use tools and science to see them.

The secret to solving performance problems is in gaining a deeper understanding of the technology and knowing what happens at the lower levels. You should appreciate what the framework is doing with your instructions at the network level. It's also important to have a basic grasp of how these commands run on the underlying hardware, and how they are affected by the infrastructure that they are deployed to.

When performance matters

Performance is not always important in every situation. Learning when performance does and doesn't matter is an important skill to acquire. A general rule of thumb is that if the user has to wait for something to happen, then it should perform well. If this is something that can be performed asynchronously, then the constraints are not as strict, unless an operation is so slow that it takes longer than the time window for it; for example, an overnight batch job on an old financial services mainframe.

A good example from a web application standpoint is rendering user view versus sending e-mail. It is a common, yet naïve, practice to accept a form submission and send an e-mail (or worse, many e-mails) before returning the result. Yet, unlike a database update, an e-mail is not something that happens almost instantly. There are many stages over which we have no control that will delay an e-mail in reaching a user. Therefore, there is no need to send an e-mail before returning the result of the form. You can do this offline and asynchronously after the result of the form submission is returned.

The important thing to remember here is that it is the perception of performance that matters and not absolute performance. It can be better to not do some work (or at least defer it) rather than speed it up.

This may be counterintuitive, especially considering how individual computer operations can be too quick to perceive. However, the multiplying factor is scale. One operation may be relatively quick, but millions of them may accumulate to a visible delay. Optimizing these will have a corresponding effect due to the magnification. Improving code that runs in a tight loop or for every user is better than fixing a routine that runs only once a day.

Slower is sometimes better

In some situations, processes are designed to be slow, and this is essential to their operation and security. A good example of this, which may be hit in profiling, is **password hashing** or **key stretching**. A secure password hashing function should be slow so that the password, which (despite being bad practice) may have been reused on other services, is not easily recovered.

We should not use generic hashing functions, such as **MD5**, **SHA1**, and **SHA256**, to hash passwords because they are too quick. Some better algorithms that are designed for this task are **PBKDF2** and **bcrypt**, or even **Argon2** for new projects. Always remember to use a unique salt per password too. We won't go into any more details here, but you can clearly see that speeding up password hashing would be bad, and it's important to identify where to apply optimizations.

Why issues are missed

One of the main reasons that performance issues are not noticed in development is that some problems are not perceivable on a development system. Issues may not occur until latency increases. This may be because a large amount of data was loaded into the system and retrieving a specific record takes longer. This may also be because each piece of the system is deployed to a separate server, increasing the network latency. When the number of users accessing a resource increases, then the latency will also increase.

For example, we can quickly insert a row into an empty database or retrieve a record from a small table, especially when the database is running on the same physical machine as the web server. When a web server is on one virtual machine and the big database server is on another, then the time taken for this operation can increase dramatically.

This will not be a problem for one single database operation, which appears just as quick to a user in both cases. However, if the software is poorly written and performs hundreds or even thousands of database operations per request, then this quickly becomes slow.

Scale this up to all the users that a web server deals with (and all of the web servers) and this can be a real problem. A developer may not notice that this problem exists if they're not looking for it, as the software performs well on their workstation. Tools can help in identifying these problems before the software is released.

Measuring

The most important takeaway from this book is the importance of measuring. You need to measure problems or you can't fix them. You won't even know when you have fixed them. Measurement is the key to fixing performance issues before they become noticeable. Slow operations can be identified early on, and then they can be fixed.

However, not all operations need optimizing. It's important to keep a sense of perspective, but you should understand where the chokepoints are and how they will behave when magnified by scale. We'll cover measuring and profiling in the next chapter.

The benefits of planning ahead

By considering performance from the very beginning, it is cheaper and quicker to fix issues. This is true for most problems in software development. The earlier you catch a bug, the better. The worst time to find a bug is once it is deployed and then being reported by your users.

Performance bugs are a little different when compared to functional bugs because often, they only reveal themselves at scale, and you won't notice them before a live deployment unless you go looking for them. You can write integration and load tests to check performance, which we will cover later in this book.

Understanding hardware

Remember that there is a computer in computer science. It is important to understand what your code runs on and the effects that this has, this isn't magic.

Storage access speeds

Computers are so fast that it can be difficult to understand which operation is a quick operation and which is a slow one. Everything appears instant. In fact, anything that happens in less than a few hundred milliseconds is imperceptible to humans. However, certain things are much faster than others are, and you only get performance issues at scale when millions of operations are performed in parallel.

There are various different resources that can be accessed by an application, and a selection of these are listed, as follows:

- CPU caches and registers:
    - L1 cache
    - L2 cache
    - L3 cache
- RAM
- Permanent storage:
    - Local **Solid State Drive (SSD)**
    - Local **Hard Disk Drive (HDD)**
- Network resources:
    - **Local Area Network (LAN)**
    - Regional networking
    - Global internetworking

Virtual Machines (**VM**s) and cloud infrastructure services could add more complications. The local disk that is mounted on a machine may in fact be a shared network disk and respond much slower than a real physical disk that is attached to the same machine. You may also have to contend with other users for resources.

In order to appreciate the differences in speed between the various forms of storage, consider the following graph. This shows the time taken to retrieve a small amount of data from a selection of storage mediums:

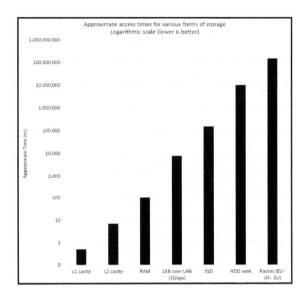

This graph has a logarithmic scale, which means that the differences are very large. The top of the graph represents one second or one billion nanoseconds. Sending a packet across the Atlantic Ocean and back takes roughly 150 milliseconds (ms) or 150 million nanoseconds (ns), and this is mainly limited by the speed of light. This is still far quicker than you can think about, and it will appear instantaneous. Indeed, it can often take longer to push a pixel to a screen than to get a packet to another continent.

The next largest bar is the time that it takes a physical HDD to move the read head into position to start reading data (10 ms). Mechanical devices are slow.

The next bar down is how long it takes to randomly read a small block of data from a local SSD, which is about 150 microseconds. These are based on Flash memory technology, and they are usually connected in the same way as a HDD.

The next value is the time taken to send a small datagram of 1 KB (1 kilobyte or 8 kilobits) over a gigabit LAN, which is just under 10 microseconds. This is typically how servers are connected in a data center. Note how the network itself is pretty quick. The thing that really matters is what you are connecting to at the other end. A network lookup to a value in memory on another machine can be much quicker than accessing a local drive (as this is a log graph, you can't just stack the bars).

This brings us on to main memory or RAM. This is fast (about 100 ns for a lookup), and this is where most of your program will run. However, this is not directly connected to the CPU, and it is slower than the on die caches. RAM can be large, often large enough to hold all of your working dataset. However, it is not as big as disks can be, and it is not permanent. It disappears when the power is lost.

The CPU itself will contain small caches for data that is currently being worked on, which can respond in less than 10 ns. Modern CPUs may have up to three or even four caches of increasing size and latency. The fastest (less than 1 ns to respond) is the Level 1 (L1) cache, but this is also usually the smallest. If you can fit your working data into these few MB or KB in caches, then you can process it very quickly.

Scaling approach changes

For many years, the speed and processing capacity of computers increased at an exponential rate. This was known as Moore's Law, named after Gordon Moore of Intel. Sadly, this era is no Moore (sorry). Single-core processor speeds have flattened out, and these days increases in processing ability come from scaling out to multiple cores, multiple CPUs, and multiple machines (both virtual and physical). Multithreaded programming is no longer exotic, it is essential. Otherwise, you cannot hope to go beyond the capacity of a single core. Modern CPUs typically have at least four cores (even for mobiles). Add in a technology such as **hyper-threading**, and you have at least eight logical CPUs to play with. Naïve programming will not be able to fully utilize these.

Traditionally, performance (and redundancy) was provided by improving the hardware. Everything ran on a single server or mainframe, and the solution was to use faster hardware and duplicate all components for reliability. This is known as vertical scaling, and it has reached the end of its life. It is very expensive to scale this way and impossible beyond a certain size. The future is in distributed-horizontal scaling using commodity hardware and cloud computing resources. This requires that we write software in a different manner than we did previously. Traditional software can't take advantage of this scaling like it can easily use the extra capabilities and speed of an upgraded computer processor.

There are many trade-offs that have to be made when considering performance, and it can sometimes feel like more of a black art than a science. However, taking a scientific approach and measuring results is essential. You will often have to balance memory usage against processing power, bandwidth against storage, and latency against throughput.

An example is deciding whether you should compress data on the server (including what algorithms and settings to use) or send it raw over the wire. This will depend on many factors, including the capacity of the network and the devices at both ends.

Tools and costs

Licensing of Microsoft products has historically been a minefield of complexity. You can even sit for an official exam on it and get a qualification. Microsoft's recent move toward open source practices is very encouraging, as the biggest benefit of open source is not the free monetary cost but that you don't have to think about the licensing costs. You can also fix issues, and with a permissive license (such as **MIT**), you don't have to worry about much. The time costs and cognitive load of working out licensing implications now and in the future can dwarf the financial sums involved (especially for a small company or startup).

Tools

Despite the new .NET framework being open source, many of the tools are not. Some editions of Visual Studio and SQL Server can be very expensive. With the new licensing practice of subscriptions, you will lose access if you stop paying, and you are required to sign in to develop. Previously, you could keep using existing versions licensed from a **Microsoft Developer Network** (**MSDN**) or BizSpark subscription after it expired and you didn't need to sign in.

With this in mind, we will try to stick to the free (community) editions of Visual Studio and the Express version of SQL Server unless there is a feature that is essential to the lesson, which we will highlight when it occurs. We will also use as many free and open source libraries, frameworks, and tools as possible.

There are many alternative options for lots of the tools and software that augments the ASP.NET ecosystem, and you don't just need to use the default Microsoft products. This is known as the ALT.NET (alternative .NET) movement, which embraces practices from the rest of the open source world.

Looking at some alternative tools

For version control, git is a very popular alternative to **Team Foundation Server** (TFS). This is integrated into many tools (including Visual Studio) and services, such as GitHub or GitLab. Mercurial (hg) is also an option. However, git has gained the most developer mindshare. Visual Studio Online offers both git and TFS integration.

PostgreSQL is a fantastic open source relational database, and it works with many **Object Relational Mappers** (**O/RMs**), including **Entity Framework** (**EF**) and NHibernate. Dapper is a great, and high-performance, alternative to EF and other bloated O/RMs. There are plenty of NoSQL options that are available too; for example, Redis and MongoDB.

Other code editors and **Integrated Development Environments** (IDEs) are available, such as Visual Studio Code by Microsoft, which also works on Apple Mac OS X. ASP.NET Core 1.0 (previously ASP.NET 5) runs on Linux (on Mono and CoreCLR). Therefore, you don't need Windows (although Nano Server may be worth investigating).

RabbitMQ is a brilliant open source message queuing server that is written in Erlang (which WhatsApp also uses). This is far better than **Microsoft Message Queuing** (**MSMQ**), which comes with Windows. Hosted services are readily available, for example, CloudAMQP.

The author has been a long time Mac user (since the PowerPC days), and he has run Linux servers since well before this. It's positive to see OS X become popular and to observe the rise of Linux on Android smartphones and cheap computers, such as the Raspberry Pi. You can run Windows 10 on a Raspberry Pi 2 and 3, but this is not a full operating system and only meant to run **Internet of Things** (**IoT**) devices. Having used Windows professionally for a long time, developing and deploying with Mac and Linux, and seeing what performance effects this brings is an interesting opportunity.

Although not open source (or always free), it is worth mentioning JetBrains products. TeamCity is a very good build and **Continuous Integration** (**CI**) server that has a free tier. ReSharper is an awesome plugin for Visual Studio, which will make you a better coder. They're also working on a C# IDE called Project Rider that promises to be good.

There is a product called Octopus Deploy, which is extremely useful for the deployment of .NET applications, and it has a free tier. Regarding cloud services, **Amazon Web Services** (**AWS**) is an obvious alternative to Azure, even if the AWS Windows support leaves something to be desired. There are many other hosts available, and dedicated servers can often be cheaper for a steady load if you don't need the dynamic scaling of the cloud.

Much of this is beyond the scope of this book, but you would be wise to investigate some of these tools. The point is that there is always a choice about how to build a system from the huge range of components available, especially with the new version of ASP.NET.

The new .NET

The new ASP.NET and the .NET Framework that it relies upon were rewritten to be open source and cross-platform. This work was called ASP.NET 5 while in development, but this has since been renamed to ASP.NET Core 1.0 to reflect that it's a new product with a stripped down set of features. Similarly, .NET Core 5 is now .NET Core 1.0, and Entity Framework 7 is now Entity Framework Core 1.0.

The web application framework that was called ASP.NET MVC has been merged into ASP.NET Core, although it's a package that can be added like any other dependency. The latest version of MVC is 6 and, along with **Web API 2**, this has been combined into a single product, called ASP.NET Core. MVC and Web API aren't normally referred to directly any more as they are simply NuGet packages that are used by ASP.NET Core. Not all features are available in the new Core frameworks yet, and the focus is on server-side web applications to start with.

All these different names can be perplexing, but naming things is hard. A variation of Phil Karlton's famous quote goes like this:

> *"There are only two hard things in Computer Science: cache invalidation, naming things, and off-by-one errors."*

We've looked at naming here, and we'll get to caching later on in this book.

It can be a little confusing understanding how all of these versions fit together. This is best explained with a diagram like the following, which shows how the layers interact:

ASP.NET Core 1.0 can run against the existing .NET Framework 4.6 or the new .NET Core 1.0 framework. Similarly, .NET Core can run on Windows, Mac OS X, and Linux, but the old .NET only runs on Windows.

There is also the Mono framework, which has been omitted for clarity. This was a previous project that allowed .NET to run on multiple platforms. Mono was recently acquired by Microsoft, and it was open sourced (along with other Xamarin products). Therefore, you should be able to run ASP.NET Core using Mono on any supported operating system.

.NET Core focuses on web-application development and server-side frameworks. It is not as feature filled as the existing .NET Framework. If you write native-graphical desktop applications, perhaps using **Windows Presentation Foundation** (**WPF**), then you should stick with .NET 4.6.

As this book is mainly about web-application development, we will use the latest Core versions of all software. We will investigate the performance implications of various operating systems and architectures. This is particularly important if your deployment target is a computer, such as the Raspberry Pi, which uses a processor with an ARM architecture. It also has limited memory, which is important to consider when using a managed runtime that includes garbage collection, such as .NET.

Summary

Let's sum up what we covered in this introductory chapter and what we will cover in the next chapter. We introduced the concept of treating performance as a feature, and we covered why this is important. We also briefly touched on some common performance problems and why we often miss them in the software development process. We'll cover these in more detail later on in this book.

We showed the performance differences between various types of storage hardware. We highlighted the importance of knowing what your code runs on and, crucially, what it will run on when your users see it. We talked about how the process of scaling systems has changed from what it used to be, how scaling is now performed horizontally instead of vertically, and how you can take advantage of this in the architecting of your code and systems.

We showed you the tools that you can use and the licensing implications of some of them. We also explained the new world of .NET and how these latest frameworks fit in with the stable ones. We touched upon why measurement is vitally important. In the next chapter, we'll expand on this and show you how to measure your software to see whether it's slow.

2
Measuring Performance Bottlenecks

Measurement is the most crucial aspect of building high performance systems. You can't change what you can't measure, because you won't know what effect your change has had, if any. Without measuring your application you won't know if it's performing well.

If you only go by when your software feels slow then you have left it too late. You are reactively fixing a problem rather than proactively avoiding one. You must measure to achieve good performance even though it's the feel that matters to a user.

Some books leave measurement, analysis, and profiling until the end. Yet this is the first thing that should be considered. It's easy to fix the wrong problem and optimize areas that are not having performance difficulties.

In this chapter we will cover the following topics.

- **Structured Query Language** (**SQL**) database profiling
    - SQL Server Profiler
    - MiniProfiler
- Web application profiling
    - Glimpse
    - **Integrated Development Environment** (**IDE**) profilers
- HTTP monitoring
    - Browser developer tools
    - Fiddler proxy

- Network monitoring
    - Microsoft message analyzer
    - Wireshark
- Scientific method and repeatability

This chapter will show you how to measure if there are performance issues and where they are occurring. We will describe the tools that can give you this information and demonstrate how to use them effectively and correctly. We'll also show you how to repeat your experiments consistently so that you can tell if you have fixed a problem once you've identified it.

We will cover measurement again towards the end of the book, but there we'll focus on continuous automated monitoring to avoid regressions. This chapter will focus more on manual testing to identify potential performance problems during development and debugging.

Tools

Good debugging tools are essential in discovering where problems lie. You can write your own crude timing code and we will show you how. However, purpose built tools are much nicer to work with.

Many of the tools in this chapter help examine areas external to your code. We will cover profiling of code too, but it's hard to identify problems this way unless the work is purely computational. Slowdowns often happen because of actions your app initiates outside of its immediate stack, and these can be hard to debug by simply stepping through the code.

Moving through your program line-by-line slows down execution so much that it can be difficult to identify which lines are fast and which are slow. The same approach taken for fixing functional bugs cannot always be applied to fix performance issues.

One of the problems with adopting a new framework (such as ASP.NET Core) early is that it can take a while for the existing tools to be updated to work with it. We will point out when this is the case but these compatibility problems should improve over time. As many of the tools are open source, you could help out and contribute to the community.

SQL

First off we will cover SQL related issues, so if you're not using a relational database then you can skip this bit, perhaps if you're using a NoSQL store or a document database instead. Relational databases are a very mature technology and are flexible in their uses. However, it is essential to have a basic knowledge of the SQL syntax and how databases work in order to use them effectively.

It can be tempting when using an O/RM such as **Entity Framework** (**EF**) to ignore SQL and stay in a C# world, but a competent developer should be able to write a high performance SQL query. Ignoring the realities of how a database engine works will often lead to performance issues. It's easy to write code with an O/RM that's too chatty with the database and issues far too many queries for an operation. Not having the correct indexes on a table will also result in poor performance.

During development you may not notice these mistakes, unless you use tools to identify the inefficient events occurring. Here we will show you a couple of ways of doing this.

SQL Server Profiler

SQL Server Profiler is a tool that allows you to inspect what commands are being executed on your SQL Server database. If you have the management tools installed then you should already have it on your machine.

1. If you are using Microsoft SQL Server, then **SQL Server Profiler** can be accessed from the **Tools** menu of **SQL Server Management Studio** (**SSMS**).

2. Load SQL Server Profiler and connect to the database that you are using. Name your trace and select the **Tuning** profile template.

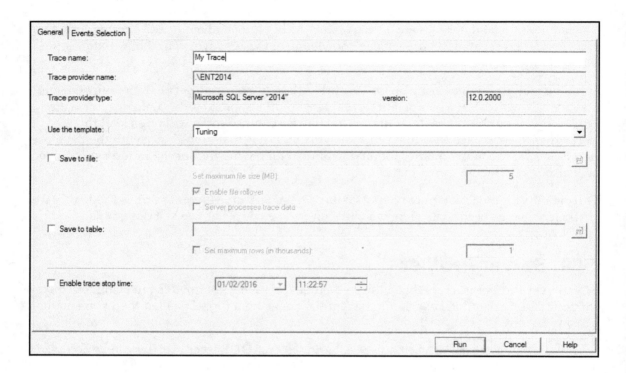

3. Click **Run** and you should see that the trace has begun. You are now ready to run your code against the database to see what queries it's actually executing.

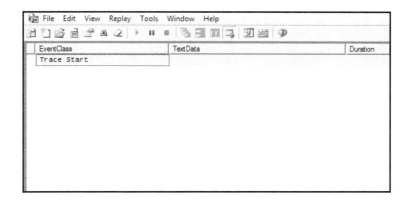

Executing a simple query

As a test you can execute a simple select query with Management Studio and the profile window should be flooded with entries. Locate the query that you just executed among the noise. This is easier if it starts with a comment, as shown in the following screenshot.

The **Duration** column shows the time taken for the query in milliseconds (ms). In this example, selecting the top 1000 rows from a table containing over a million entries took **246** ms. This would appear very quick, almost instantaneous, to the user. Modifying the query to return all rows makes it much slower, as shown in the following screenshot:

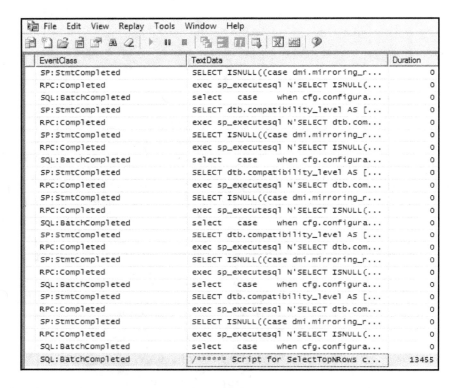

The query has now taken over 13 seconds (**13455** ms) to complete, which is noticeably slow. This is an extreme example, but it is quite a common mistake to request more data than needed and to filter or sort it in application code. The database is often much better suited to this task and is usually the correct location to select the data you want.

We will cover specific SQL mistakes and remedies in the following chapters. However, the first step is knowing how to detect what is going on with the communication between your application and the database. If you can't detect that your app is making inefficient queries then it will be difficult to improve performance.

MiniProfiler

MiniProfiler is an excellent open source tool for debugging data queries. It supports SQL databases and some NoSQL databases, such as Mongo and Raven. It came out of Stack Exchange, the people who run the Stack Overflow Q&A site. It embeds a widget into your web pages that shows you how long they take to get their data. It also shows you the SQL queries and warns you about common mistakes. Although MiniProfiler started with .NET, it is also available for Ruby, Go, and Node.js.

The biggest benefit of MiniProfiler over SQL Server Profiler is that it's always there. You don't need to explicitly go looking for SQL problems and so it can highlight issues much earlier. It's even a good idea to run it in production, only visible to logged in admins. This way, every time you work on the website you will see how the data access is performing. Make sure you test for the performance impacts of this before deploying it though.

Unfortunately MiniProfiler doesn't yet support ASP.NET Core 1.0. It relies on the `System.Web` library and doesn't tie into the **Open Web Interface for .NET (OWIN)** style lifecycle used by the new framework. Hopefully it will soon support ASP.NET Core (and may do by the time you read this) as it's a very useful tool.

> If you're using a supported version of ASP.NET then MiniProfiler is highly recommended. ASP.NET Core support is planned, so keep an eye on `ANCLAFS.com` for the latest support details.

Due to these limitations, we won't cover MiniProfiler in too much detail but you can get more information at `miniprofiler.com`. If you are using a previous version of ASP.NET then you can install it into your project with the NuGet package manager. Type `Install-Package MiniProfiler` into the package manager PowerShell console window in Visual Studio. Then follow the rest of the setup instructions from the website.

Application profiling

Often you will want a breakdown of where all the time is being taken up within your application. There are various tools available for this and we will cover a couple of them here.

Glimpse

Glimpse is a fantastic open source add-on for your web application. Like MiniProfiler, it adds a widget to your web pages so that you can see problems as you navigate around and work on your site. It provides information similar to your browser developer tools but also delves inside your server side application to show you a trace of what actions are taking the most time.

Glimpse is available from `getglimpse.com` and you can install it with NuGet for the web framework and O/RM you're using. For ASP.NET Core we will need to use Glimpse version 2. This is currently a beta prerelease, but by the time you read this it may be stable.

Using Glimpse

Installing Glimpse is really simple, there are only three steps.

1. Install with NuGet.
2. Add lines to `Startup.cs`.
3. Build and run the app.

Let's have a look at these steps.

Installing the package

Right-click on your web application project in the Solution Explorer and select **Manage NuGet Packages...** to open the graphical package manager window. Search for Glimpse, select it, and then click on the **Install** button. If you want to install the beta version of Glimpse 2, then make sure the **Include prerelease** checkbox is selected:

Add code

You need to add three snippets of code to your `Startup.cs` file. In the `using` directives at the top of the file, add the following:

```
using Glimpse;
```

In the `ConfigureServices` function, add the following:

```
services.AddGlimpse();
```

In the `Configure` function, add the following:

```
app.UseGlimpse();
```

Running your web application

Build and run your web application by pressing *F5*. If you encounter a duplicate type error when running then simply clean the solution and do a full rebuild. You may need to apply migrations to the database, but this is just a button click in the browser. However, if you add this to an existing project with data, then you should take more care.

You should then look at your web application with the Glimpse bar at the bottom of the browser window, which looks like the following screenshot. The bar is one long strip, but it has been broken up in this screenshot to display it more clearly:

 The first page load may take much longer than subsequent ones, so you should refresh for more representative data. However, we won't worry about this for the purposes of this demo.

Mouse over each section in the Glimpse toolbar to expand it for more information. You can minimize and restore each section (HTTP, HOST, or AJAX) by clicking on its title.

If you used the default web application template (and left the authentication as the default individual user accounts), then you can register a new user to cause the application to perform some database operations. You will then see some values in the **DB queries** field, as shown in the following screenshot:

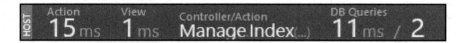

Click on the Glimpse logo to see a history of all the page requests. Select one to view the details and expand the SQL queries by clicking on them, which is displayed in the following screenshot:

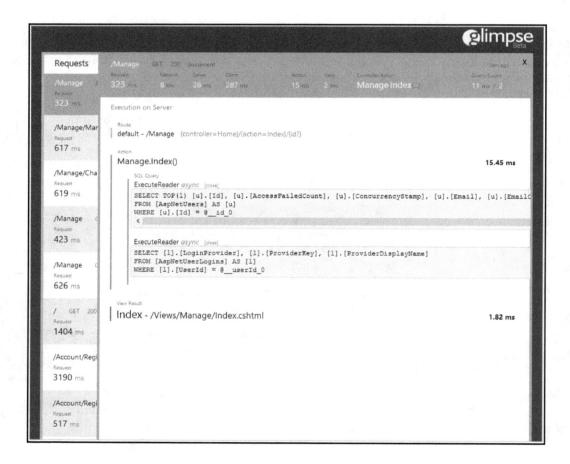

Glimpse shows you how much time is spent in each layer of your application and exactly which SQL queries are being run. In this case, EF Core 1.0 generates the SQL.

Glimpse is very useful to track down where performance problems lie. You can easily see how long each part of the page pipeline takes and identify slow parts.

IDE

Using the profiling tools that are built into **Visual Studio (VS)** can be very informative to understand the CPU and memory usage of your code. You can also see the time taken for certain operations.

When running your application, open the diagnostic tools window in VS, as shown in the following screenshot:

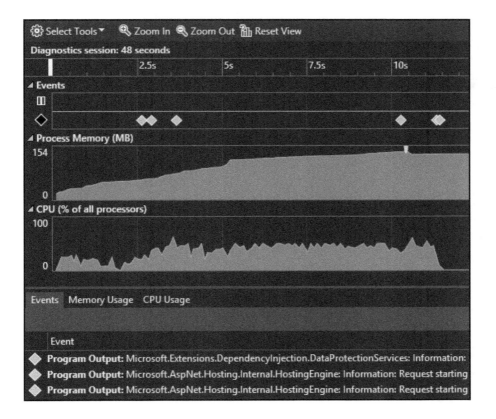

You can see the CPU and memory profiles, including the automatic Garbage Collection events that are used to free up memory (the marker just prior to memory use decreasing). You will be able to see breakpoint events and, if you have the enterprise version of VS, IntelliTrace events as well.

 IntelliTrace is only available in the enterprise edition of Visual Studio. However, you can still use the performance and diagnostic tools in the free community edition.

If you have **IntelliTrace**, then you can find it in the VS options, as shown in the following screenshot. However, the diagnostic tools are still useful without this premium feature:

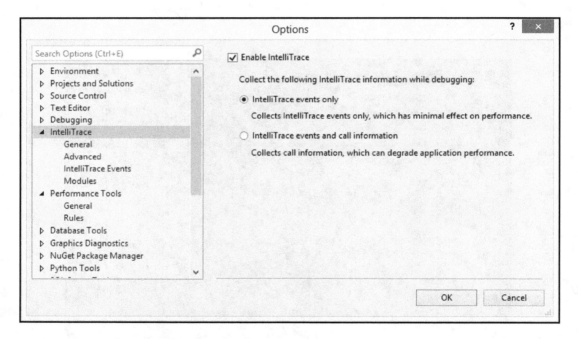

When you put in a breakpoint and your code hits it, then VS will tell you how long it was since the previous event. This is shown in the events list and also overlaid near the breakpoint.

You can't install the community edition and enterprise edition of Visual Studio on the same machine. Use a **Virtual Machine** (**VM**), for example, with **Hyper-V** or VirtualBox, if you wish to run both.

Alternatives to VStools are Redgate ANTS and Telerik JustTrace. JetBrains also have dotTrace and dotMemory. However, all of these tools can be quite expensive and we won't cover them here.

Monitoring HTTP

When dealing with a web application, you will normally use HTTP as the application protocol. It's very useful to know what requests occur between the browsers and your servers.

Browsers

Most modern browsers have excellent developer tools, which include a network tab to monitor requests to and responses from the web server. You can normally access the dev tools by pressing *F12*. These are handy to view the web traffic and you can still see encrypted communications without messing about with certificates.

The dev tools in both Chrome and Firefox are superb. We'll focus on the network and timing component, but we highly recommend that you learn all of the features. If you know how to get the best out of them, then web development is much easier.

Chrome

The network dev tools in Chrome are very useful. They provide a good visualization of the request timings, and you can throttle the connection to see how it behaves over various different internet connections. This is particularly important for mobile devices.

A selection of network requests from the Chrome dev tools are shown in the following screenshot. Additional columns are available if you right-click on the **Headers** bar:

Name Path	Method	Status Text	Type	Initiator	Size Content	Time Latency
localhost	GET	200 OK	document	Other	2.8 KB 8.5 KB	49 ms 43 ms
bootstrap.css /lib/bootstrap/dist/css	GET	200 OK	stylesheet	(index):9 Parser	31.8 KB 151 KB	397 ms 147 ms
site.css /css	GET	200 OK	stylesheet	(index):10 Parser	873 B 618 B	140 ms 139 ms
ASP-NET-Banners-01.png /images	GET	200 OK	png	(index):52 Parser	8.5 KB 8.1 KB	214 ms 150 ms

You can disable the cache with a simple checkbox so that the browser will always load assets fresh from your web server. You can also click on a resource for more information and the timing tab is very useful to provide a breakdown of the connection components, for example, **Time To First Byte** (**TTFB**). Some basic timing details from a local web server are shown in the following screenshot:

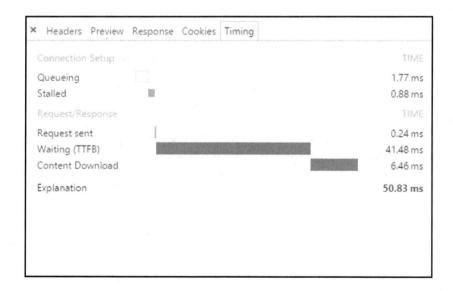

On a local web server, this breakdown won't contain much extra information, but on a remote server it will display other things, such as the **Domain Name System** (**DNS**) hostname lookup, and SSL/TLS handshake. These additional components are shown in the next screenshot:

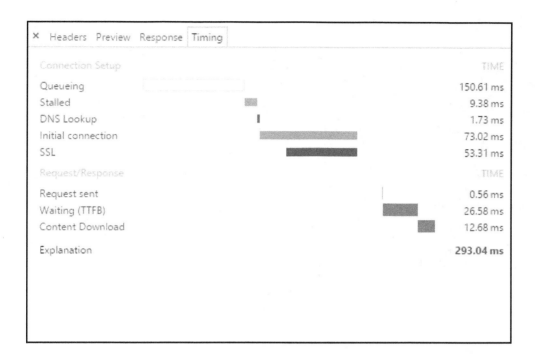

Firefox

Firefox has similar dev tools to Chrome but with some added features. For example, you can edit a request and resend it to the web server. The **Network** tab presents the same sort of information as Chrome does, as shown in the following screenshot:

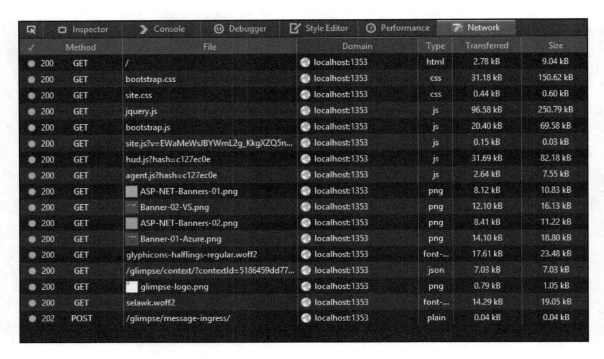

The detail view is also very similar, including the **Timings** tab. This tab is shown in the following screenshot:

Fiddler

Sometimes, browser tools aren't enough. Perhaps, you are debugging a native application, backend web client, or mobile browser. Fiddler is a free debugging proxy that can capture all HTTP traffic between the client and server. With a little bit of work, it can also intercept HTTPS traffic. Fiddler is available at `www.telerik.com/fiddler`.

As this book focuses on web development we won't go into more detail. The browser dev tools are suitable for most work these days. They now fulfil a large part of the role that Fiddler used to play before they acquired the same features. Fiddler is still there if you need it and it can be handy if your web server calls an external HTTP API. Although this can also often be debugged directly inside VS.

Network

Occasionally, you will need to debug at a lower level than HTTP or SQL. This is where network monitors or packet sniffers come in. Perhaps, you want to debug a **Tabular Data Stream** (**TDS**) message to a SQL Server DB or a TLS handshake to an SSL terminating load balancer. Or maybe you want to analyze a SOAP web service envelope or **Simple Mail Transfer Protocol** (**SMTP**) e-mail connection to see why it's not working correctly.

Microsoft Message Analyzer

Microsoft Message Analyzer supersedes Microsoft Network Monitor (**Netmon**) and is a tool to capture network traffic on Windows systems. Netmon requires you to log out and back in again after installation, whereas Wireshark doesn't. You can read more about these two Microsoft tools online, but, for clarity and brevity, we will focus on Wireshark for low-level network monitoring.

Wireshark

Wireshark (previously called Ethereal) is an open source and cross-platform packet capture and network analysis application. It is probably the most popular tool of its kind and has many uses. You can install Wireshark without needing to restart or log out which makes it great to debug a live problem that's hard to recreate. You can download Wireshark from `www.wireshark.org` and it runs on Windows, Mac OS X, and Linux.

Wireshark isn't particularly useful for local development as it only captures traffic going over the network, not to localhost. The only thing you are likely to see if you run it against a local web application is VS reporting what you do back to Microsoft.

You can turn off the **Customer Experience Improvement Program** (CEIP) by clicking on the button next to the quick launch box and selecting **Settings...**. By default, it is on (it's now opt-out rather than the opt-in of previous products).

Click on the fin icon button at the top-left of Wireshark to start a trace. Then perform some network actions, such as loading a webpage from a test server. Once you capture some packets, click on the stop button and you can then examine the collected data at your leisure.

Ask your IT administrator before running Wireshark. It can often pick up sensitive information off of the LAN, which may be against your IT acceptable use policy.

The following screenshot shows part of the results from a Wireshark capture.

There can be a lot of noise when using Wireshark. You will see low-level network packets, such as **Address Resolution Protocol** (**ARP**) traffic, which you can filter out or ignore. You may also see data from VoIP phones and other networked devices or data that is intended for other computers on the network.

Select the packet that you are interested in from the top pane. The middle pane will display the contents of the packet. You can normally ignore the lower layers of the network stack, such as Ethernet and TCP/IP (presented at the top of the list).

Dive straight into the application layer that is listed last. If this is a protocol that Wireshark recognizes, then it will break it down into the fields that it's made up of.

The bottom pane displays a hex dump of the raw packet. This is not normally as useful as the parsed data in the middle pane.

If you use TLS/SSL (hint: you should), then you won't see the contents of HTTP traffic. You would need a copy of the server's private key to see inside the TLS connection, which wraps and encrypts the HTTP application data. You will only be able to see the domain that was connected to via the DNS lookup and TLS certificate, not the full URL or any payload data.

Using Wireshark is a huge topic, and there are many great resources available to learn about it, both online and offline. We won't go into much more detail here because it's usually not necessary to go down to this low level of network scrutiny. However, this is a good tool to have in your back pocket.

Roll your own

Sometimes, you may want to write your own performance measurement code. Make sure that you have exhausted all other options and investigated the available tools first.

 Perhaps, you want to record the execution time of some process to write to your logs. Maybe you want to send this to a system such as Logstash then visualize the changes over time with **Kibana**. Both are great open source products from Elastic, and they store data in the Elasticsearch search server. You can read more about both of these tools at `elastic.co`

You can easily record the length of time for a task by storing the current time before it starts and comparing this to the current time after it finishes, but this approach has many limitations. The act of measuring will affect the result to some extent, and the clock is not accurate for short durations. It can be useful for really slow events if you need to share states between processes or multiple runs, but, to benchmark, you should normally use the `Stopwatch` class.

It is usually best to store timestamps in **Coordinated Universal Time (UTC)**, which is otherwise known as **Greenwich Mean Time (GMT)**, and name timestamps in UTC. You will avoid many issues with time zones and daylight saving if you use `DateTimeOffset.UtcNow` (or at least `DateTime.UtcNow`). Name variables and columns to indicate this, for example, `TimestampUtc`.

Use `TimeSpan` for lengths of time, but, if you must use primitives (such as integers), then include the units in the variable or column name. For example, `DurationInMilliseconds` or `TimeoutInSeconds`. This will help to avoid confusion when another developer (or your future self) comes to use them.

However, to benchmark quick operations, you should use a `Stopwatch`. This class is in the `System.Diagnostics` namespace.

If you try to measure a single quick event, then you will not get accurate results. A way around this is to repeat the task many times and then take an average. This is useful to benchmark, but it is not usually applicable to real applications. However, once you identify what works quickest with a test, then you can apply it to your own programs.

Let's illustrate this with a small experiment to time how long it takes to hash a password with the PBKDF2 algorithm (in the `System.Security.Cryptography` namespace). In this case, the operation under test is not important, as we are simply interested in the timing code. A naÃ¯ve approach may look like the following code:

```
var s = Stopwatch.StartNew();
pbkdf2.GetBytes(2048);
s.Stop();
Console.WriteLine($"Test duration = {s.ElapsedMilliseconds} ms");
```

This code will output a different value every time it is run, due to the flaws in the measurement process. A better way would be to repeat the test many times and average the output, like the following code:

```
var s = Stopwatch.StartNew();
for (var ii = 0; ii < tests; ii++)
{
    pbkdf2.GetBytes(2048);
}
s.Stop();
var mean = s.ElapsedMilliseconds / tests;
Console.WriteLine($"{tests} runs mean duration = {mean} ms");
```

This code will output very similar results every time. The higher the value of `tests`, the more accurate it will be, but the longer the test will take.

We use the new concise string-formatting method here, but you can use the traditional overloads to `Console.WriteLine` if you prefer.

Let's write a quick example application that demonstrates the differences by running these two different versions multiple times. We'll extract the two tests into methods and call them each a few times:

```
var pbkdf2 = new Rfc2898DeriveBytes("password", 64, 256);
SingleTest(pbkdf2);
SingleTest(pbkdf2);
SingleTest(pbkdf2);

Console.WriteLine();
var tests = 1000;
AvgTest(pbkdf2, tests);
AvgTest(pbkdf2, tests);
AvgTest(pbkdf2, tests);

Console.WriteLine();
Console.WriteLine("Press any key...");
Console.ReadKey(true);
```

The output will look something like the following screenshot. You can find the full application listing in the code that accompanies this book if you want to run it for yourself:

You can see that the three individual tests can give wildly different results and yet the averaged tests are identical.

Detailed steps to download the code bundle are mentioned in the Preface of this book. Please have a look. The code bundle for the book is also hosted on GitHub at https://github.com/PacktPublishing/ASP.NET-Core-1.0-High-Performance. We also have other code bundles from our rich catalog of books and videos available at https://github.com/PacktPublishing/. Check them out!

Your results will vary. This is due to the inherent variability in computer systems. Embedded systems that are time sensitive usually use a real time OS. Normal software systems typically run on a time-sharing OS, where your instructions can easily get interrupted, and VMs make the problem even worse.

You will get different results, depending on whether you build in debug or release mode and if you run with or without debugging. Release mode without debugging (*Ctrl + F5*) is the fastest.

The following screenshot shows the same benchmarking demo application running with debugging. You can tell because the dotnet executable is shown in the title bar of the command prompt. If it ran without debugging, then this would display cmd.exe (on Windows), as in the previous screenshot.

```
C:\Program Files\dotnet\dotnet.exe

Test duration = 34 ms
Test duration = 39 ms
Test duration = 29 ms

1000 runs mean duration = 26 ms
1000 runs mean duration = 26 ms
1000 runs mean duration = 26 ms

Press any key...
```

Unit testing is very valuable and you may even practice **Test-Driven Development (TDD)**, but you should be careful about including performance tests as unit tests. Unit tests must be quick to be valuable, and tests that accurately measure the time taken for operations are often slow. You should set a timeout on your unit tests to make sure that you don't write slow ones with external dependencies. You can still test performance, but you should do it in the integration testing stage along with tests that hit an API, DB, or disk.

Science

We dealt with the computer in computer science by showcasing some hardware in the previous chapter. Now, it's time for the science bit.

It's important to take a scientific approach if you wish to achieve consistently reliable results. Have a methodology or test plan and follow it the same way every time, only changing the thing that you want to measure. Automation can help a lot with this.

It's also important to always measure for your use case on your systems with your data. What worked well for someone else may not work out great for you.

We will talk more about science and statistics later in the book. Taking a simple average can be misleading but it's fine to use it as a gentle introduction. Read `Chapter 8`, *The Downsides of Performance Enhancing Tools*, for more on concepts such as medians and percentiles.

Repeatability

Results need to be repeatable. If you get wildly different results every time you test, then they can't be relied upon. You should repeat tests and take the average result to normalize out any variability in the application or hardware under test.

It is also important to clearly record the units of measurement. When you compare a new value to a historic one, you need to know this. NASA famously lost a Mars probe because of unit confusion.

Only change one thing

When testing, you aim to measure the impact of a single change. If you change more than one thing at a time, then you cannot be sure which one has made the difference.

The aim is to minimize the effects of any other changes apart from the one you are interested in. This means keeping external factors as static as possible and performing multiple tests, taking the average result.

Summary

Let's sum up what we covered about measurement in this chapter and what we'll cover in the next chapter. We covered the importance of measurement in solving performance problems. Without measuring, you cannot hope to write high-performance software; you will be coding in the dark.

We highlighted some of the tools that you can use to measure performance. We showed you how to use a selection of these and how to write your own.

We also covered the value of taking a scientific approach to measurement. Making sure that your results are repeatable and that you record the correct units of measurement are important concerns.

In the next chapter, we will learn how to fix common performance problems. You will gain the skills to speed up the low-hanging fruit and make yourself look like a performance wizard to your colleagues. No longer will it be a case of it worked in test, it's an operations problem now.

3
Fixing Common Performance Problems

This chapter gets into the meat of optimization, once you identify and locate performance problems. It covers a selection of the most common performance issues across a variety of areas and explains simple solutions to some of the mistakes people often make. When using these techniques, you'll look like a wizard to your clients and colleagues by quickly speeding up their software.

Topics covered in this chapter include the following:

- Network latency
- **Select N+1** problems
- Disk I/O issues on virtual machines
- Asynchronous operations in a web application
- Performing too many operations in one web request
- Static site generators
- Pragmatic solutions with hardware
- Shrinking overly-large images

Most of the problems in this chapter center on what happens when you add latency to common operations or when throughput is reduced from what it was in development. Things that worked fine in test when everything was on one physical machine with minimal data are now no longer quite as speedy when you have an API on a different continent, a full database on a different machine to your web server, and its virtual disk somewhere else on the network entirely.

You will learn how to identify and fix issues that are not always apparent when everything is running on a single machine. You'll see how to identify when your O/RM or framework behaves badly and is too chatty with the database, which can easily happen if it's not used correctly.

We will see how to ensure that work is performed in the most appropriate place, and we'll look at some ways of keeping your images small using the correct resolution and format. These techniques will ensure that your application is efficient and that data is not sent over the wire unnecessarily.

We'll also discuss how to mitigate performance issues with an alternative approach by improving the underlying hardware to reduce the factors that amplify issues in bad software. This can be a good temporary measure if the software is already deployed to production and in use. If you already have live performance problems then this can buy you some time to engineer a proper fix.

Latency

As covered in previous chapters, latency is the delay that occurs before an operation can complete, sometimes also known as **lag**. You may not be able to control the latency of the infrastructure that your software runs on, but you can write your application in such a way that it can cope with this latency in a graceful manner.

The two main types of latency that we will discuss here are **network latency** and **disk latency**. As the names suggest these are, respectively, the delay in performing an operation over the network and the delay to read from or write to a persistent storage medium. You will often deal with both at the same time, for example, a **database** (**DB**) query to a server on a remote virtual machine will require the following operations:

- A network operation from web server to DB server
- A network operation from DB server to remote disk on a **Storage Area Network** (**SAN**)
- A disk operation to look up data on the physical drive

 Although **Solid State Drives** (**SSDs**) have much lower latency than spinning platter disks, they are still relatively slow. When we talk about disk I/O here, we refer to both types of drive.

You can clearly see that, if you issue too many DB operations, the latency present in typical production infrastructure will compound the problem. You can fix this by minimizing the number of DB operations so that they can't be amplified as much.

Let's illustrate this with an example. Let's suppose you wish to return 200 records from your DB and the round trip latency is 50 milliseconds (ms). If you retrieve all of the records at once, then the total time will be 50 ms plus the time to transfer the records. However, if you first retrieve a list of the record identifiers and then retrieve all of them individually, the total time will be at least *201 * 50 ms = 10.05 seconds*!

Unfortunately, this is a very common mistake. In a system where latency dominates throughput, it is important to keep requests to a minimum.

Asynchronous operations

Most new .NET framework APIs that have significant latency will have **asynchronous (async)** methods. For example, the .NET HTTP client (superseding the web client), SMTP client, and **Entity Framework (EF)** all have async versions of common methods. In fact, the async version is usually the native implementation and the non-async method is simply a blocking wrapper to it. These methods are very beneficial and you should use them. However, they may not have the effect that you imagine when applied to web application programming.

 We will cover async operations and asynchronous architecture later in this book. We'll also go into **Message Queuing (MQ)** and worker services. This chapter is just a quick introduction and we will simply show you some tools to go after the low-hanging fruit on web applications.

An async API returns control to the calling method before it completes. This can also be awaited so that on completion, execution resumes from where the asynchronous call was made. With a native desktop or mobile application, awaiting an async method returns control to the **user interface (UI)** thread, which means that the software remains responsive to user input. The app can process user interactions rather than blocking on your method. Traditionally, you may have used a background worker for these tasks.

You should never perform expensive work on the UI thread. Therefore, this technique does increase performance for native applications. However, for a web application this UI blocking problem does not exist because the browser is the UI. Therefore, this technique will not increase performance for a single user in isolation.

Awaiting asynchronous API methods in a web application is still good practice, but it only allows the software to scale better and handle more concurrent users. A web request typically cannot complete until the async operation also completes. Therefore, although the thread is surrendered back into the thread pool and you can use it for other requests, the individual web request will not complete quicker.

Simple asynchronous tools

As this book deals with web application programming, we won't go into much more detail on native application UIs in this chapter. Instead, we will showcase some simple tools and techniques that can help with async tasks in web applications.

The tools we are about to cover offer some simple solutions that are only suitable for very small applications. They may not always be reliable, but sometimes they can be good enough. If you are after a more robust solution, then you should read the later chapters about distributed architecture.

Background queuing

Background queuing is a useful technique when you have an operation that does not need to occur straight away. For example, logging stats to a database, sending an e-mail, or processing a payment transaction. If you perform too much work in a single web request, then background queuing may offer a convenient solution, especially if you don't require the operation to always succeed.

If you use ASP.NET 4.6 (or any version from 4.5.2 onwards), then you can use `HostingEnvironment.QueueBackgroundWorkItem` to run a method in the background. This is preferable to simply setting a task running, as if ASP.NET shuts down then it will issue a cancellation request and wait for a grace period before killing the item. However, this still does not guarantee completion because the application can die at any point due to an unexpected reboot or hardware failure. If the task needs to complete, then it should be **transactional** and make a record of success upon completion. It can then be retried if it failed. Queuing a background work item is okay for fire-and-forget events, if you genuinely don't care whether they succeed or not.

Unfortunately, `HostingEnvironment.QueueBackgroundWorkItem` is not part of ASP.NET Core. Therefore, if you want to use this, then you will have to simply queue a job. We will show you how to do this later, but if you use the full version of ASP.NET, then you can do the following to send an e-mail in the background:

```
var client = new SmtpClient();
HostingEnvironment.QueueBackgroundWorkItem(ct =>
    client.SendMailAsync(message));
```

Assuming that you already have your message, this will create an SMTP client and send the e-mail message in the background without blocking further execution. This does not use the `ct` (cancellation token) variable. Keep in mind that the e-mail is not guaranteed to be sent. Therefore, if you need to definitely dispatch it, then consider using another method.

If you use ASP.NET Core, then this functionality is not available. However, you can manually create something similar with `Task.Run` as in the following example. However, this is probably not the best approach for anything nontrivial:

```
Task.Run(() => asyncMethod(cancellationToken));
```

If you can cancel your task, then you can get the `ApplicationStopping` token from an injected instance of the `IApplicationLifetime` interface to pass in as your cancellation token. This will let your task know when the application is about to stop, and you can also block shutdown with it while you gracefully clean up.

You should use this technique with caution, so we won't give you a full example here. Although, you should now have enough pointers to dig deeper and understand the ASP.NET Core application lifecycle if you wish.

Hangfire

Hangfire is an excellent library to run simple background jobs. It does not support ASP.NET Core yet, but this is planned (refer to `ANCLAFS.com` for the latest information). If you use the full .NET, then you should consider it and you can read more at `hangfire.io`.

You need persistent storage, such as SQL Server, to use Hangfire. This is required so that it can ensure that tasks are completed. If your tasks are very quick, then this overhead can outweigh the benefits. You can reduce the latency using **message queues** or the in-memory store **Redis**, but these are advanced topics.

As this book focuses on ASP.NET Core and Hangfire does not support it yet, we won't cover its use in more detail. It is also beyond the scope of this chapter in terms of quick and easy solutions.

Select N+1 problems

You may have heard of Select N+1 problems before. It's a name for a class of performance problems that relate to inefficient querying of a DB. The pathological case is where you query one table for a list of items and then query another table to get the details for each item, one at a time. This is where the name comes from. Instead of the single query required, you perform *N* queries (one for the details of each item) and the one query to get the list to begin with. Perhaps a better name would be Select 1+N.

You will hopefully not write such bad-performing queries by hand, but an O/RM can easily output very inefficient SQL if used incorrectly. You might also use some sort of business objects abstraction framework, where each object lazily loads itself from the DB. This can become a performance nightmare if you want to put a lot of these objects in a list or calculate some dashboard metrics from a large set.

 We will go into detail about SQL and O/RM optimization in `Chapter 5`, *Optimizing I/O Performance*. This chapter will simply offer some quick fixes to common problems.

If you have a slow application that has performance issues when retrieving data, then Select N+1 may be the problem. Run a SQL profiler tool, as described in the previous chapter, to discover if this is the case. If you see lots of SQL queries for your data instead of just one, then you can move on to the solution stage. For example, if your screen fills with queries on a page load, then you know you have a problem.

In the following example, we will use the micro-O/RM Dapper (made by the team at Stack Overflow) to better illustrate what occurs. However, you are more likely to encounter these problems when using a large lazy loading library or O/RM (such as EF or NHibernate).

 Entity Framework Core 1.0 (previously EF 7) does not support lazy loading, so you are unlikely to encounter Select N+1 problems when using it. Previous versions of EF do support this and it may be added to EF Core in the future.

You currently need to use a beta pre-release version of Dapper to work with ASP.NET Core. As with Glimpse, this may be stable by the time you read this (check `ANCLAFS.com`). To use Glimpse with Dapper, you need to use the `Glimpse.ADO` package, which unfortunately does not yet support .NET Core.

Consider a simple blog website. On the home page, we would like a list of the posts along with the number of comments each post has. Our blog post model may look something like the following:

```
namespace SelectNPlusOne.Models
{
    public class BlogPost
    {
        public int BlogPostId { get; set; }
        public string Title { get; set; }
        public string Content { get; set; }
        public int CommentCount { get; set; }
    }
}
```

We also have a model for a comment, which may look like this.

```
namespace SelectNPlusOne.Models
{
    public class BlogPostComment
    {
        public int BlogPostCommentId { get; set; }
        public string CommenterName { get; set; }
        public string Content { get; set; }
    }
}
```

 As this is an example, we kept things simple and only used a single set of models. In a real application, you will typically have separate **view models** and **data access layer models**. The controller will map between these, perhaps assisted by a library, such as AutoMapper (`automapper.org`).

Our view to render this into HTML may look something like the following:

```
@model IEnumerable<SelectNPlusOne.Models.BlogPost>
<table class="table">
    <tr>
        <th>Title</th>
        <th># Comments</th>
    </tr>
    @foreach (var post in Model)
    {
        <tr>
            <td>@post.Title</td>
            <td>@post.CommentCount</td>
        </tr>
```

```
    }
</table>
```

We want to populate these models and view from our database. We have two tables, which look like this:

The relationship between the two tables in question looks like the following:

In our controller, we can write code, such as the following to query the database, populate the model from the database results, and return the view to render it:

```
using (var connection = new SqlConnection(connectionString))
{
    await connection.OpenAsync();
    var blogPosts = await connection.QueryAsync<BlogPost>(@"
        SELECT * FROM BlogPost");
    foreach (var post in blogPosts)
    {
        var comments = await
            connection.QueryAsync<BlogPostComment>(@"
            SELECT * FROM BlogPostComment
            WHERE BlogPostId = @BlogPostId",
            new { BlogPostId = post.BlogPostId });
        post.CommentCount = comments.Count();
    }
    return View(blogPosts);
}
```

We test this and it works! We feel pretty happy with ourselves. It completes quickly on our local test database that contains a handful of rows. We used the async methods everywhere, which must be what makes this so quick. We even only get the comments for each blog in question, not all comments everytime. We also used a parameterized query to avoid **SQL injection**, and everything looks good. Ship it!

 As this is an example, we kept it simple for clarity. In a real application, you will want to use techniques such as dependency injection (such as the DI built into ASP.NET Core) to make it more flexible.

Unfortunately, when the data starts to increase (as posts and comments are added), the blog starts to get much slower with pages taking a longer time to load. Our readers get bored waiting and give up. Audience figures drop along with revenue.

Let's profile the database to see what the problem might be. We run SQL Server Profiler filtering on the database in question, and look at the SQL being executed.

The following screenshot shows the filter dialog in SQL Server Profiler:

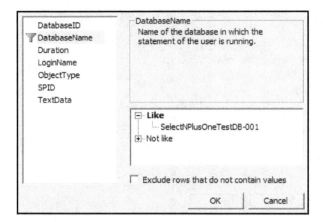

The trace that we capture reveals that lots of queries are being executed; far too many for the data that we need. The problem is that our code is not very efficient because it uses multiple simple queries rather than one slightly more complicated one.

Our code first gets a list of blog posts and then gets the comments for each post, one post at a time. We also bring back way more data than we need. `Async` does not speed up an individual request because we still need all of the data before we can render the page.

 The bad coding is obvious in this example because Dapper has the SQL right in your code. However, if you use another O/RM, then you wouldn't typically see the SQL in Visual Studio (or your editor of choice). This is an additional benefit of using Dapper because you see the SQL where it's used, so there are no surprises.

However, the main benefit of Dapper is that it's fast, very fast, and much faster than EF. It's a great choice for performance and you can read more about it at `github.com/StackExchange/dapper-dot-net`.

We only want a count of the comments for each post and we can get everything that we need (and only what we need) in one query. Let's alter our previous code to use a slightly more complicated SQL query rather than two simpler queries, one of which was inside a `foreach` loop:

 A SQL query inside a loop is an obvious **code smell** that indicates things may not be as well thought-out as they can be.

```
using (var connection = new SqlConnection(connectionString))
{
    await connection.OpenAsync();
    var blogPosts = await connection.QueryAsync<BlogPost>(@"
        SELECT
            bp.BlogPostId,
            bp.Title,
            COUNT(bpc.BlogPostCommentId) 'CommentCount'
        FROM BlogPost bp
        LEFT JOIN BlogPostComment bpc
            ON bpc.BlogPostId = bp.BlogPostId
        GROUP BY bp.BlogPostId, bp.Title");
    return View(blogPosts);
}
```

This more efficient code only performs a single query against the database and gets all of the information that we need. We join the comments table to the posts in the database and then aggregate by grouping. We only request the columns that we need and add the count of the comments to our selection.

Let's profile the new code to see whether we fixed the problem. The following image shows that we now only have a single query being executed rather than the thousands being executed before:

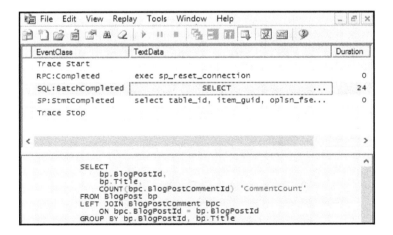

The number of queries has been dramatically reduced. Therefore, the page loads much faster. However, the page is still very big because all the blog posts are listed on it and there are a lot. This slows down rendering and increases the time to deliver the page to a browser.

Efficient paging

In a real application, you want to implement paging so that your list is not too long when a lot of data is in the table. It's a bad idea to list thousands of items on a single page.

You may want to do this with LINQ commands because they are very convenient. However, you need to be careful. If your O/RM is not LINQ aware or you accidentally cast to the wrong type a little too early, then the filtering may occur inside the application when the best place to perform this filtering is actually in the database. Your code may be retrieving all of the data and throwing most of it away without you realizing it.

Perhaps you are tempted to modify the action method `return` statement to look something like the following:

```
return View(blogPosts.OrderByDescending(bp => bp.CommentCount)
                .Skip(pageSize * (pageNumber - 1))
                .Take(pageSize));
```

This works and will speed up your application considerably. However, it may not have the effect that you think it has. The application is quicker because the view rendering is speedier due to generating a smaller page. This also reduces the time to send the page to the browser and for the browser to render the HTML.

Yet, the application still gets all of the blog posts from the database and loads them into memory. This can become a problem as the amount of data grows. If you want to use LINQ methods such as this, then you need to check that they are handled all the way to the database. It's a very good idea to read the documentation for your O/RM or framework and double-check the SQL that is generated using a profiler.

Let's have a look at what the SQL should look like. For example, if you use SQL Server, starting with the preceding query, you can take only the top ten most-commented posts by altering it like the following:

```sql
SELECT TOP 10
    bp.BlogPostId,
    bp.Title,
    COUNT(bpc.BlogPostCommentId) 'CommentCount'
FROM BlogPost bp
LEFT JOIN BlogPostComment bpc
    ON bpc.BlogPostId = bp.BlogPostId
GROUP BY bp.BlogPostId, bp.Title
ORDER BY COUNT(bpc.BlogPostCommentId) DESC
```

We order by comment count in descending order. However, you can sort by descending ID to get a rough reverse chronological order if you like. From this ordered set, we select (or take) only the top ten records.

If you want to skip records for paging, the SELECT TOP clause is not good enough. In SQL Server 2012 and onward, you can use the following instead:

```
SELECT
    bp.BlogPostId,
    bp.Title,
    COUNT(bpc.BlogPostCommentId) 'CommentCount'
FROM BlogPost bp
LEFT JOIN BlogPostComment bpc
    ON bpc.BlogPostId = bp.BlogPostId
GROUP BY bp.BlogPostId, bp.Title
ORDER BY COUNT(bpc.BlogPostCommentId) DESC
OFFSET 0 ROWS
FETCH NEXT 10 ROWS ONLY
```

You can adjust the value for OFFSET to get the correct entries for your page number. The FETCH NEXT value will change the page size (the number of entries on a page). You can pass these values in with a parameterized query, as follows:

```
using (var connection = new SqlConnection(connectionString))
{
    await connection.OpenAsync();
    var blogPosts = await connection.QueryAsync<BlogPost>(@"
        SELECT
            bp.BlogPostId,
            bp.Title,
            COUNT(bpc.BlogPostCommentId) 'CommentCount'
        FROM BlogPost bp
        LEFT JOIN BlogPostComment bpc
            ON bpc.BlogPostId = bp.BlogPostId
        GROUP BY bp.BlogPostId, bp.Title
        ORDER BY COUNT(bpc.BlogPostCommentId) DESC
        OFFSET @OffsetRows ROWS
        FETCH NEXT @LimitRows ROWS ONLY", new
        {
            OffsetRows = pageSize * (pageNumber - 1),
            LimitRows  = pageSize
        }
    );
    return View(blogPosts);
}
```

You can pass in the page size and number as URL parameters if you update your action method signature to the following:

```
public async Task<IActionResult> Index(int pageNumber = 1,
                                       int pageSize   = 10)
```

Here, we provided default values for both parameters, so they are optional. When no parameters are provided, then the first page of ten results is shown. We need to multiply the page size by the zero-indexed page number to calculate the correct offset. It should be zero for the first page so that no records are skipped.

 It would be a very good idea to apply some validation to the paging parameters. Don't allow users to set them to anything outside of a reasonable range. This is left as an exercise to the reader.

If we look in the profiler at the queries being executed on the database server, then we can see what SQL is now being run. We can also see the time taken and compare this to our results from previously:

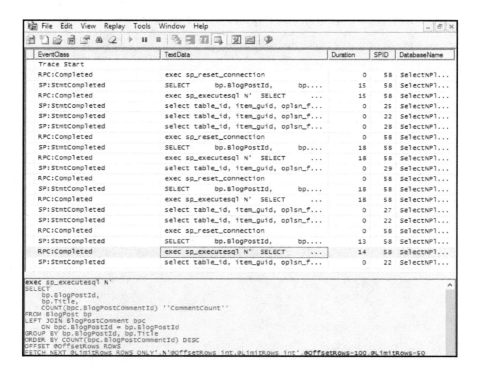

The query in the screenshot gets the data for the third page with the page size set to 50 entries. Therefore, it used an offset of 100 (to skip the first two pages of 50) and fetched the next 50 rows. The URL query string for this can look something like the following:

```
/?pagenumber=3&pagesize=50
```

We can see that the duration of the query has decreased from **24** ms previously to **14** ms now.

 Note how the SQL executes differently when parameters are passed into the query. This is much safer than concatenating user-supplied values directly into a SQL command.

If you do not use any parameters, then the default values are used and the home page shows only ten entries, which looks something like the following screenshot, depending on the data in the database:

By default, the home page only displays the top 10 most commented posts, but you can easily add page navigation with hyperlinks. Simply add the pagenumber and pagesize query string parameters to the URL.

You can use the example URL query string shown previously on either the home page or the bad paging path, for example, `/Home/BadPaging/?pagenumber=3&pagesize=50`.

The links in the navigation bar load the examples that we just walked through. The best is the same as the home page and is the default. Top 10 and bad paging should be fairly self-explanatory. Bad will take a long time to load, especially if you use the DB creation script included with the project. You can time it with your browser developer tools.

For previous versions of SQL Server (prior to 2012), there are paging workarounds using `ROW_NUMBER()` or nested `SELECT` statements, which invert the sort order. If you use another database, such as PostgreSQL, MySQL, or SQLite, then you can easily implement paging with the `LIMIT` clause. These free databases often have more features than SQL Server, such as the `Limit` clause mentioned here and a **concatenation aggregator** to name just one other.

 One of the touted benefits of big O/RMs is the layer of abstraction that they offer. This allows you to change the database that you use. However, in practice, it is rare to change something as core as a database. As you can see from the simple paging example, syntax varies between databases for anything other than simple standard SQL. To get the best performance, you really need to understand the features and custom syntax of the database that you use.

Static site generators

The database is the logical place to perform any work to filter and sort data. Doing this in the application is a waste. However, for a simple blog that is updated infrequently, a database may be unnecessary in the first place. It may even become the bottleneck and slow the whole blog down. This is a typical problem of blog engines, such as **WordPress**. A better approach may be to use a static site generator.

A static site generator prerenders all of the pages and saves the resulting HTML. This can easily be served by a simple web server and scales well. When a change is made and pages need updating, then this site is regenerated and a new version is deployed. This approach doesn't include dynamic features, such as comments, but third-party services are available to provide these added extras.

A popular static site generator is **Jekyll**, which is written in **Ruby**. **GitHub** provides a free static site-hosting service called **GitHub Pages**, which supports Jekyll, and you can read more about it at `pages.github.com`. Another static site generator (written in **Go**) is **Hugo**, which you can read about at `gohugo.io`. These tools are basically a form of extreme caching. We'll cover caching in the next section and later on in this book.

It's often worth taking a step back to see whether the problem that you're trying to solve is even a problem. You may well improve database performance by removing the database.

Pragmatic solutions with hardware

The best approach to take with a poorly performing application is usually to fix the software. However, it is good to be pragmatic and try to look at the bigger picture. Depending on the size and scale of an application, it can be cheaper to throw better hardware at it, at least as a short term measure.

Hardware is much cheaper than developer time and is always getting better. Installing some new hardware can work as a quick fix and buy you some time. You can then address the root causes of any performance issues in software as part of the ongoing development. You can add a little time to the schedule to **refactor** and improve an area of the code base as you work on it.

Once you discover that the cause of your performance problem is latency, you have two possible approaches:

- Reduce the number of latency-sensitive operations
- Reduce the latency itself using faster computers or by moving the computers closer together

With the rise of cloud computing, you may not need to buy or install new hardware. You can just pay more for a higher-performing instance class or you can move things around inside your cloud provider's infrastructure to reduce latency.

A desktop example

To borrow an example from native desktop applications, it is quite common to have poorly-performing **Line of Business** (**LoB**) applications on corporate desktops. The desktop will probably be old and underpowered. The networking back to the central database may be slow because the connection might be over a remote link to a regional office.

With a badly-written application that is too chatty with the DB, it can be better, performance-wise, to run the application on a server close to (or on the same server as) the DB. Perhaps the application workspace and DB servers can be in the same **server rack** at the **data center** and connected by Gigabit (or ten Gigabit) **Ethernet**.

The user can then use a remote desktop connection or **Citrix** session to interact with the application. This will reduce the latency to the DB and can speed things up, even taking into consideration the lag of the remote UI. This effectively turns the desktop PC into a **thin client**, similar to how old mainframes are used.

For example, you can build a high-performance server with RAID SSDs and lots of RAM for much less than the cost of the developer time to fix a large application. Even badly-written software can perform well if you run the application and DB together on the same machine, especially if you run it on **bare metal** with no virtual machines in the way. This tactic would buy you time to fix things properly.

These remote application and virtualization technologies are usually sold as tools to aid deployment and maintenance. However, the potential performance benefits are also worth considering.

Due to the rise of web applications, **thick client** desktop applications are now less common. Architecture seems to oscillate between computation on the server and doing work on the client, as the relative progress of networking speed and processing power race each other.

Web applications

The same relocation approach does not typically work as well for web applications, but it depends on the architecture used. The good news is that, for web applications, you usually control the infrastructure. This is not normally the case for native application hardware.

If you use a **three-tier architecture**, then you can move the application servers closer to the DB server. Whether this is effective or not depends on how chatty the web servers are with the application servers. If they issue too many web API requests, then this won't work well.

A **two-tier architecture** (where the web servers talk directly to the database) is more common for typical web applications. There are solutions using **clustered** databases or read-only mirrors to place the data close to the web servers, but these add complexity and cost.

What can make a significant difference are **proxy servers**. A popular open source proxy server is Varnish and you can also use the NGINX web server as a proxy. Proxy servers cache the output of web servers so that a page doesn't have to be regenerated for each user. This is useful for shared pages but caching is hard; typically, you should not cache personalized pages. You don't want to accidentally serve someone's authenticated private information to another user.

Proxies such as Varnish can also route different parts of your website to different servers. If you have a small area of your site that performs badly due to DB chatter, then you could host that part from web servers on (or very close to, such as on the same VM host) the DB machines and route requests for it to there. The rest of the site could remain on the existing web server farm.

This isn't a long term solution, but it allows you to split off a poorly performing part of your program so that it doesn't impact the rest of your system. You're then free to fix it once it's been decoupled or isolated. You can even split off the data required to a separate DB and synchronize it with a background process.

There are also **Content Delivery Networks (CDNs)**, such as **CloudFlare**, **Amazon CloudFront**, and **Azure CDN**, which are good to cache static assets. CDNs cache parts of your site in data centers close to your users, reducing the latency. CloudFlare can even add HTTPS to your site for free, including automatically issuing certificates.

 You can read more about the CDN offerings of CloudFlare (including HTTP/2 server push and WebSockets on the free plan) at `www.cloudflare.com`.

We will cover caching in more detail in `Chapter 7`, *Learning Caching and Message Queuing*, so we won't go into more detail here. Caching is a challenging subject and needs to be understood well so that you can use it effectively.

Oversized images

While we're on the subject of static assets, we should briefly mention image optimization. We'll cover this in much more detail in the next chapter, but it's worth highlighting some common problems here. As you have very little control over network conditions between your infrastructure and the user, low throughput may be a problem in addition to high latency.

Web applications heavily use images, especially on landing pages or home pages, where they might form a fullscreen background. It is regrettably common to see a raw photo from a camera simply dropped straight in. Images from cameras are typically many megabytes in size, far too big for a web page.

You can test whether there are problems on a web page using a tool, such as Google's PageSpeed Insights. Visit `developers.google.com/speed/pagespeed/insights`, enter a URL, and click on ANALYZE to view the results. Google use this information as part of their search engine ranking, so you would do well to take its advice up to a point. Slow sites rank lower in search results.

You can also use the browser developer tools to view the size of images. Press *F12* and look at the network tab after a page load to view how much data was transferred and how long it took. You can often miss these performance issues on a local machine or test server because the image will load quickly. After the first load, it will also be stored in the browser's cache, so make sure you do a full hard reload and empty or disable the cache. In Chrome (when the dev tools are open), you can right-click or long click on the reload button for these extra options. It's also a good idea to use the built-in throttling tools to see how a user will experience the page loading.

The most basic image optimization problems typically fall into two categories:

- Images that are overly large for the display area they are displayed in
- Images that use the wrong compression format for the subject matter

Image resolution

The most common issue is that an image has too high a resolution for the area that displays it. This forces the browser to resize the image to fit the screen or area. If the size of the file is unnecessarily large, then it will take longer to be transferred over an internet connection. The browser will then throw away most of the information. You should resize the image ahead of time before adding it to the site.

There are many image manipulation tools available to resize pictures. If you run Windows, then **Paint.NET** (`www.getpaint.net`) is an excellent free piece of software. This is much better than the Paint program that comes with Windows (although this will work if you have no other option).

For other platforms, GIMP (www.gimp.org) is very good. If you prefer using the command line, then you may like ImageMagick (imagemagick.org), which can perform lots of image manipulation tasks programmatically or in batches. There are also cloud-hosted image management services, such as **Cloudinary** (cloudinary.com).

You should shrink images to the actual size that they will be displayed on the user's screen. There can be complications when dealing with responsive images, which scale with the size of the user's screen or browser window. Also keep in mind **high DPI** or Retina displays, which may have more than one physical pixel to every logical pixel. Your images may have to be bigger to not look blurry, but the upper bound is still likely to be lower than the raw size. It is rare to need an image at more than twice the size of the displayed resolution. We will discuss responsive images in more detail later in this book, but it is worth keeping them in mind.

The following image displays the resizing dialog from Paint.NET:

When resizing an image, it is usually important to keep the **aspect ratio** of the image the same. This means changing the horizontal and vertical sizes in proportion to each other.

For example, reducing the **Height** from **600** px to **300** px and reducing the **Width** from **800** px to **400** px (meaning both dimensions are reduced by 50%) keeps the image looking the same, only smaller. Most image-manipulation software will assist with this process. Keeping the aspect ratio the same will avoid images looking stretched. If images need to fit a different shape, then they should be cropped instead.

Image format

The next most common problem is using images in the wrong file format for the content. You should never use raw uncompressed images, such as **bitmap (BMP)**, on the web.

For natural images such as photos, use the JPEG file format. JPEG is a lossy codec, which means that information is lost when using it. It is very good for pictures with a lot of gradients in them, such as images of natural scenes or people. JPEG looks poor if there is any text in the image because there will be **compression artifacts** around the edges of the letters. Most mid- and low-end cameras natively save images as JPEG, so you do not lose anything by staying with it. However, you should resize the images to make them smaller, as mentioned previously.

For artificial images such as diagrams or icons, use **PNG**. PNG is a lossless codec, which means that no information is discarded. This works best for images with large blocks of solid color, such as diagrams drawn in painting software or screenshots. This also supports transparency, so you can have images that don't appear rectangular or are translucent. You can also have animated PNGs, which are of superior quality to **GIFs**, but we won't go into the details of them in this chapter.

You can alter the format of images using the same tools that you use to resize them, as mentioned previously, by simply changing the file format when saving the image. As always, you should test for what works best in your specific use case. You can perform experiments by saving the same image in different formats (and different resolutions) then observing the sizes of the files on disk.

The following image displays the available image options in Paint.NET. Additional formats are available and we will go into more detail in `Chapter 4`, *Addressing Network Performance*:

Even when you only choose between **JPEG** and **PNG**, you can still make a significant difference. The following screenshot displays the difference in the size of the file of the same image in two resolutions and two formats.

The following test image is the one used in the experiment. Due to the hard edges it looks best as a PNG, but the gradient background makes it more difficult to compress:

 The test images used here are available for download with this book, so you can try the experiment for yourself.

In a web context, this particular image may be best served with a transparent background using CSS for the gradient. However, simple shapes, such as these can better be represented as **Scalable Vector Graphics (SVG)** or with a HTML5 canvas.

Summary

In this chapter, you learned about some common performance problems and how to fix them. We covered asynchronous operations, Select N+1 problems, pragmatic hardware choices, and overly-large images.

In the next chapter, we will expand on image optimization and extend this to other forms of compression for different types of resources. We'll look at the new process for the bundling and minification of static assets in ASP.NET Core using open source tools.

Additionally, we will introduce networking topics, such as TCP/IP, HTTP, WebSockets, and encryption. We'll also cover caching, including another look at CDNs.

4
Addressing Network Performance

This chapter builds on a subset of the problems that were discussed in the previous chapter but in more detail. It deals with latency, or lag, which originates at the networking level between the user and the application. This is mostly applicable to web applications where the user interacts with the application via a web browser. You will learn how to optimize your application to cater for bandwidth and latency that is unknown and outside of your control. You'll compress your payloads to be as small as possible, and then you will deliver them to the user as quickly as possible. You will learn about the tools and techniques that can be used to achieve a fast and responsive application. You'll also see the trade-offs involved and be able to calculate whether these methods should be applied to your software.

The topics that we will cover in this chapter include the following:

- TCP/IP
- HTTP and HTTP/2
- HTTPS (TLS/SSL)
- WebSockets and push notifications
- Compression
- Bundling and minification
- Caching and CDNs

This chapter deals with how to speed up the experience for a user using your application. The skills in this chapter are just as applicable to a static site or client-side web app as they are to a dynamic web application.

These topics apply to any web application framework. However, we will focus on how they are implemented with ASP.NETâ®®in particular with the new ASP.NET Core implementation, and how this differs from the existing full ASP.NET.

Internet protocols

It's important to know about how your HTML and other assets are delivered from the web server to your user's browser. Much of this is abstracted away and transparent to web development, but it's a good idea to have at least a basic understanding in order to achieve high performance.

TCP/IP

Transmission Control Protocol / Internet Protocol (TCP/IP) is the name for a pair of communication protocols that underpin the internet. **IP** is the lower-level protocol of the two, and this deals with routing *packets* to their correct destinations. IP can run on top of many different lower-level protocols (such as Ethernet), and this is where IP addresses come from.

TCP is a layer above IP, and it is concerned with the reliable delivery of packets and *flow control*. TCP is where ports come from, such as port 80 for HTTP, and port 443 for HTTPS. There is also the **User Datagram Protocol** (**UDP**), which can be used instead of TCP, but it provides fewer features.

HTTP runs on top of TCP, and it is usually what you will deal with in a web application. You may occasionally need to directly use **Simple Mail Transfer Protocol** (**SMTP**) to send e-mails, the **Domain Name System** (**DNS**) to resolve hostnames to IP addresses, or **File Transfer Protocol** (**FTP**) to upload and download files.

The basic unencrypted versions of these protocols run directly on TCP, but the secure encrypted versions (HTTPS, SMTPS, and FTPS) have a layer in between them. This layer is called **Transport Layer Security(TLS)**, and this is the modern successor to the **Secure Sockets Layer(SSL)**. SSL is insecure and deprecated, and it should no longer be used. However, the term SSL is still commonly and confusingly used to describe TLS. All browsers require the use of TLS encryption to support HTTP/2.

You may not often think about the lower-level protocols when you build web applications. Indeed, you may not need to consider even HTTP/HTTPS that much. However, the protocol stack below your application can have significant performance implications.

The following diagram shows how the protocols are typically stacked:

Slow-start

TCP implements an algorithm called *slow-start* for congestion-control purposes. This means that the connection from a browser to a web server is initially slow and ramps up over time to discover the available bandwidth. You can alter the settings for this so that the ramp up is more aggressive, and connections get quicker faster. If you increase the initial *congestion window*, then performance can improve, especially on connections with good bandwidth but high latency, such as mobile **4G** or servers on other continents.

As usual, you should test for your use case perhaps using Wireshark, as described previously in Chapter 2, *Measuring Performance Bottlenecks*. There are downsides to altering this window, and it should be considered carefully. Although this may speed up websites, it can cause buffers in networking equipment to fill, which can generate latency problems for VoIP applications and games if no **Quality of Service (QoS)** is in use end to end.

You can change this value on Windows Server 2008 R2 with a hotfix (KB2472264) and higher. You can also easily adjust this on Linux, and ASP.NET Core enables you to run your .NET web app on Linux (and Mac OS X) in addition to Windows.

We won't provide detailed instructions here because this should be a cautiously considered decision, and you shouldn't apply advice blindly. You can easily find instructions online for the operating system that you use on your web server.

TCPslow-start is just one example of why you can't ignore the lower levels of Internet technology on the shoulders of which web applications stand. Let's move up the stack a little to the application layer.

HTTP

As a web application developer who wants to deliver high performance, it's important to understand Hypertext Transfer Protocol. You should know what version of HTTP you use, how it works, and how this affects things, such as **request pipelining** and encryption.

HTTP/1.1 is the version that you will probably be most familiar with today because it has been in use for some time. HTTP/2 is becoming more popular, and it changes the best way to do many things.

Headers

HTTP uses headers to provide metadata about a request along with the main payload in the body of the message, much like e-mails do. You won't see these headers when you view the source, but you can observe them using the browser developer tools. You can use headers for many things, such as cache control and authentication. Cookies are also sent and received as headers.

Browsers will only open a limited number of HTTP/1.1 connections at one time to a single host. If you require a lot of requests to retrieve all the assets for a page, then they are queued, which increases the total time taken to fully load it. When combined with the TCP slow-start mentioned previously, this effect can be amplified, degrading the performance. This is less of a problem with HTTP/2, which we will cover shortly. You can reduce the impact of this problem by allowing the browser to reuse connections. You can do this by ensuring that your web server doesn't send a `Connection: close` header with HTTP responses.

HTTP methods

There are multiple methods (or verbs) that HTTP uses. The most common are GET and POST, but there are many more. Typically, we use GET requests to retrieve data from a server, and we use POST to submit data and make changes. GET should not be used to alter data.

Other useful verbs are HEAD and OPTIONS. HEAD can check the headers for a GET request without the overhead of downloading the body. This is useful to check caching headers to see whether the resource has changed. OPTIONS is commonly used for **Cross Origin Resource Sharing** (**CORS**) to perform a preflight check to validate a domain.

Other often used verbs are PUT, DELETE, and PATCH. We mainly use these for **Representational State Transfer** (**REST**) APIs because they can mimic operations on resources or files. However, not all software (such as some proxy servers) understands them, so sometimes, we emulate them using POST. You may even have problems with OPTIONS being blocked by proxies and web servers.

Status codes

HTTP uses numeric response codes to indicate a status. You are probably familiar with 200 (OK) and 404 (Not Found), but there are many others. For example, 451 indicates that the content has been blocked by a government-mandated censorship filter.

The 451 status code is in reference to the book *Fahrenheit 451* (whose title is the purported temperature at which paper burns). You can read the official document (RFC 7725) at tools.ietf.org/html/rfc7725. If this code is not used, then it can be tricky to discover if and why a site is unavailable. For example, you can find out whether the UK government is blocking your site at blocked.org.uk, but this is just a volunteer effort run by the Open Rights Group the British version of the **Electronic Frontier Foundation** (**EFF**).

We commonly use 3xx codes for redirection (perhaps to HTTPS). There are various forms of redirection with different performance characteristics (and other effects). You can use a 302 to temporarily redirect a page, but then the browser has to request the original page every time to see whether the redirect has ended. It also has bad implications for **Search Engine Optimization** (**SEO**), but we won't discuss these here.

A better approach is to use a 301 to indicate a permanent redirect. However, you need to be careful, as this can't be undone and clients won't look at the original URL again. If you use redirects to upgrade users from HTTP to HTTPS, then you should also consider using **HTTP Strict Transport Security (HSTS)** headers. Again, do this carefully.

Encryption

HTTP encryption is very important. It not only secures data in transit to prevent eavesdropping, but it also provides authentication. This ensures that users actually connect to the site that they think they are and that the page wasn't tampered with. Otherwise, unscrupulous internet connection providers can inject or replace adverts on your site, or they can block internet access until you have opted out of a parental filter. Or, these can be worse things, such as stealing your user's data, which you are usually required by law to protect.

There is really no good reason today to not use encryption everywhere. The overheads are tiny, although we will still consider them and show you how to avoid potential issues. Arguments against using HTTPS are usually hangovers from a time long ago when computation was expensive.

Modern computing hardware is very capable and often has special acceleration for common encryption tasks. There are many studies that show that the processing overheads of encryption are negligible. However, there can be a small delay in initially setting up a secure connection for the first time. In order to understand this, it is useful to illustrate a simple model of how TLS works.

There are two parts to secure communication: the initial key exchange and the ongoing encryption of the channel. Session ciphers, such as the **Advanced Encryption Standard (AES)**, can be very quick, and they can operate at close to line speed. However, these ciphers are *symmetrical* and both parties need to know the key. This key needs to be distributed securely so that only the two communicating parties possess it. This is called *key exchange*, and it uses asymmetric encryption. This usually also requires a third party to vouch for the server, so we have a system of certificates. This initial setup is the slow part, although we will show you an alternative for devices that lack the AES acceleration later.

Key exchange

As mentioned previously, key exchange is the process of securely sharing an encryption key between two parties without being intercepted. There are various methods of doing this, which mostly rely on asymmetric encryption. Unlike symmetric encryption (that we exchange this key for), this can only be performed in one direction with a single key. In other words, the key that is used to encrypt cannot be used to decrypt, and a different key is required. This is not the case for the majority of the data once we have shared a key. The reason that we do this is that symmetric encryption is faster than asymmetric encryption. Therefore, it is not used for everything and is only needed to encrypt another key.

In addition to exchanging a key, the browser (or other HTTPS client) should check the certificate to ensure that the server belongs to the domain that it claims to. Some programmatic clients fail to do this by default, so this is worth checking out. You can also implement certificate pinning (even in the browser with **HTTP Public Key Pinning**) to improve security, but this is beyond the scope of this book.

We will illustrate two variations of key exchange by analogy in simplified forms to show you how the process works. You can look up the technical details if you wish.

RSA

RSA is traditionally the most common key-exchange mechanism that is used for TLS. Until recently, we used it on most HTTPS connections.

RSA stands for Rivest-Shamir-Adleman after the names of its creators, and it is probably the most popular form of public key cryptography. The British snooping agency, **Government Communications Headquarters (GCHQ)**, supposedly conceived public key cryptography at around the same time, but as it was only made public in 1997, it's impossible to prove this. The invention credit goes to Whitfield Diffie and Martin Hellman, who recently picked up a Turing Award for it. We'll talk more about their work shortly.

 The Turing Award is the Nobel Prize of computing. It's named after Alan Turing, the legendary computing pioneer who helped the allies win WWII while working for the nascent GCHQ, but who was later betrayed by the British government.

RSA uses large prime numbers to generate a public and private key pair. The public key can be used to encrypt information that can only be decrypted with the private key. In addition to this, the private key can be used to sign information (usually a **hash** of it), which can be verified with the public key. RSA is often used to sign TLS certificates even if another algorithm is used as the key exchange mechanism (this is negotiated during the initial TLS handshake).

 This hashing and signing of certificates is where you may have heard of **SHA-1** certificates being deprecated by browsers. SHA-1 is no longer considered secure for hashing and, like **MD5** before it, should not be used. Certificate chains must now use at least an **SHA-2** hashing algorithm (such as **SHA-256**) to sign.

An analogy to help explain how RSA works is to think of sending a lock instead of sending a key. You can post an open padlock to someone, retaining the key to it. They can then use your lock to secure a case with a key of theirs inside and send it back to you. Now, only you can open the case to get the new key.

In reality, this is more complicated. You can't be sure that someone didn't intercept your lock and then use their own lock to get the key and copy it before sending it on to you. Typically, we solve this with **Public Key Infrastructure** (**PKI**). A trusted third party will sign your certificate and verify that it is indeed your public key and that you own the lock. Browsers typically display a warning if a **Certificate Authority** (**CA**) does not countersign the certificate in this way.

Diffie-Hellman (**D-H**) key exchange is another method of gaining a shared key. Invented shortly before RSA, it has only recently become popular on the web. This is partly due to the reduced computational cost of the **elliptic curve** variant. However, another reason is that the ephemeral versions provide a quality called **Perfect Forward Secrecy** (**PFS**). Unlike RSA, the session key for the symmetric encryption never needs to be transmitted. Both parties can calculate the shared key without it needing to be sent on the wire (even in an encrypted state) or permanently stored. This means that an eavesdropped encrypted exchange cannot be decrypted in the future if the keys were recovered. With RSA key exchange, you can recover a recorded communication in plain text if you obtain the private keys later. PFS a is useful countermeasure against mass surveillance, where all communication is caught in a dragnet and permanently stored.

D-H is better explained with a color mixing analogy, where paints represent numbers. The two parties choose a shared color, and each party chooses a secret color of their own. Both mix the shared color with their secret color and send the result to the other. Each party then mixes the color that they received with their secret color again. Both parties now have the same color without ever having to send this color anywhere where it could be observed.

As this is not a book about security, we won't go into any more detail on encryption algorithms. If you are interested, there is a huge amount of information available that we can't cover here. Encryption is a large subject, but security is an even broader concern.

TLS handshake

The point of briefly explaining how TLS key exchange works for various methods is to show that it is complex. Many messages need to be sent back and forth to establish a secure connection, and no matter how fast the connection, latency slows down every message. This all occurs in the TLS handshake, where the client (usually a web browser) and server negotiate common capabilities and agree on what ciphers they should use. There is also **Server Name Indication** (**SNI**) to consider, which is similar to the HTTP host header in that it allows multiple sites to use the same IP address. Some older clients don't support SNI.

We can observe the TLS handshake using Wireshark. We won't go into a huge amount of detail, but you can see that at least four messages are exchanged between the client and server. These are client hello, server hello (including the certificate and server key exchange), client key exchange, and cipher agreement. The browser may send more messages if we do not optimally configured things, such as requesting an intermediate certificate. This may also check a revocation list to see whether the certificate was revoked.

The following screenshot shows a TLS handshake captured with Wireshark:

```
TLSv1     223 Client Hello
TCP      1502 [TCP segment of a reassembled PDU]
TCP      1502 [TCP segment of a reassembled PDU]
TCP        54 2697 → 443 [ACK] Seq=170 Ack=2897 Win=66048 Len=0
TLSv1    1002 Server Hello, Certificate, Server Key Exchange, Server Hello Done
TLSv1     220 Client Key Exchange, Change Cipher Spec, Encrypted Handshake Message
TLSv1     113 Change Cipher Spec, Encrypted Handshake Message
TLSv1     283 Application Data
```

All these network operations happen quickly. However, if the connection has a high latency, then these extra messages can have an amplified effect on performance. The computational delays are typically much smaller than the network delays, so we can discount these, unless you use very old hardware. Fortunately, there are some simple things you can do that will help speed things up and let you enjoy high performance while still being secure.

Delay diagnostics

There are various mechanisms that are built into TLS that can you can use to speed it up. However, there are also things that will slow it down if you don't do them correctly. Some great free online tools to assess your TLS configuration are available from Qualys SSL Labs at `ssllabs.com`. The server test at `ssllabs.com/ssltest` is very useful. You enter a URL, and they give you a grade along with lots of other information.

For example, if we analyze the `packtpub.com` site, we can see that on the date of the test it got a **B** grade. This is due to supporting weak Diffie-Hellman parameters and the obsolete and insecure **RC4** cipher. However, it is not always as simple as removing old ciphers. You can have a very secure site, but you might exclude some of your customers, who use older clients that don't support the latest standards. This will, of course, vary depending on the nature of your client base, and you should measure your traffic and consider your options carefully.

The following screenshot shows some of the report from SSL Labs for `packtpub.com`.

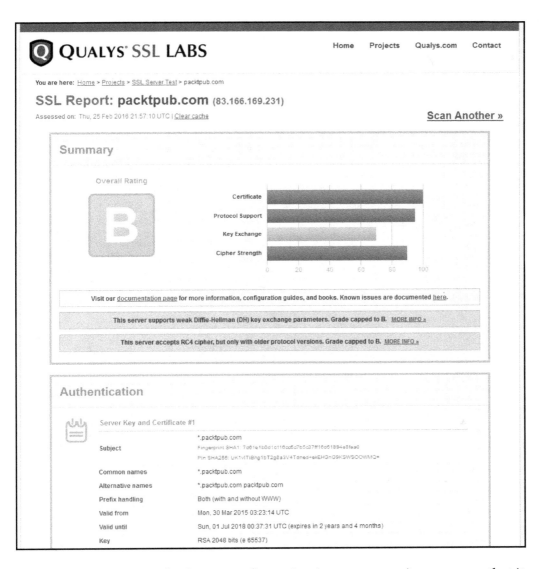

If we have a look at a site with a better configuration (`emoncms.org`), we can see that it gets an **A** grade. You can get an A+ grade using HSTS headers. Additionally, these headers avoid the overhead of a redirect. You may also be able to get your site embedded in a preloaded list shipped with browsers if you submit the domains to the vendors.

The following screenshot shows some of the report from SSL Labs for `emoncms.org`:

The options chosen by modern browsers would typically be an **Elliptic Curve Diffie-Hellman Ephemeral key exchange (ECDHE)** with an RSA SHA-256 signature and AES session cipher. The ephemeral keys provide PFS because they are only held in memory for the session. You can see what connection has been negotiated by looking in your browser.

In Firefox, you can do this by clicking on the lock icon in the URL bar and then clicking on the **More Information** button, as shown in the following image:

In the **Technical Details** section, you will see the cipher suite used. The following image from Firefox shows ECDHE key exchange and RSA certificate signing:

Technical Details
Connection Encrypted (TLS_ECDHE_RSA_WITH_AES_128_GCM_SHA256, 128 bit keys, TLS 1.2)

You can also view the certificate details by clicking on the **View Certificate** button. The domain is usually included as the **Common Name (CN)** in the **Subject** field. Alternative domains can also be included under the **Certificate Subject Alt Name** extension:

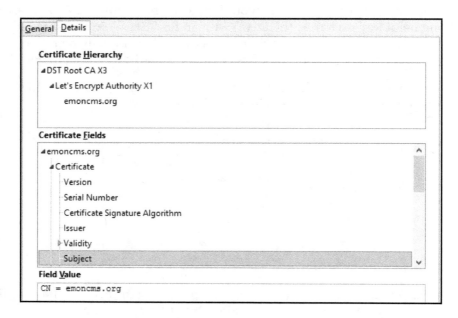

In Chrome, you can look at the TLS connection information in the **Security** tab of the developer tools. For example, the following image displays the security details for `huxley.unop.uk`:

The following screenshot displays the same window for emoncms.org:

You may need to refresh the page to see TLS information if the site was already loaded when you opened the developer tools. You can access the same tab by clicking on the padlock in the Chrome URL bar and then clicking on the **Details** link.

You can view the certificate (in the native operating system certificate store) by clicking on the **Open full certificate details** button. A link with the same function exists on the equivalent screen of Chrome for Android, although the certificate information is reduced.

Performance tweaks

We already discussed the most important performance tweak for TLS because it is not about TLS. You should ensure that your HTTP connections are reusable, because if this is not the case, then you will incur the added penalty of the TLS negotiation along with the TCP overhead. Caching is also very important, and we will talk more about this later.

TLS and HTTP both support compression, but these have security implications. Therefore, consider them carefully. They can leak information, and a determined adversary can use an analysis of them to recover encrypted data. TLS compression is deprecated, and it will be removed in TLS 1.3. Therefore, do not use it. We will discuss HTTP compression later on in this chapter.

In regard to specific advice for TLS, there are a few things, which you can do to improve performance. The main technique is to ensure that you use **session resumption**. This is different to reusing HTTP connections, and this means that clients can reuse an existing TLS connection without having to go through the whole key exchange.

 You can implement sessions with IDs on the server or with encrypted tickets (in a similar manner to ASP.NET cookies that are encrypted with the machine key). There was a bug in the Microsoft client implementation around ticket encryption key rotation, but the **KB3109853** patch fixed it. Make sure that you install this update, especially if you see exceptions thrown when connecting to secure endpoints from your .NET code.

It is important to not overdo things and bigger is not always better, especially when it comes to key size. It is a trade-off between performance and security, and this will depend on your specific situation. In general, a good balance is not using 256 bit AES keys when 128 bit will do.

A 2048 bit RSA key is big enough, lower is insecure and larger is too slow. You can use the **Elliptic Curve Digital Signature Algorithm** (**ECDSA**) to sign instead of RSA, as it is much quicker. However, support is limited, so you would need to deploy RSA in parallel.

If you use ECDSA, then a 256 bit key is sufficient. For ECDHE, 256 bit is also fine, and for the slower version without elliptic curves (DHE), 2048 bit is sufficient. If you use ECDSA, then you will see this listed instead of the RSA signing in the connection details. For example, when visiting `huxley.unop.uk`, the details in the following screenshots are displayed in Firefox. This difference is also displayed in the previous Chrome screenshots:

Technical Details

Connection Encrypted (TLS_ECDHE_ECDSA_WITH_AES_128_GCM_SHA256, 128 bit keys, TLS 1.2)

Additionally, it is important to include the full certificate chain with your certificate. If you fail to include all intermediate certificates, then the browser will need to download them until it finds one in its trusted root store. You can also use a technique called **Online Certificate Status Protocol** (**OCSP**) stapling, by embedding revocation data so browsers don't need to check a certificate revocation list.

Both of these certificate techniques may increase the size of payloads, which can be an issue if bandwidth is a concern. However, they will reduce the number of messages, which will increase performance if latency is the main problem, which is usually the case. Keeping key sizes small also helps a little with bandwidth. It is hard to recommend one generic approach. Therefore, as always, test for your unique situation.

There is also an alternative stream cipher called **ChaCha/Poly**, which is especially useful for mobile devices. This uses the **ChaCha20**stream cipher and the **Poly1305 Message Authentication Code** (**MAC**) algorithm to create a secure alternative to RC4. AES is a block cipher and is fast with hardware support, but many mobile devices and some older computers don't have this acceleration. ChaCha/Poly is faster when using just software. Therefore, this is better for battery life. This is supported in Chrome, including Chrome for Android, and in Firefox (from version 47).

 As all algorithms are different, you can't directly compare key sizes as a measure of how secure they are. For example, a 256 bit ECDHE key is equivalent to a 3072 bit RSA key. AES is very secure with relatively small keys, but you cannot use it for key exchange. ChaCha/Poly is more comparable to the security of AES 256 than AES 128.

In the following screenshot of Chrome on Android, you can see that when connecting to `huxley.unop.uk`, Chrome uses **CHACHA20_POLY1305** as the stream cipher, ECDHE for the key exchange, and ECDSA for the signature:

The new version of TLS (1.3) is still a draft, but it may be finalized soon. It looks like it will only allow **Authenticated Encryption with Additional Data** (**AEAD**) ciphers. AES-GCM and ChaCha/Poly are the only two ciphers that currently meet these criteria. It will also remove some other obsolete features, such as TLS compression.

It may sometimes sound like using TLS is not always worth it, but it is an excellent idea to use HTTPS on your entire site, including any third-party resources that you load in. By doing this, you will be able to take advantage of the performance enhancing features of HTTP/2, which include techniques that mean that it is no longer crucial to serve resources (such as JavaScript libraries) from multiple domains. You can securely host everything yourself and avoid the DNS, TCP, and TLS overhead of additional requests. All of this can also be free because *Let's Encrypt* and *CloudFlare* provide certificates at zero cost. Let's look at HTTP/2 in detail now.

HTTP/2

As the name suggests, HTTP/2 is the new version of HTTP. It contains some significant performance improvements for the modern web. It was predated by **SPDY**, which has since been deprecated in favor of HTTP/2.

As mentioned previously, the first step toward using HTTP/2 is to use HTTPS on your entire site. Although not technically required, most clients (all the major browsers) mandate the use of TLS to enable HTTP/2. This is mainly due to the **Application-Layer Protocol Negotiation** (**ALPN**) that TLS provides, which allows easy support for HTTP/2. It also stops proxy servers from messing up the data, which many ISPs use to reduce their costs and record what their customers do online.

HTTP/2 improves performance in a number of ways. It uses compression even for the headers, and multiplexing, which allows multiple requests to share the same connection. It also allows the server to push resources that it knows the client will need before the client has realized it needs them. Although, this requires some configuration to set the correct headers and it can waste bandwidth if it is overused.

Multiplexing has implications for bundling and image concatenation (**sprites**), which we will talk about in the compression section later on in this chapter. This also means that you don't need to split assets over multiple domains (**shards**), where the extra overheads may even slow things down. However, you may still wish to use a cookie-free subdomain to serve static assets without cookies, even though the new header compression means that the bandwidth savings will be smaller. If you use a naked domain (without a www), then you may need a new domain name for cookie-less use.

You can identify what version of HTTP is used to deliver your assets using the browser developer tools. In Firefox, you can see this on the details panel of the network tab. You will see the version listed as HTTP/1.1 when the old protocol is in use.

The following screenshot shows that `packtpub.com` uses **HTTP/1.1**:

In Chrome, you can right-click on the column headers in the network inspector and add a **Protocol** column. You can also see more detailed network information by entering `chrome://net-internals` into the address bar. This displays things, such as sessions for HTTP/2 and **Quick UDP Internet Connections** (**QUIC**)âⓔⓔan experimental multiplexed stream transport.

The following screenshot shows that `emoncms.org` also uses **HTTP/1.1**, even though TLS is configured differently. The encrypted transport layer is transparent to HTTP:

When HTTP/2 is used, you will see the version listed as **HTTP/2.0**. The following screenshot displays this for `huxley.unop.uk`, and it also displays CORS, caching, and content compression headers:

WebSockets

WebSockets is a different protocol to HTTP. However, HTTP initiates it and it uses the same ports, so we'll discuss it briefly here. This HTML5 feature is useful for **push notifications** and **Real Time Communication (RTC)** applications. WebSockets use the `ws://` and `wss://` protocol prefixes instead of `http://` and `https://`. Once established by an existing HTTP connection, the protocol is full-duplex and binary in contrast to HTTP/1.

Before WebSockets, if your web server wanted to notify a client of a change, then you would have to use a technique, such as long polling. This is where a web request is held open by the server in case it wants to send something. When the request gets a response or it times-out, it is re-established. Needless to say, polling is never very efficient.

Push notifications can improve performance from a user's point of view because they receive updates as soon as they occur. They don't need to refresh anything or keep checking. You can immediately respond to the user when a long running process starts, run it asynchronously, and notify them immediately upon its completion.

Socket.IO is a popular WebSocket library for Node.js. To see it in action, you can look in the browser developer tools on a site that uses it. For example, if you open the dev tools and go to `https://www.opentraintimes.com/maps/signalling/staines`, you will see the connection being upgraded from HTTPS to WSS (or from HTTP to WS if you use the insecure version).

WebSockets predate HTTP/2, but they are still relevant despite the new server push technology. These two features appear similar, but they serve different purposes. WebSockets are for real-time and two-way data transfers, and server push is currently just to preload.

 In addition to HTTP/2 server push preloading, there is a new browser feature that is currently supported in Android, Chrome, and Opera, which allows you to declare resource preloading in markup using `rel="preload"` on a `link` tag. You can read the spec at `w3c.github.io/preload` and check the current state of browser support at `caniuse.com/#feat=link-rel-preload`.

In Chrome, the protocol switch will look something like the following screenshot. You can't see the contents of a WebSocket connection, so you won't be able to view the data being transferred from within the dev tools:

```
▼ General
    Request URL: wss://data.opentraintimes.com/socket.io/?EIO=3&transport=websocket
    Request Method: GET
    Status Code: ● 101 Switching Protocols
▼ Response Headers          view source
    Connection: upgrade
    Date: Sat, 27 Feb 2016 16:19:09 GMT
    Sec-WebSocket-Accept: GfOqW7FtWTX9yflqYhgJ1z2VJ8g=
    Sec-WebSocket-Extensions: permessage-deflate
    Server: nginx/1.8.1
    Upgrade: websocket
▼ Request Headers           view source
    Accept-Encoding: gzip, deflate, sdch
    Accept-Language: en-US,en;q=0.8,en-GB;q=0.6
    Cache-Control: no-cache
    Connection: Upgrade
```

There is a Microsoft library for ASP.NET, which is called `SignalR`. This library allows you to perform push notifications with WebSockets. It also falls back to long polling if the client or server does not support them. You will need a fairly recent version of Windows Server (2012 or later) and IIS (8.0 and above) to use WebSockets.

Unfortunately, the latest stable version (`SignalR 2`) does not support .NET Core. The new version (`SignalR 3`) is not planned for release until after the **Release to manufacturing** (**RTM**) of ASP.NET Core, but this is a top priority. You can try a beta version, but it may be stable by the time you read this.

 You may also wish to look at `StackExchange.NetGain` as a WebSocket server.

Compression

Data compression is a broad topic, and we can't hope to cover it all. Here, we will learn about lossless compression and how to use it in HTTP. We will also cover lossy image compression of pictures later in the chapter. Compression is important because if we can make files smaller, we can shorten the time that it takes to transfer them over a network.

Lossless compression algorithms

You may have noticed HTTP headers from some of the previous screenshots were related to encoding. The most common compression algorithms for HTTP are gzip and **DEFLATE**, which are very similar. These are both related to the algorithm used in ZIP files. If you do not already use HTTP compression, then this is a quick win, and it will improve the performance of your site if you enable it.

There are many other more advanced compression algorithms, such as **xz**, which is similar to the **7-Zip (7z)** format and uses the **Lempel-Ziv-Markov chain Algorithm (LZMA/LZMA2)**. However, there are currently only two additional algorithms in common use in major browsers. These are **Brotli** and **Shared Dictionary Compression for HTTP (SDCH)**. Both are from Google, but only Chrome supports SDCH, and it requires a large dictionary.

Brotli is more interesting, and Opera and Chrome (currently behind a `chrome://flags/#enable-brotli` flag), and Firefox by default (version 44 or higher) support it. Both browsers require the use of HTTPS to support Brotli (yet another good reason to use TLS), and the encoding token used in the headers is `br`. Brotli promises significant performance improvements, especially for mobile devices on slow connections.

If you access a site over HTTP, you will see the following for the request headers in the Chrome dev tools network inspector in the details of a request:

```
Accept-Encoding: gzip, deflate, sdch
```

However, if you use HTTPS then you will see this instead (after enabling the flag):

```
Accept-Encoding: gzip, deflate, sdch, br
```

The server can then respond with Brotli-encoded content using this response header:

```
Content-Encoding: br
```

For example, if you visit `https://www.bayden.com/test/brotliimg.aspx` in a supported browser, then Brotli will deliver the content (an image of a star). Here is a subset (for clarity and brevity) of the request headers from Chrome:

```
GET /test/brotliimg.aspx HTTP/1.1
Host: www.bayden.com
Connection: keep-alive
Accept-Encoding: gzip, deflate, sdch, br
```

This is a subset of the corresponding response headers:

```
HTTP/1.1 200 OK
Content-Type: image/png
Content-Encoding: br
Server: Microsoft-IIS/7.5
X-AspNet-Version: 4.0.30319
YourAcceptEncoding: gzip, deflate, sdch, br
```

Fiddler (the awesome HTTP debugging proxy by Eric Lawrence that we mentioned previously) also supports Brotli with a simple add-on (drop `https://bayden.com/dl/Br otli.exe` into `fiddler2\tools` and restart it). You can use this to easily test the impact on your site without deploying anything to your web servers.

Bundling and minification

Bundling and minification are techniques that you may already be familiar with. They speed up the delivery of static assets. They are usually used for text files, such as JavaScript and CSS content.

Bundling

Bundling is the technique of combining or concatenating multiple files together so that they can be delivered as one. This is a good idea when using HTTP/1.1 because the number of concurrent connections is limited. However, bundling is less necessary with HTTP/2, and in fact, it can reduce performance. The new multiplexing in HTTP/2 means that there is no longer a large penalty when you request many files instead of one that contain all of the same content. You can take advantage of this by only delivering what is needed for a page rather than the entire client side codebase for every page. Even if you selectively bundle per page, this could be inefficient.

For example, you may include a validation library for use with forms. However, because this is bundled, it will be sent to all pages, including the ones with no forms to validate. If you have a separate bundle for validated pages, then there may be duplication in the common core code that is also sent. By keeping things separated, the client can cache them individually and reuse components. This also means that if you change something, you only need to invalidate the cache of this one part. The client can keep using the other unmodified parts and not have to redownload them.

As always, you should measure for your particular use case. You may find that bundling still reduces the total file size. The overheads for HTTP/2 are much lower but still not zero, and compression can work better on larger files. However, keep in mind the implications for caching and reusability.

Minification

Minification is the process of reducing the file size of a textual static asset. We do this by various means, including stripping out comments, removing whitespace, and shortening variable names. It can also be useful to *obfuscate* code to make it harder to reverse engineer. Minification is still useful when you use HTTP/2, but you should be careful when testing to compare preminified and postminified files size after the lossless compression has also been applied.

As discussed previously, you should use HTTP content compression with at least the gzip or DEFLATE algorithms. These are pretty efficient; so, you may find that when compressed, your minified file is not much smaller than the compressed raw source file.

Changes in ASP.NET Core

In the full .NET Framework and previous versions of MVC, there was an integrated bundling and minification system. This has changed for ASP.NET Core, and there are new tools to perform this work.

The new tools that were adopted include the task runner gulp, although you can use Grunt if you prefer to. Also, a generator tool called Yeoman is used for scaffolding. There are now package managers, such as **Bower** and **npm**, which are similar to NuGet, but for frontend libraries. For example, NuGet no longer delivers jQuery and Twitter Bootstrap, and they use Bower instead by default.

Most of these tools are written in JavaScript, and they run on Node.js. The package manager for Node.js is npm. These tools are popular in other open source web frameworks, and they are well established. They're not new to the scene, only new to .NET.

Gulp packages come from npm and are responsible for the minification of your static assets. This is now done at build time, as opposed to request time, as was previously the case. It works much more like a static site generator than a dynamic web application. A gulp file (`gulpfile.js`) in the root of your project configures these tasks using JavaScript.

The new tooling is not only restricted to ASP.NET Core, and you can use these features with traditional ASP.NET applications in Visual Studio. This is a good example of the cross-pollination and benefits that the new frameworks can provide to the existing ones.

Image optimization

Digital media compression is much more complicated than the lossless file compression that we talked about previously even if we just stick to images. We briefly mentioned when to use PNG and when to use JPEG in the previous chapter. Here, we'll go into much more detail and explore some other exotic options.

We covered the rule of thumb, which says that PNG is the best image format for icons and JPEG is better for photos. These two formats are the most common for lossless and lossy image compression, respectively.

We will talk more about other image formats later, but you are usually constrained to the popular formats by what browsers support. So, how can you get more out of the common choices?

PNG

Portable Network Graphics (**PNG**) is a lossless image compression format that internally works similarly to a ZIP file (using the DEFLATE algorithm). It's a good choice for images that contain solid blocks of color, and it has a better quality (with more colors) than the old **Graphics Interchange Format** (**GIF**).

PNG supports transparency in all modern browsers, so you should use it instead of GIF for static images. This is not a problem unless you need to support Internet Explorer 6, in which case this is probably the least of your troubles. PNG also supports animation with **Animated PNG** (**APNG**) files. These are like animated GIFs but of a much higher quality. Unfortunately, only Firefox and Safari support APNGs.

 A great site to look up which browsers support a particular feature is caniuse.com. You can search for feature support, then check this against the user agent analytics of your site. For example, you could search for PNG-alpha, Brotli, or APNG.

Some ZIP algorithm implementations are better than others, and they produce smaller files that can still be decoded by everyone. For example, 7-Zip is much more efficient than most other zip compression software on Windows, even when using the ZIP format, not its native 7z format. Likewise, you can compress a PNG more compactly without losing any data and still have it work in all browsers. This usually comes with a higher upfront computational cost. However, if you compress static assets, which rarely change, then it can be well worth the effort.

You may already use the PNGOUT tool to losslessly reduce the size of your PNG images. If you're not, then you probably should. You can read more about it and download it at `advsys.net/ken/utils.htm`.

However, there is a new algorithm called Zopfli that offers better compression, but it is very slow to compress. Decompression is just as quick, so it's only a single optimization cost for precompiled resources. Zopfli is a precursor to Brotli, but it's compatible with DEFLATE and gzip, as it's not a new format.

You can get Zopfli from `github.com/google/zopfli`, but you should always test with your images and verify that there is indeed a file size reduction. You will find that these tools can help you deliver your assets quicker and achieve higher performance.

You may also use the practice of combining many sprites into one image. As with bundling, this is less necessary when using HTTP/2. However, the same caveats apply as with compression, and you should always test for your set of images.

JPEG

JPEG is a lossy image compression format, which means that it usually discards data from the picture to make it smaller. It is best suited to natural gradients and continuous tones, such as those found in photographs. JPEG does not support transparency like PNG does, so if you want to use one on different backgrounds, then you will need to prerender them.

 It's a good space saving idea to remove the **Exchangeable image file format (Exif)** metadata from your JPEG files for the web. This contains information about the camera used and geographic data of where the photo was taken.

JPEG has a quality setting, which affects the image file size and the level of detail. The lower the quality, the smaller the file, but the worse it will look. You can perform tests on your images to see what settings provide an acceptable trade-off. Crucially, the best value for this quality setting will vary per image, depending on the content. There are tools that allow you to automatically detect the optimal quality level, such as Google's butteraugli.

There is an interesting project from Mozilla (the makers of the Firefox browser) called **mozjpeg**. This aims to better compress JPEG images and is similar to what PNGOUT and Zopfli do for PNG images. You can use mozjpeg to compress your JPEG images to a smaller size than normal, without affecting decompression or quality. It is available at `github.com/mozilla/mozjpeg`, but you will need to compile it yourself. As always, results may vary, so test it for the photos on your site.

JPEG Archive (`github.com/danielgtaylor/jpeg-archive`) is a handy tool that uses mozjpeg to compress JPEG images, using various comparison metrics. Another similar tool is imgmin (`github.com/rflynn/imgmin`), which is slightly older.

Other image formats

Many other image formats are available, but you are usually limited on the web by what browsers support. As discussed in the previous chapter, you shouldn't scale images in the browser, or you will get poor performance. This usually means having to save multiple separate copies of smaller images, for example, when displaying thumbnails. Clearly this results in duplication, which is inefficient. Some of these new image formats have clever solutions to the problem of responsive and scalable images.

BPG is an image format by the talented Fabrice Bellard, and you can read more about it at `bellard.org/bpg`. It has a JavaScript polyfill to support browsers before native support is added to any of them.

WebP is an image format from Google, and only Chrome, Android, and Opera support it. It has impressive space savings over JPEG, and it will be a good choice if it becomes more widely supported, so check `caniuse.com` for the latest adoption stats.

JPEG2000 is an improved version of JPEG, although it may be encumbered by software patents, so it hasn't seen widespread adoption outside of medical imaging. Only Safari supports JPEG2000, and there is also JPEG XR, which is only supported in IE.

Whereas JPEG uses a **Discrete Cosine Transform** (**DCT**), JPEG2000 is based on a Wavelet Transform. One of the properties this provides is a *progressive* download. This means that the image is stored in such a way that if you download a small part from the beginning of the file, then you have a smaller and lower quality version of the full image. This has obvious applications for responsive and scalable images. The browser would only need to download enough of the image to fill the area it is rendering to, and the file need only be stored once. No resizing and no duplication for thumbnails would be required. This technique is also used in the **Free Lossless Image Format** (**FLIF**).

FLIF is one of the more exciting upcoming image formats, as it is progressive and responsive, but free and not patented. FLIF is still in development, but it promises to be very useful if browsers support it, and you can read more about it at `flif.info`.

 JPEG and PNG can support progressive download, but this isn't normally useful for responsive images. Progressive JPEG subjectively loads more gracefully and can even make files smaller, but interlaced PNG usually makes files bigger.

The problem is that most of these progressive image formats are not yet ready for the mainstream because all of the major browsers do not support them. It's a good idea to keep an eye on the future, but for now, we need to resize images for high performance.

Resizing images

Until new image formats gain widespread adoption, resizing is still required, and you may need to do this dynamically for different devices. Perhaps, you also have user-submitted image content, although you need to be very careful with this from a security point of view. Some image libraries are not safe, and a specially-crafted image can exploit your system. In fact, many image-processing libraries have issues when they are used in a web context.

If you are not extremely diligent and careful, then you can easily end up with memory leaks, which can take down your web server. It is always a good idea to separate and sandbox a process that deals with large media files.

Coming from a .NET standpoint, it can be tempting to use WinForms `System.Drawing` or its WPF successor (`System.Windows.Media`). However, these were designed for desktop software, and Microsoft strongly recommends against using them in a service or web application. Microsoft recommends the **Windows Imaging Component** (**WIC**), but this is a **Component Object Model** (**COM**) API that is meant for use from C or C++ apps. In addition to this, none of these imaging libraries are cross-platform, so they are not suitable for use in .NET Core.

If you use Windows, then you could try using ImageResizer by Imazen (`imazen.io`), from `imageresizing.net`. While it still uses the **GDI+** `System.Drawing`, it is pretty battle hardened, so most of the bugs should have been worked out. There's also **DynamicImage**, which wraps the newer WPF image functions and uses shaders. You can read more about it at `dynamicimage.apphb.com`, although it hasn't been updated in a while, and it doesn't support .NET Core.

A popular option in open source circles is ImageMagick, which we've mentioned previously, and a fork called **GraphicsMagick**, which claims to be more efficient. Another popular image library is **LibGD**, and it's suitable for server use. You can read more at `libgd.github.io`. Although it's written in C, there are wrappers for other programming languages, for example, **DotnetGD** targeting .NET Core.

One of the features that .NET Core lacks is that there is not yet a compelling option for image processing. ImageResizer 5 may help with this when released, so it is worth keeping an eye on it. Native code support is now much better in .NET Core, as it was a pain to do in classic .NET, which may help with integrating native cross-platform imaging libraries.

There is also a new cross-platform version of the open source **ImageProcessor** libraries (`imageprocessor.org`), called **ImageProcessorCore**, which shows promise. However, this is still a work in progress, and it is not yet stable. If you want to try it out, then you can get the nightly packages from MyGet or build it from source.

 Platform support and compatibility changes rapidly, so check `ANCLAFS.com` for the latest information. Feel free to contribute to this list or to the projects.

For now, it may be easier to install an open source service, such as Thumbor, or use a cloud-based imaging service, such as ImageEngine (`WURFL.io`) or Cloudinary, which we've already mentioned. Image manipulation is a common task, and it is effectively a solved problem. It may be better to use an existing solution and not reinvent the wheel, unless it's part of your core business or you have very unusual requirements.

 Once you have your resized images, you can load them responsively with the `picture` and `source` tags using the `srcset` and `sizes` attributes. You can also use this technique to provide newer image formats (such as WebP), with a fallback for browsers that don't yet support them. Or you can use **Client Hints** (refer to `httpwg.org/http-extensions/client-hints.html` and `caniuse.com/#feat=client-hints-dpr-width-viewport`).

Caching

It is often said (originally by Phil Karlton) that caching is one of the hardest problems in computer science, along with naming things. This may well be an exaggeration, but caching is certainly difficult. It can also be very frustrating to debug if you are not methodical and precise in your approach.

Caching can apply at various different levels from the browser to the server using many diverse technologies. You rarely use just a single cache even if you don't realize it. Multiple caches don't always work well together, and it's vexing if you can't clear one.

We briefly touched upon caching in the previous chapter, and we'll go into much more detail in Chapter 7, *Learning Caching and Message Queuing*. However, as caching has an impact on network performance, we'll cover it here as well.

Browser

A lot of caching happens in the web browser, which is inconvenient because as you don't have direct control over it (unless it's your browser). Asking users to clear their cache is unsatisfactory and confusing to many. Yet, you can exert influence on how browsers cache resources by carefully controlling the HTTP headers that you set and the URLs that you use.

If you fail to declare what resources are cacheable and for how long, then many browsers will just guess this. The heuristics for this can be wildly different between implementations. Therefore, this will result in suboptimal performance. You should be explicit and always declare cache information even (and especially) for assets that shouldn't be cached by marking them as noncacheable.

 You need to be vigilant with what you advertise as cacheable because if you are careless, then you can get yourself into a situation where you're unable to update a resource. You should have a cache-busting strategy in place, and tested, before using caching.

There are various technologies that are used are to cache in browsers. Many different HTTP headers can be set, such as Age, Cache-Control, ETag (Entity Tag), Expires, and Last-Modified. These come from a few different standards, and the interactions can be complex, or they vary between browsers. We will explain these in more detail in Chapter 7, *Learning Caching and Message Queuing*.

Another technique is to use a unique URL for content. If a URL changes, then a browser will treat it as a different resource, but if it is the same, then it may load it from its local cache. Some frameworks calculate a hash of the file contents, and then they use this as a query string parameter. This way, when the contents of the file changes, so does the URL.

There are other and more modern features that you can use to cache, such as the **HTML5 Application Cache** (or **AppCache**). This was designed for offline web applications and wasn't very flexible. Busting the cache was complicated to put it mildly. AppCache is already deprecated, and you should use **Service Workers** instead. These provide much more flexibility, although support is pretty recent.

There are many improvements coming, in the latest browsers that give you more control, and we'll also show you how to use them in `Chapter 7`, *Learning Caching and Message Queuing*.

Server

The web server is a great place to cache because it is usually under your complete control. However, it's not really part of network performance, apart from generating the correct headers. There can be other great performance benefits with server-side caching in terms of improving the speed to generate pages, but we will cover these in later chapters.

If you use the traditional .NET Framework on Microsoft's **Internet Information Services (IIS)** web server, then you can use **output caching** from within your application. This will take care of setting the correct headers and sending 304 (Not Modified) responses to browser requests. It will also cache the output on the server in memory, on disk or using Memcached/Redis. You can add attributes to your controller action methods to control the caching options, but other ways of doing this are available, for example, in the configuration files.

`OutputCache` is not available in ASP.NET Core, but you can use `ResponseCache` to set the correct headers. The output is not cached on the server, but you can install a caching proxy in front of it. Again, we will cover this more and demonstrate server-side caching in `Chapter 7`, *Learning Caching and Message Queuing*.

If you want to disable caching on an ASP.NET Core page, then add this annotation to your controller action:

```
[ResponseCache(NoStore = true, Duration = 0)]
```

This will set the following header on the HTTP response and ensure that it is not cached:

```
Cache-Control: no-store
```

To cache a page for an hour, add the following instead, `Duration` is in seconds:

```
[ResponseCache(Duration = 3600, VaryByHeader = "Accept")]
```

The cache control header will then look like the following:

```
Cache-Control: public,max-age=3600
```

There's plenty more to say about other caching configuration options and profiles. Therefore, if you're interested, then read the later chapters. It's a complex topic, and we've only scratched the surface here.

You can read documentation about response caching in ASP.NET Core at `docs.asp.net/en/latest/performance/caching/response.html`.

These caching directives not only instruct the browser, but they also instruct any proxies on the way. Some of these may be in your infrastructure if you have a caching proxy, such as Squid, Varnish, or HAProxy. Or perhaps, you have a TLS-terminating load balancer (such as **Azure Application Gateway**) to reduce the load on your web servers that also caches. You can forcibly flush the caches of servers that you control, but there may be other caches in between you and your users where you can't do this.

Proxy servers between you and your users

There can be many proxy servers between you and your users over which you have no direct control. They may ignore your caching requests, block parts of your site, or even modify your content. The way to solve these problems is to use TLS, as we have already discussed. TLS creates a secure tunnel so that the connection between your infrastructure and the browser can't easily be tampered with.

Corporate proxies commonly **Man in the Middle attack** (**MitM**) your connection to the user so that they can spy on what employees are doing online. This involves installing a custom-trusted root certificate on users' workstations so that your certificate can be faked. Unfortunately, there isn't much you can do about this, apart from educating users. **Certificate pinning** is effective in native apps, but it's not so useful for web applications. **HTTP Public Key Pinning** (**HPKP**) is available but, as it is a **Trust on First Use** (**TOFU**) technique, the initial connection could be intercepted. Client certificates are another option, but they can be difficult to distribute, and they aren't commonly used.

MitM can be useful if you trust the third party and remain in control. This is used by some **Content Delivery Networks** (**CDNs**) to speed up your site.

CDNs

CDNs can improve the performance of your site by storing copies of your content at locations closer to your users. Services, such as the ones provided by CloudFlare, perform a MitM on your connection and save copies at data centers around the world. The difference from an unauthorized proxy is that you control the configuration, and you can purge the cache whenever you like.

You should be careful because if you don't use the caching features, then this can reduce the responsiveness of your site due to the extra hops involved. Make sure that you monitor the response times with and without a CDN, and you need a fallback plan in case they go down.

Another common use case for CDNs is to distribute popular libraries, for example, the jQuery JavaScript library. There are free CDNs from jQuery (MaxCDN), Google, Microsoft, and cdnjs (CloudFlare) that do this. The hypothesis is that a user may already have the library from one of these in their cache. However, you should be extremely careful that you trust the provider and connection. When you load a third-party script into your site, you are effectively giving them full control over it or at least relying on them to always be available.

If you choose to use a CDN, then ensure that it uses HTTPS to avoid tampering with scripts. You should use explicit `https://` URLs on your secure pages or at least protocol agnostic URLS (`//`), and never `http://`. Otherwise, you will get mixed content warnings, which some browsers display as totally unencrypted or even block.

You will need a fallback that is hosted on your own servers anyway in case the CDN goes down. If you use HTTP/2, then you may find that there is no advantage to using a CDN. Obviously, always test for your situation.

There are some useful new features in ASP.NET Core views to easily enable local fallback for CDN resources. We'll show you how to use them and other features in later chapters.

Summary

In this chapter, you learned how to improve performance at the network level between the edge of your infrastructure and your users. You now know more about the internet protocols under your application and how to optimize your use of them for best effect.

You learned how to take advantage of compression to shrink text and image files. This will reduce bandwidth and speed up delivery of assets. We also highlighted caching, and you should now see how important it is. We'll cover caching more in `Chapter 7`, *Learning Caching and Message Queuing*.

In the next chapter, you will learn how to optimize the performance inside your infrastructure. You will see how to deal with I/O latency, and how to write well-performing SQL.

5
Optimizing I/O Performance

This chapter addresses issues that often occur when you take your functionally tested application and split it up into parts for deployment. Your web servers host the frontend code, your database is somewhere else in the data center, you may have a **Storage Area Network (SAN)** for centralized files, an app server for APIs, and the virtual disks are all on different machines as well.

These changes add significant latency to many common operations and your application now becomes super slow, probably because it's too chatty over the network. In this chapter, you will learn how to fix these issues by batching queries together, and performing work on the best server for the job. Even if everything runs on one machine, the skills that you'll learn here will help to improve performance by increasing efficiency.

The topics covered in this chapter include the following:

- The operations that can be slow
- Select N+1 problems in detail
- Returning only what you need
- Writing high-performance SQL

You will learn about the operations that you shouldn't use synchronously, and how to query for getting only the data that you need in an efficient manner. You'll also see how to tame your O/RM, and learn to write high-performance SQL with **Dapper**.

We briefly covered some of these topics in Chapter 3, *Fixing Common Performance Problems*, but here we'll dive into greater detail. The first half of this chapter will focus on background knowledge and using diagnostic tools, while the second half will show you solutions to issues you may come across. You'll also learn about some more unusual problems, and how to fix or alleviate them.

We'll initially focus on understanding the issues, because if you don't appreciate the root cause of a problem, then it can be difficult to fix. You shouldn't blindly apply advice that you read, and expect it to work successfully. Diagnosing a problem is normally the hard part, and once this is achieved, it is usually easy to fix it.

Input/output

I/O is a general name for any operation in which your code interacts with the outside world. There are many things that count as I/O, and there can be plenty of I/O that is internal to your software, especially if your application has a distributed architecture.

The recent rise in popularity of the .io **Top Level Domain** (**TLD**) can be partly attributed to standing for I/O, but that is not its real meaning. As is the case for some other TLDs, it is actually a country code. Other examples include .ly for Libya and .tv for Tuvalu (which, like the neighboring Kiribati, may soon be submerged beneath the Pacific Ocean due to climate change).
The TLD .io is intended for the **British Indian Ocean Territory** (**BIOT**), a collection of tiny but strategic islands with a shameful history. The .io TLD is therefore controlled by a UK-based registry. BIOT is nothing more than a military base, and also happens to be a hop on the proposed AWE fiber optic cable between Australia and Djibouti.

In this chapter, we will focus on improving the speed of I/O, not on avoiding it. Therefore, we won't cover caching here. Both I/O optimizing and caching are powerful techniques on their own, and when they're combined, you can achieve impressive performance. See Chapter 7, *Learning Caching and Message Queuing* for more on caching.

Categories of I/O

The first challenge is to identify the operations that trigger I/O. A general rule of thumb in .NET is that if a method has an asynchronous API (MethodAsync() variants), then it is declaring that it can be slow, and may be doing I/O work. Let's take a closer look at some of the different kinds of I/O.

Disks

The first type of I/O we will cover is reading from, and writing to, persistent storage. This will usually be some sort of a disk drive such as a spinning platter **Hard Disk Drive (HDD)**, or as is more common these days, a flash memory-based **Solid State Drive (SSD)**.

HDDs are slower than SSDs for random reads and writes, but are competitive for large block transfers. The reason for this is that the arm on the HDD has to physically move the head to the correct location on the magnetic platter before it can begin the read or write operations. If the disk is powered down, then it can take even longer, as the platters will have to **Spin-up** from a stationary position to the correct **revolutions per minute (rpm)** beforehand.

You may have heard the term "Spin-up" in reference to provisioning a generic resource. This historically comes from the time taken to spin the platters on a rotating disk up to the operational speed. The term is still commonly used, even though these days there may not be any mechanical components present.

Terminology like this often has a historical explanation. As another example, a floppy disk icon is normally used to represent the save function. Yet floppy disks are no longer in use, and many younger users may never have encountered one.

Knowing what type of drive your code is running on is important. HDDs perform badly if you make lots of small reads and writes. They prefer to have batched operations, so writing one large file is better than many smaller ones.

The performance of disks is similar to that of a network, in that there is both latency and throughput, often called bandwidth in networking parlance. The latency of an HDD is high, as it takes a relatively long time to get started, but once started, the throughput can be respectable. You can read data rapidly if it's all in one place on the disk, but it will be slower if it is spread all over, even if the total data is less. For example, copying a single large file disk-to-disk is quick, but trying to launch many programs simultaneously is slow.

SSDs experience fewer of these problems as they have lower latency, but it is still beneficial to keep random writes to a minimum. SSDs are based on **flash memory** (similar to the chips used in memory cards for phones and cameras), and they can only be written to a fixed number of times. The controller on the SSD manages this for you, but the SSD's performance degrades over time. Aggressive writing will accelerate this degradation.

Multiple disks can be combined to improve their performance and reliability characteristics. This is commonly done using a technology called **Redundant Array of Independent Disks (RAID)**. Data is split across multiple disks to make it quicker to access, and more tolerant to hardware failures. RAID is common in server hardware, but can increase the startup time, as Spin-up is sometimes staggered to reduce the peak power draw.

HDDs offer much larger capacity than SSDs, and so are a good choice for storage of infrequently used files. You can get hybrid drives, which combine an HDD with an SSD. These claim to offer the best of both worlds, and are cheaper than SSDs of an equivalent size. However, if you can afford it, and if you can fit all of your data on an SSD, then you should use one. You will also decrease your power and cooling requirements, and you can always add an additional HDD for mass storage or backups.

Virtual file systems

File access can be slow at the best of times due to the physical nature of the disks storing the data, as mentioned previously. This problem can be compounded in a virtualized environment such as a cloud-hosted infrastructure. The storage disks are usually not on the same host server as the virtual machine, and will generally be implemented as network shares even if they appear to be mounted locally. In any case, there is always an additional problem, which is present whether the disk is on the VM host or somewhere else on the network, and that is contention.

On a virtualized infrastructure, such as those provided by AWS and Azure, you share the hardware with other users, but a physical disk can only service a single request at once. If multiple tenants want to access the same disk simultaneously, then their operations will need to be queued and timeshared. Unfortunately, this abstraction has much the same detrimental effect on performance as reading lots of random files. Users are likely to have their data on disk stored in locations different from other customers. This will cause the arm on the drive to frequently move to different sectors, reducing throughput and increasing latency for everyone on the system.

All this means that on shared virtual hosting, using an SSD can have a bigger positive performance impact than normal. Even better is to have a local SSD, which is directly attached to the VM host, and not to another machine on the network. If disks must be networked, then the storage machine should be as close as possible to the VM using it.

You can pay extra for a dedicated VM host where you are the only tenant. However, you may as well then be running on bare metal, and reaping the benefits of reduced costs and higher performance. If you don't require the easy provisioning and maintenance of VMs, then a bare metal dedicated server may be a good option.

Many cloud hosting providers now offer SSDs, but most only offer ephemeral local disks. This means that the local disk only exists while your VM is running, and vanishes when it is shutdown, making it unsuitable for storing the OS if you want to bring a VM back up in the same state.

You have to write your application in a different way to take advantage of an ephemeral local drive, as it could disappear at any time, and so can only be used for temporary working storage. This is known as an **immutable server**, which means it doesn't change and is disposable. This normally works better when the OS is Linux, as it can be tricky to bootstrap new instances when running Windows.

Databases

Databases can be slow, because they rely on disks for the storage of their data, but there are other overheads as well. However, DBs are usually a better way of storing significant data than flat files on disk. Arbitrary data can be retrieved quickly if it is indexed, much quicker than scanning a file by brute force.

Relational databases are a mature and very impressive technology. However, they only shine when used correctly, and how you go about querying them makes a massive difference to performance. DBs are so convenient that they're often overused, and are typically the bottleneck for a web application.

An unfortunately common *anti-pattern* is requiring a database call in order to render the homepage of a website. An example is when you try to visit a website mentioned on live TV, only to discover that it has crashed due to the MySQL DB being overloaded. This sort of a website would be better architected as a static site with the client-side code hitting cached and queued web APIs.

The pathological case for a slow DB is where the web server is in one data center, the database server is in another, and the disks for the DB are in a third. Also, all the servers may be shared with other users. Obviously, it's best not to end up in this situation, and to architect your infrastructure in a sane way, but you will always have some latency.

There are application programming techniques that allow you to keep your network and DB chatter to a minimum. These help you to improve the performance and responsiveness of your software, especially if it is hosted in a high-latency virtualized environment. We will demonstrate some of these skills later on in this chapter.

APIs

Modern web application programming generally involves using third-party services and their associated APIs. It's beneficial to know where these APIs are located, and what the latency is. Are they in the same data center, or are they on the other side of the planet? Unless you've discovered some exciting new physics, then light only travels so fast.

 Today, almost all intercontinental data travels by fiber optics cables. Satellites are rarely used anymore, as the latency is high, especially for geostationary orbits. Many of these cables are under the oceans, and are hard to fix. If you rely on an API on a different continent, not only can it slow you down, but it also exposes you to additional risk.
You probably shouldn't build an important workflow that can be disrupted by a fisherman trawling in the wrong place. You also need to further secure your data, as some countries (such as the UK) are known to tap cables and store the communications, if they cross their borders.

One of the issues with APIs is that latency can compound. You may need to call many APIs, or maybe an API calls another API internally. These situations are not normally designed this way, but can grow organically as new features are added, especially if no refactoring is performed periodically to tidy up any mess.

One common form of latency is startup time. Websites can go to sleep if not used, especially if using the default **Internet Information Services** (**IIS**) settings. If a website takes a non-negligible amount of time to wake up, and all the required APIs also need to wake up, then the delays can quickly add up to a significant lag for the first request. It may even time-out.

There are a couple of solutions to this initial lag problem. If you use IIS, then you can configure the application pool to not go to sleep. The defaults in IIS are optimized for shared hosting, so they will need tweaking for a dedicated server. The second option is to keep the site alive by regularly polling it with a health check or uptime monitoring tool. You should be doing this anyway so that you know when your site goes down, but you should also ensure that you are exercising all the required dependencies (such as APIs and DBs). If you are simply retrieving a static page or just checking for a 200 status code, then services may go down without you realizing.

Similarly, scaling can have a lag. If you need to scale up, then you should preheat your load balancers and web servers. This is especially important if using an AWS **Elastic Load Balancer** (**ELB**). If you're expecting a big peak in traffic, then you can ask AWS to have your ELBs prewarmed. An alternative would be using **Azure Load Balancer**, **Azure Application Gateway**, or running HAProxy yourself so that you have more control. You should also be running load tests, which we'll cover in Chapter 9, *Monitoring Performance Regressions*.

Network diagnostics tools

As we discovered earlier, practically all I/O operations in a virtualized or cloud-hosting infrastructure are now network operations. Disks and databases are rarely local, as this would prevent scaling out horizontally. There are various command-line tools that can help you discover where the API, DB, or any other server you're using is located, and how much latency is present on the connection.

While all of these commands can be run from your workstation, they are most useful when run from a server via a **Secure Shell** (**SSH**) or **Remote Desktop Protocol** (**RDP**) connection. This way, you can check where your databases, APIs, and storage servers are, in relation to your web servers. Unfortunately, it is common for hosting providers to geographically separate your servers, and put them in different data centers.

For example, if using AWS, then you would want to configure your servers to be in at least the same region, and preferably in the same Availability Zone (**AZ**), which usually means the same data center. You can replicate (cluster) your DB or file server across AZs (or even across regions) so that your web servers are always talking to a server on their local network. This also adds redundancy, so in addition to increasing performance, it will make your application more resilient to hardware faults or power supply failures.

Ping

Ping is a simple networking diagnostics tool, available on almost all operating systems. It operates at the IP level and sends an **Internet Control Message Protocol** (**ICMP**) echo message to the host specified.

Not all machines will respond to pings, or requests may be blocked by firewalls. However, it's good netiquette to allow servers to respond for debugging purposes, and most will oblige. For example, open a command prompt or terminal, and type the following:

```
ping ec2.eu-central-1.amazonaws.com
```

This will ping an **Amazon Web Services** (**AWS**) data center in Germany. In the response, you will see the time in milliseconds. From the UK, this **round-trip time** (**RTT**) may be something like 33ms, but your results will vary.

 On Windows, by default, ping performs four attempts, then exits. On a Unix-like OS (such as Mac OS X, BSD, or Linux), by default, it continues indefinitely. Press *Ctrl+C* to stop and quit.

Try this command next, which will do the same, but for an AWS data center in Australia:

```
ping ec2.ap-southeast-2.amazonaws.com
```

From the UK, the latency now goes up, by almost an order of magnitude, to around 300 ms. AWS doesn't have any data centers in the UK, and neither do Microsoft and Google (read into that what you will). So to ping a UK hosting provider, enter the following:

```
ping bytemark.co.uk
```

The latency now decreases to an average of 23ms, as our connection has (probably) not left the country. Obviously, your results will vary depending on where you are. Next we'll see how to discover what route our data is taking, as it's not always only distance that's important. The number of hops can likewise be significant.

The following image shows the output of the three ping operations that we have just performed to Germany, the UK, and Australia. Note the difference in the timings; however, your results will be different, so try this for yourself.

```
C:\Users\James>ping ec2.eu-central-1.amazonaws.com

Pinging ec2.eu-central-1.amazonaws.com [54.239.54.36] with 32 bytes of data:
Reply from 54.239.54.36: bytes=32 time=33ms TTL=241
Reply from 54.239.54.36: bytes=32 time=33ms TTL=241
Reply from 54.239.54.36: bytes=32 time=33ms TTL=241
Reply from 54.239.54.36: bytes=32 time=33ms TTL=241

Ping statistics for 54.239.54.36:
    Packets: Sent = 4, Received = 4, Lost = 0 (0% loss),
Approximate round trip times in milli-seconds:
    Minimum = 33ms, Maximum = 33ms, Average = 33ms

C:\Users\James>ping ec2.ap-southeast-2.amazonaws.com

Pinging ec2.ap-southeast-2.amazonaws.com [54.240.195.29] with 32 bytes of data:
Reply from 54.240.195.29: bytes=32 time=297ms TTL=237
Reply from 54.240.195.29: bytes=32 time=298ms TTL=237
Reply from 54.240.195.29: bytes=32 time=297ms TTL=237
Reply from 54.240.195.29: bytes=32 time=297ms TTL=237

Ping statistics for 54.240.195.29:
    Packets: Sent = 4, Received = 4, Lost = 0 (0% loss),
Approximate round trip times in milli-seconds:
    Minimum = 297ms, Maximum = 298ms, Average = 297ms

C:\Users\James>ping bytemark.co.uk

Pinging bytemark.co.uk [80.68.81.80] with 32 bytes of data:
Reply from 80.68.81.80: bytes=32 time=22ms TTL=53
Reply from 80.68.81.80: bytes=32 time=22ms TTL=53
Reply from 80.68.81.80: bytes=32 time=27ms TTL=53
Reply from 80.68.81.80: bytes=32 time=22ms TTL=53

Ping statistics for 80.68.81.80:
    Packets: Sent = 4, Received = 4, Lost = 0 (0% loss),
Approximate round trip times in milli-seconds:
    Minimum = 22ms, Maximum = 27ms, Average = 23ms
```

IPv4 addresses starting with 54 (the ones in the form `54.x.x.x`) are a clue that the server may be running on an AWS **Elastic Compute Cloud (EC2)** virtual server. Perform a reverse DNS lookup with `nslookup` or `ping` (covered later in this chapter) to confirm if this is the case. AWS provides IP address ranges at the following link:
`docs.aws.amazon.com/general/latest/gr/aws-ip-ranges.html`

Tracert

Tracert (or traceroute on a Unix-like OS) is a tool which, as the name suggests, traces the route to a destination host. Enter the following command:

```
tracert www.google.com
```

You should be able to see the connection leaving the network of your **Internet Service Provider (ISP)**, and entering the domain `1e100.net`, which is Google's domain. *1.0 x 10^{100}* is a **googol**, which is their namesake. The following image shows the output that you might see for this trace:

```
C:\Users\James>tracert www.google.com

Tracing route to www.google.com [173.194.112.180]
over a maximum of 30 hops:

  1     1 ms     1 ms     1 ms  BThomehub.home [192.168.1.254]
  2     *        *        *     Request timed out.
  3    16 ms    18 ms    15 ms  31.55.186.181
  4    16 ms    16 ms    17 ms  31.55.186.180
  5    17 ms    16 ms    16 ms  core4-hu0-6-0-3.faraday.ukcore.bt.net [195.99.127.202]
  6    19 ms    17 ms    17 ms  peer1-xe0-1-0.faraday.ukcore.bt.net [213.121.193.173]
  7    17 ms    16 ms    16 ms  109.159.253.67
  8    16 ms    16 ms    16 ms  209.85.244.182
  9    17 ms    17 ms    17 ms  209.85.250.184
 10    22 ms    23 ms    23 ms  209.85.253.108
 11    26 ms    27 ms    28 ms  74.125.37.102
 12    75 ms    74 ms    73 ms  66.249.95.38
 13   231 ms    29 ms    28 ms  216.239.57.148
 14    37 ms    28 ms    38 ms  72.14.238.57
 15    68 ms    71 ms    70 ms  fra07s32-in-f20.1e100.net [173.194.112.180]

Trace complete.
```

Next, let's trace a route to Australia by running the following command with the same AWS host name as our earlier example, as follows:

```
tracert ec2.ap-southeast-2.amazonaws.com
```

This may take some time to run, especially if some hosts don't respond to pings and traceroute has to timeout. If you get asterisks (* * *), then this could indicate the presence of a firewall. Your results may look something like the following image:

```
C:\Users\James>tracert ec2.ap-southeast-2.amazonaws.com

Tracing route to ec2.ap-southeast-2.amazonaws.com [54.240.195.144]
over a maximum of 30 hops:

  1     1 ms     3 ms     3 ms  BThomehub.home [192.168.1.254]
  2     *        *        *     Request timed out.
  3     *        *        *     Request timed out.
  4    16 ms    16 ms    16 ms  31.55.186.180
  5    16 ms    16 ms    16 ms  195.99.127.42
  6    26 ms   235 ms    17 ms  peer2-et-9-3-0.faraday.ukcore.bt.net [62.6.201.195]
  7   198 ms    19 ms    15 ms  213.137.183.98
  8    16 ms    16 ms    16 ms  82.112.115.185
  9   175 ms   174 ms   174 ms  ae-1.r03.londen05.uk.bb.gin.ntt.net [129.250.6.230]
 10   173 ms   173 ms   171 ms  ae-15.r03.amstn102.nl.bb.gin.ntt.net [129.250.6.25]
 11    22 ms    23 ms    23 ms  ae-4.r25.amstn102.nl.bb.gin.ntt.net [129.250.2.146]
 12   100 ms   100 ms   101 ms  ae-5.r23.asbnva02.us.bb.gin.ntt.net [129.250.6.162]
 13   101 ms   101 ms   102 ms  ae-0.r22.asbnva02.us.bb.gin.ntt.net [129.250.3.84]
 14   167 ms   166 ms   166 ms  ae-5.r23.lsanca07.us.bb.gin.ntt.net [129.250.3.189]
 15   176 ms   175 ms   176 ms  ae-2.r00.lsanca07.us.bb.gin.ntt.net [129.250.3.238]
 16   167 ms   168 ms   168 ms  ae-1.amazon.lsanca07.us.bb.gin.ntt.net [129.250.198.98]
 17     *        *        *     Request timed out.
 18     *        *        *     Request timed out.
 19     *        *        *     Request timed out.
 20   305 ms   305 ms   304 ms  54.240.203.85
 21   305 ms   305 ms   305 ms  54.240.192.115
 22   305 ms   305 ms   305 ms  54.240.192.181
 23   305 ms   305 ms   305 ms  54.240.195.144

Trace complete.
```

In the preceding example, we can see the connection leaving the **British Telecom** (**BT**) network, and entering the **Nippon Telegraph and Telecom** (**NTT**) Global IP Network. We can even see the route taken from London to Sydney, via Amsterdam, Ashburn (east US, in Virginia), and Los Angeles. The hostnames suggest that the connection has gone via the Faraday telephone exchange building, near St. Paul's Cathedral in London (named after electrical pioneer Michael Faraday), and entered Amazon's network in LA.

This isn't the whole story as it only shows the IP level. At the physical level, the fiber likely comes back to the UK from the Netherlands (possibly via Porthcurno, Goonhilly Satellite Earth Station, or more likely, Bude where GCHQ conveniently have a base). Between LA and Australia, there will also probably be a stopover in Hawaii (where the NSA base that Edward Snowden worked at is located).

There are maps of the connections available at submarinecablemap.com and www.us.ntt.net/about/network-map.cfm. It's good idea to have at least a basic understanding of how the internet is physically structured, in order to achieve high performance.

If we now trace the routes to the AWS data centers in Korea and Japan, we can see that, initially, they both take the same route as each other. They go from London to New York and then to Seattle, before reaching Osaka in Japan. The Korean trace then carries on for another eleven hops, but the Japanese trace is done in six, which makes logical sense.

The following image shows the typical results of a trace to Korea first, then the results of a second trace to Japan.

```
C:\Users\James>tracert ec2.ap-northeast-2.amazonaws.com

Tracing route to ec2.ap-northeast-2.amazonaws.com [52.95.192.85]
over a maximum of 30 hops:

  1     1 ms     1 ms     1 ms  BThomehub.home [192.168.1.254]
  2     *        *        *     Request timed out.
  3     *        *        *     Request timed out.
  4    36 ms    16 ms    16 ms  31.55.186.188
  5    16 ms    16 ms    15 ms  core4-hu0-6-0-1.faraday.ukcore.bt.net [195.99.127.200]
  6    25 ms    15 ms    15 ms  peer2-et-10-3-0.faraday.ukcore.bt.net [62.6.201.199]
  7    19 ms    15 ms    15 ms  213.137.183.100
  8    17 ms    17 ms    16 ms  82.112.115.185
  9   273 ms   274 ms   273 ms  ae-13.r02.londen03.uk.bb.gin.ntt.net [129.250.2.118]
 10    17 ms    16 ms    16 ms  ae-4.r22.londen03.uk.bb.gin.ntt.net [129.250.5.24]
 11    87 ms    87 ms    88 ms  ae-5.r24.nycmny01.us.bb.gin.ntt.net [129.250.2.18]
 12   172 ms   179 ms   157 ms  ae-1.r21.sttlwa01.us.bb.gin.ntt.net [129.250.4.13]
 13   250 ms   250 ms   250 ms  ae-2.r20.osakjp02.jp.bb.gin.ntt.net [129.250.3.86]
 14   252 ms   248 ms   311 ms  ae-4.r22.osakjp02.jp.bb.gin.ntt.net [129.250.6.188]
 15   280 ms   275 ms   274 ms  ae-1.r00.osakjp02.jp.bb.gin.ntt.net [129.250.2.253]
 16   255 ms   256 ms   254 ms  ae-0.amazon.osakjp02.jp.bb.gin.ntt.net [61.200.82.122]
 17   261 ms   261 ms   261 ms  54.239.52.142
 18   286 ms   286 ms   286 ms  54.239.52.149
 19     *        *        *     Request timed out.
 20   294 ms   291 ms   298 ms  54.239.122.238
 21   322 ms   289 ms   295 ms  54.239.122.245
 22   422 ms   335 ms   295 ms  54.239.122.38
 23     *        *        *     Request timed out.
 24     *        *        *     Request timed out.
 25     *        *        *     Request timed out.
 26     *        *        *     Request timed out.
 27   292 ms   296 ms   295 ms  52.95.192.85

Trace complete.

C:\Users\James>tracert ec2.ap-northeast-1.amazonaws.com

Tracing route to ec2.ap-northeast-1.amazonaws.com [27.0.1.195]
over a maximum of 30 hops:

  1     2 ms     1 ms     1 ms  BThomehub.home [192.168.1.254]
  2     *        *        *     Request timed out.
  3     *        *        *     Request timed out.
  4    16 ms    16 ms    16 ms  31.55.186.180
  5    16 ms    16 ms    16 ms  core3-hu0-6-0-1.faraday.ukcore.bt.net [195.99.127.192]
  6    15 ms    16 ms    16 ms  peer2-et-9-3-0.faraday.ukcore.bt.net [62.6.201.195]
  7    15 ms    15 ms    16 ms  213.137.183.96
  8    16 ms    16 ms    16 ms  82.112.115.185
  9   273 ms   274 ms   274 ms  ae-13.r02.londen03.uk.bb.gin.ntt.net [129.250.2.118]
 10    16 ms    17 ms    17 ms  ae-4.r22.londen03.uk.bb.gin.ntt.net [129.250.5.24]
 11    82 ms    83 ms    83 ms  ae-5.r24.nycmny01.us.bb.gin.ntt.net [129.250.2.18]
 12   153 ms   153 ms   152 ms  ae-1.r21.sttlwa01.us.bb.gin.ntt.net [129.250.4.13]
 13   242 ms   243 ms   242 ms  ae-2.r20.osakjp02.jp.bb.gin.ntt.net [129.250.3.86]
 14   294 ms   309 ms   283 ms  ae-4.r23.osakjp02.jp.bb.gin.ntt.net [129.250.6.188]
 15   273 ms   273 ms   273 ms  ae-2.r00.osakjp02.jp.bb.gin.ntt.net [129.250.3.197]
 16   247 ms   246 ms   246 ms  ae-0.amazon.osakjp02.jp.bb.gin.ntt.net [61.200.82.122]
 17   259 ms   259 ms   259 ms  27.0.0.250
 18   255 ms   412 ms   306 ms  54.239.52.135
 19   261 ms   262 ms   260 ms  27.0.0.67
 20   254 ms   254 ms   254 ms  27.0.0.155
 21   255 ms   255 ms   255 ms  27.0.0.175
 22   255 ms   255 ms   255 ms  27.0.1.195

Trace complete.
```

You can use the difference in time between hops to work out the approximate geographic distance. However, there are occasionally anomalies if some systems respond quicker than others.

If you're on a flight with free Wi-Fi, then a traceroute is an interesting exercise to perform. The internet connection is likely going via satellite, and you'll be able to tell the orbit altitude from the latency. For example, a geostationary orbit will have a large latency of around 1,000 ms, but a **Low Earth Orbit (LEO)** will be much smaller. You should also be able to work out where the ground station is located.

Nslookup

Nslookup is a tool for directly querying a DNS server. **Dig** is another similar tool, but we won't cover it here. Both `ping` and traceroute have performed DNS lookups, but you can do this directly with `nslookup`, which can be very useful. You can call `nslookup` with command-line parameters, but you can also use it interactively. To do this, simply type the name of the tool into a console or a command prompt, as follows:

```
nslookup
```

You will now get a slightly different command prompt from within the program. By default, the DNS name servers of the computer you're on are used, and it bypasses any entries in your local *hosts file*.

A hosts file can be very useful for testing changes prior to adding them to DNS. It can also be used as a crude blocker for adverts and trackers by setting their addresses to `0.0.0.0`. There are local DNS servers you can run to do this for your whole network. One such project is `pi-hole.net`, which is based on **dnsmasq**, but which simplifies setting it up and updating the hosts on **Raspberry Pi**.

Enter the hostname of a server to resolve its IP address; for example, type the following:

```
polling.bbc.co.uk
```

The results show that this hostname is a CNAME (an alias for the real Canonical Name) of `polling.bbc.co.uk.edgekey.net`, which resolves to `e3891.g.akamaiedge.net`, and this currently has an IP address of `23.67.87.132`. We can perform a reverse DNS lookup on the IP address by entering it:

```
23.67.87.132
```

We then get the hostname of that machine, conveniently containing the IP address, which is `a23-67-87-132.deploy.static.akamaitechnologies.com`. The domain name is owned by Akamai, which is a **Content Delivery Network (CDN)** used to distribute load.

If you are using a DNS server on your local network, possibly with your router running dnsmasq, then it may cache results, and give you stale data. You can see more up-to-date information by changing the server to a core one that propagates changes quicker. For example, to use one of Google's public DNS servers, enter the following (but be aware that Google will log all the internet sites you visit if you use this normally):

```
server 8.8.8.8
```

Then run the same query again. Notice how the hostname now resolves to a different IP address. This is a common behavior for CDNs, and the record will change over time, even on the same DNS server. It is often used as a technique to balance network load. Changing DNS servers can also sometimes be used to get around naïve content filters or location restrictions.

To exit the nslookup interactive mode, type exit and press *return*. The following image shows the output for the previous commands:

```
C:\Users\James>nslookup
Default Server:  BThomehub.home
Address:  192.168.1.254

> polling.bbc.co.uk
Server:  BThomehub.home
Address:  192.168.1.254

Non-authoritative answer:
Name:     e3891.g.akamaiedge.net
Address:  23.67.87.132
Aliases:  polling.bbc.co.uk
          polling.bbc.co.uk.edgekey.net

> 23.67.87.132
Server:  BThomehub.home
Address:  192.168.1.254

Name:     a23-67-87-132.deploy.static.akamaitechnologies.com
Address:  23.67.87.132

> server 8.8.8.8
Default Server:  google-public-dns-a.google.com
Address:  8.8.8.8

> polling.bbc.co.uk
Server:  google-public-dns-a.google.com
Address:  8.8.8.8

Non-authoritative answer:
Name:     e3891.g.akamaiedge.net
Address:  23.65.37.43
Aliases:  polling.bbc.co.uk
          polling.bbc.co.uk.edgekey.net

> exit
```

IPv4 is the version of IP that you will probably be most familiar with. It uses 32-bit addresses that are usually represented as four dotted decimal octets, such as `192.168.0.1`. However, we have run out of IPv4 addresses, and the world is (slowly) moving to the new version of IP, called **IPv6**. The address length has increased fourfold, to 128-bit, and is usually represented in hexadecimal such as `2001:0db8:0000:0000:0000:ee00:0032:154d`. Leading zeros can be omitted, like `2001:db8::ee00:32:154d`, to make them easier to write. Localhost loopback (`127.0.0.1`) is now simply `::1` in IPv6.

On Windows, you can use `ping -a x.x.x.x` to do a reverse DNS lookup, and resolve IP addresses to hostnames. On Linux (and on other Unix-like systems such as OS X), this feature is not available, and the `-a` flag serves a different purpose. You will have to use `nslookup`, or dig for reverse DNS on these OSs.

Build your own

You can build your own tools using C#, and the functions you need are provided by .NET. These are built into the full .NET Framework, but for .NET Core, you will need to add the NuGet package `System.Net.Ping` for ping, although the DNS name resolution is built-in. The underlying implementations are platform-specific, but the framework will take care of calling the native code on the OS you're using.

You won't normally need to programmatically resolve a hostname, as most networking commands will do this automatically. However, it can occasionally be useful, especially if you want to perform a reverse DNS lookup, and find the hostname for an IP address.

The .NET `Dns` class differs from `nslookup`, as it includes entries from the local hosts file rather than just querying a DNS server. It is, therefore, more representative of the IP addresses that other processes are resolving.

To programmatically perform a DNS lookup, follow these steps:

1. Add the `System.Net` namespace.

```
using System.Net;
```

2. To resolve a hostname to an IP address, use the following static method. This will return an array of IP addresses, although there will usually only be one.

```
var results = await Dns.GetHostAddressesAsync(host);
```

3. To resolve an IP address to a hostname, use the following method instead:

```
var revDns = await Dns.GetHostEntryAsync(result);
```

4. If successful, then the hostname will be available as `revDns.HostName`.

To programmatically ping a host, follow these steps:

1. Add the `System.Net.NetworkInformation` namespace.

```
using System.Net.NetworkInformation;
```

2. You can then instantiate a new `Ping` object.

```
var ping = new Ping();
```

3. With this object, you can now ping an IP address or hostname (that will perform a DNS lookup internally) by using the following method:

```
var result = await ping.SendPingAsync(host);
```

4. You can get the status of the ping with `result.Status,` and if successful, then you can get the RTT in milliseconds with `result.RoundtripTime`.

 The source code for our console application, illustrating how to use the .NET Core `Dns` and `Ping` classes, is available for download along with this book.

A reverse DNS lookup can usually reveal the hosting company being used by a website. Usually, there is only one IP address per hostname, as shown in the following image of our .NET Core console app output:

```
Enter a hostname or IP address:
emonCMS.org

Performing DNS lookup of emonCMS.org
Complete, emonCMS.org = 80.243.190.58
Performing reverse DNS lookup of 80.243.190.58
Complete, 80.243.190.58 = redstation.com

Pinging emonCMS.org 4 times
Ping attempt #1 of 4
Success
20 ms
Ping attempt #2 of 4
Success
20 ms
Ping attempt #3 of 4
Success
20 ms
Ping attempt #4 of 4
Success
20 ms

Press any key to exit...
```

In the preceding screenshot, we can see that `emoncms.org` is using `redstation.com` as a host. The low latency suggests that the server is located in the same country as our computer.

DNS is often used for load balancing. In this case, you will see many IP addresses returned for a single domain name, as shown in the following screenshot:

```
Enter a hostname or IP address:
DuckDuckGo.com

Performing DNS lookup of DuckDuckGo.com
Complete, DuckDuckGo.com = 54.229.105.92
Performing reverse DNS lookup of 54.229.105.92
Complete, 54.229.105.92 = ec2-54-229-105-92.eu-west-1.compute.amazonaws.com

Complete, DuckDuckGo.com = 54.229.105.203
Performing reverse DNS lookup of 54.229.105.203
Complete, 54.229.105.203 = ec2-54-229-105-203.eu-west-1.compute.amazonaws.com

Complete, DuckDuckGo.com = 176.34.131.233
Performing reverse DNS lookup of 176.34.131.233
Complete, 176.34.131.233 = ec2-176-34-131-233.eu-west-1.compute.amazonaws.com

Complete, DuckDuckGo.com = 176.34.155.20
Performing reverse DNS lookup of 176.34.155.20
Complete, 176.34.155.20 = ec2-176-34-155-20.eu-west-1.compute.amazonaws.com

Complete, DuckDuckGo.com = 46.51.197.89
Performing reverse DNS lookup of 46.51.197.89
Complete, 46.51.197.89 = ec2-46-51-197-89.eu-west-1.compute.amazonaws.com

Complete, DuckDuckGo.com = 176.34.135.167
Performing reverse DNS lookup of 176.34.135.167
Complete, 176.34.135.167 = ec2-176-34-135-167.eu-west-1.compute.amazonaws.com

Pinging DuckDuckGo.com 4 times
Ping attempt #1 of 4
Success
27 ms
Ping attempt #2 of 4
Success
27 ms
Ping attempt #3 of 4
Success
27 ms
Ping attempt #4 of 4
Success
27 ms

Press any key to exit...
```

We can see in the preceding screenshot that the privacy-focused search engine **DuckDuckGo** (which doesn't track its users like Google does) is using AWS. DNS is being used to balance the load across various instances—in this case, they're all in the Dublin data center, because that's the closest one. Notice how the ping times are now slightly higher than the UK-based host in the previous example.

It's likely that they're using the AWS DNS service **Route 53** (so named because DNS uses port 53). This can balance load across regions, whereas an ELB (which DuckDuckGo doesn't appear to be using) can only balance inside a region (but both inside and across AZs). Azure offers a similar service called **Traffic Manager** for DNS load balancing.

Solutions

Now that you understand a bit more about the causes of latency-based problems, and how to analyze them, we can demonstrate some potential solutions. The measurements that you have taken using the previously illustrated tools will help you quantify the scale of the problems, and choose the appropriate fixes to be applied.

Batching API requests

Rendering a typical web page may require calls to many different APIs (or DB tables) to gather the data required for it. Due to the style of object-oriented programming encouraged by C# (and many other languages), these API calls are often performed in series. However, if the result of one call does not affect another, then this is suboptimal, and the calls could be performed in parallel. We'll cover DB tables later in this chapter, as there are better approaches for them.

Concurrent calls can be more pertinent if you implement a **microservices** architecture (as opposed to the traditional monolith, or big ball of mud), and have lots of different distributed endpoints. Message queues are sometimes a better choice than HTTP APIs in many cases, perhaps using a publish and subscribe pattern. However, maybe you're not responsible for the API, and are instead integrating with a third party. Indeed, if the API is yours, then you could alter it to provide all the data that you need in one shot anyway.

Consider the example of calling two isolated APIs that have no dependencies on each other. The sequence diagram for this may look something like the following:

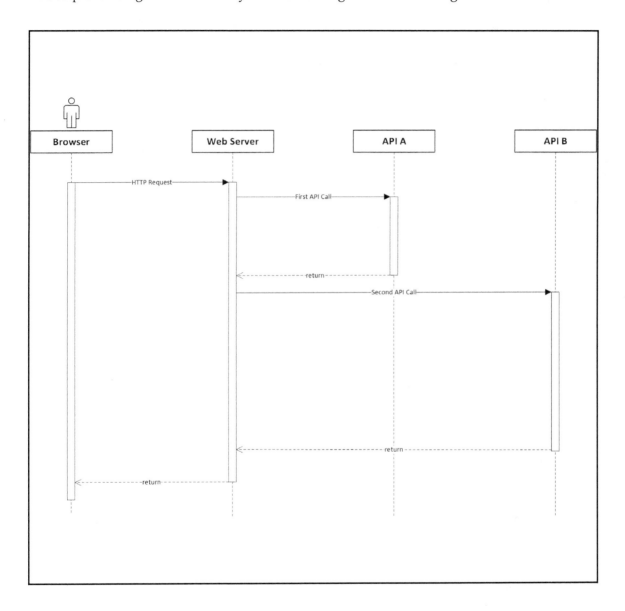

This linear process of calling A, and then calling B when A is done, is simple, as it requires no complex orchestration to wrangle the results of the API calls, but it is slower than necessary. By calling both APIs synchronously and in sequence, we waste time waiting for them to return. A better way of doing this, if we don't require the result of the first API for the request to the second, may be to call them together asynchronously. The sequence diagram for this new flow may look something like the following:

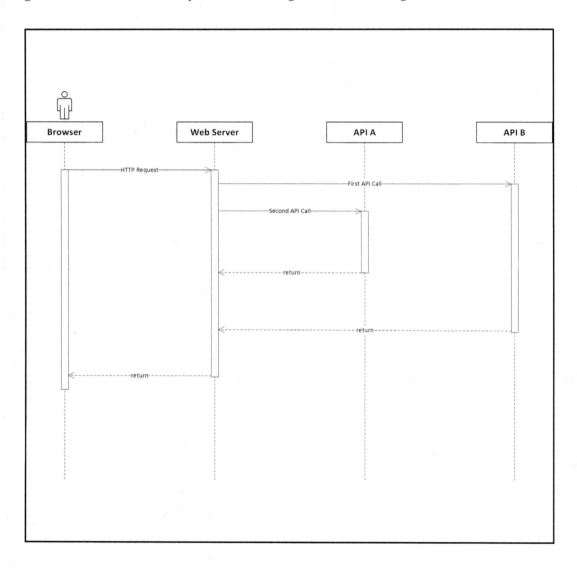

There are two changes in this new sequence, one obvious and the other subtle. We call both APIs asynchronously and in parallel so that they are simultaneously in flight. This first change will have the greatest impact, but there is a smaller tweak that can also help, which is calling the slowest API first.

In the original sequence diagram, we call **API A** and then **API B**, but B is slower. Calling A and B at the same time will have a big impact, but calling B and then A is slightly better. B dominates the timeline, and we will be killing a (relatively) large amount of time waiting for it.

We can use this downtime to call A, as there will be some small fixed overhead in any API method call. Both of these changes combined mean that we are now only waiting for B, and effectively get the call to A for free, in terms of time.

We can illustrate this principle with a simple console application. There are two methods that simulate the APIs, and both are similar. API A has the following code:

```
private static async Task CallApiA()
{
    Thread.Sleep(10);
    await Task.Delay(100);
}
```

`Thread.Sleep` simulates the fixed overhead, and `Task.Delay` simulates waiting for the API call to return. API B takes twice as long to return as API A, but the fixed overhead is the same, and it has the following code:

```
private static async Task CallApiB()
{
    Thread.Sleep(10);
    await Task.Delay(200);
}
```

Now, if we synchronously call the methods in sequence, we discover that all of the delays add up, as expected.

```
CallApiA().Wait();
CallApiB().Wait();
```

These operations take a total of around **332 ms** on average, as there is about 10 ms of additional intrinsic overhead in the method invocation. If we call both methods simultaneously, the time reduces significantly.

```
Task.WaitAll(CallApiA(), CallApiB());
```

The operations now take an average total of **233 ms**. This is good, but we can do better if we swap the order of the methods.

```
Task.WaitAll(CallApiB(), CallApiA());
```

This now takes, on an average, a total of **218 ms**, because we have swallowed the fixed overheads of API A into the time we are waiting for API B.

 The full console application which benchmarks these three variants is available for download with this book. It uses the `Stopwatch` class to time the operations, and averages the results over many runs.

The results of these three different approaches are shown in the following image:

```
Benchmarking over an average of 20 runs
A then B mean elapsed time: 332 ms
A and B mean elapsed time: 233 ms
B and A mean elapsed time: 218 ms
Press any key to exit...
```

As is always the case, measure your results to make sure there really is an improvement. You may find that if you are making many calls to one API, or reusing the same API client, then your requests are processed sequentially, regardless.

This parallelizing of tasks not only works for I/O, but can also be used for computation, as we will discover in the next chapter. For now, we will move on, and take a deeper look at database query optimization.

Efficient DB operations

Although this isn't a book aimed at **Database Administrators** (**DBAs**), it's advantageous for you to appreciate the underlying technology that you're using. As is the case with networking, if you understand the strengths and weaknesses, then you can achieve high performance more easily.

This is additionally relevant for the recent trend of developers doing more work outside of their specialization, particularly in small organizations or startups. You may have heard the buzzwords full-stack developer or **DevOps**. These refer to roles that blur the traditional boundaries, and merge development (both frontend and backend), quality assurance, networking, infrastructure, operations, and database administration into one job. Being a developer today is no longer a case of just programming or shipping code. It helps to know something about the other areas too.

Previously, in Chapter 3, *Fixing Common Performance Problems*, we covered using the micro O/RM Dapper, and how to fix Select N+1 problems. Now, we'll build on that knowledge, and highlight a few more ways that you can consolidate queries and improve the performance of your DB operations.

As detailed in Chapter 2, *Measuring Performance Bottlenecks*, the first step is to profile your application and discover where the issues lie. Only then should you move on to applying solutions to the problem areas.

Database tuning

We're going to focus more on improving poorly performing queries, so we won't go into DB tuning too much. This is a complex topic, and there is a lot you can learn about indexes and how data is stored.

However, if you haven't run the **Database Engine Tuning Advisor** (**DETA**), then this is an easy step to identify if you have any missing indexes. Yet, you should be careful when applying the recommended changes, as there are always downsides and tradeoffs to consider. For example, indexes make retrieving data quicker, but also make it slower to add and update records. They also take up additional space, so it is best not to overdo it. It will depend on your particular business use case: if you wish to optimize upfront, or take the hit later on retrieval.

The first step is to capture a trace with **SQL Server Profiler**. See Chapter 2, *Measuring Performance Bottlenecks* for how to do this, and save the resulting file. This is one of the reasons that the tuning profile is a good choice. You should make sure that the trace is representative of a genuine DB use to get good results. You can launch the DETA from the same menu as the profiler in SSMS.

You can then load in your trace as a workload, and after processing, it will give you some recommendations. We won't cover the details of how to do this here for space reasons, and it is pretty self-explanatory. There are many good guides available online, if required.

Reporting

A common use case, which can often bring a database to its knees, is reporting. Reports usually run on large amounts of data, and can take considerable time if poorly written.

If you already have a method for retrieving a single item from a DB, then it can be tempting to reuse this for reporting purposes and for calculating metrics inside of the application. However, this is best avoided; reports should generally have their own dedicated queries.

Even better is to have another database dedicated to reporting, which is populated from the main DB or from backups. This way, intensive reports won't affect the performance of the main application at the expense of not including real-time data. This is sometimes known as a **data warehouse** or **data mart**, and the data is occasionally denormalized for simplicity or performance reasons. Populating another DB can also be a convenient way to test your backups, as database backups should always be tested to ensure that they can be restored correctly and contain all of the required data.

 In the ensuing examples, we will focus on **Microsoft SQL Server (MS SQL)** and the **Transact-SQL (T-SQL)** dialect of SQL. Other databases, such as PostgreSQL, are available as well. PostgreSQL has its own dialect called **Procedural Language / PostgreSQL (PL/pgSQL)**, which is similar to Oracle **PL/SQL**. These dialects all support basic SQL commands, but use different syntax for some operations, and contain different or additional features.

The latest version of MS SQL Server is SQL Server 2016, and it's the first edition to support running on Linux in addition to Windows. It is based on the **SQL Azure** service code, so there should now be fewer differences between a self-hosted, on-premise DB and Microsoft's cloud offering.

Aggregates

Aggregate functions are an incredibly useful feature of a RDBMS. You can compute values that summarize many records in the database, and only return the result keeping the source data rows in the DB.

You will be familiar with the COUNT aggregate function from earlier in the book, if not before. This gives you the total number of records returned by your query, but without returning them. You may have read advice that COUNT(1) performs better than COUNT(*), but this is no longer the case, as SQL Server now optimizes the latter to perform the same as the former.

 By default, SQL Server will return a message detailing the count of the records returned, along with the result of every query. You can turn this off by prefixing your query with the SET NOCOUNT ON command, which will save a few bytes in the **Tabular Data Stream** (TDS) connection, and increase performance slightly. This is significant only if a **cursor** is being used, which is bad practice anyway for locking reasons. It's good practice to re-enable row count after the query, even though it will be reset outside of the local scope anyway.

In Chapter 3, *Fixing Common Performance Problems*, we solved our Select N+1 problem by joining tables in the DB, and using COUNT instead of performing these calculations in our application code. There are many other aggregate functions available, that can be useful in improving performance, especially for reporting purposes.

Going back to our earlier example, suppose we now want to find out the total number of blog posts. We also want to find the total number of comments, the average comment count, the lowest number of comments for a single post, and the highest number of comments for a single post.

The first part is easy—just apply COUNT to the posts instead of the comments—but the second part is harder. As we already have our list of posts with a comment count for each, it may be tempting to reuse that, and simply work everything out in our C# code.

This would be a bad idea, and the query would perform poorly, especially if the number of posts is high. A better solution would be to use a query such as the following:

```
;WITH PostCommentCount AS(
SELECT
    bp.BlogPostId,
    COUNT(bpc.BlogPostCommentId) 'CommentCount'
FROM BlogPost bp
LEFT JOIN BlogPostComment bpc
    ON bpc.BlogPostId = bp.BlogPostId
GROUP BY bp.BlogPostId
) SELECT
    COUNT(BlogPostId) 'TotalPosts',
    SUM(CommentCount) 'TotalComments',
    AVG(CommentCount) 'AverageComments',
```

```
    MIN(CommentCount) 'MinimumComments',
    MAX(CommentCount) 'MaximumComments'
FROM PostCommentCount
```

This query uses a **Common Table Expression** (**CTE**), but you could also use a nested `SELECT` to embed the first query into the `FROM` clause of the second. It illustrates a selection of the aggregate functions available, and the results on the test database from before look like the following:

	TotalPosts	TotalComments	AverageComments	MinimumComments	MaximumComments
1	3000	44748	14	0	141

The semicolon at the start is simply a good practice to avoid errors and remove ambiguity. It ensures that any previous command has been terminated, as `WITH` can be used in other contexts. It isn't required for the preceding example, but might be if it were part of a larger query. CTEs can be very useful tools, especially if you require recursion. However, they are evaluated every time, so you may find that temporary tables perform much better for you, especially if querying one repeatedly in a nested `SELECT`.

Now suppose that we wish to perform the same query, but only include posts that have at least one comment. In this case, we could use a query like the following:

```
;WITH PostCommentCount AS(
SELECT
    bp.BlogPostId,
    COUNT(bpc.BlogPostCommentId) 'CommentCount'
FROM BlogPost bp
LEFT JOIN BlogPostComment bpc
    ON bpc.BlogPostId = bp.BlogPostId
GROUP BY bp.BlogPostId
HAVING COUNT(bpc.BlogPostCommentId) > 0
) SELECT
    COUNT(BlogPostId) 'TotalPosts',
    SUM(CommentCount) 'TotalComments',
    AVG(CommentCount) 'AverageComments',
    MIN(CommentCount) 'MinimumComments',
    MAX(CommentCount) 'MaximumComments'
FROM PostCommentCount
```

We have added a `HAVING` clause to ensure that we only count posts with more than zero comments. This is similar to a `WHERE` clause, but for use with a `GROUP BY`. The query results now look something like the following:

	TotalPosts	TotalComments	AverageComments	MinimumComments	MaximumComments
1	1361	44748	32	1	141

Sampling

Sometimes, you don't need to use all of the data, and can sample it. This technique is particularly applicable to any time-series information that you may wish to graph. In SQL Server, the traditional way to perform random sampling was using the `NEWID()` method, but this can be slow. For example, consider the following query:

```
SELECT TOP 1 PERCENT *
FROM [dbo].[TrainStatus]
ORDER BY NEWID()
```

This query returns exactly 1% of the rows with a random distribution. When run against a table with 1,205,855 entries, it returned 12,059 results in about four seconds, which is slow. A better way may be to use `TABLESAMPLE`, which is available in any reasonably recent version of SQL Server (2005 onwards), as follows:

```
SELECT *
FROM [dbo].[TrainStatus]
TABLESAMPLE (1 PERCENT)
```

This preceding query is much quicker, and when run against the same data as the previous example, it completes almost instantly. The downside is that it's cruder than the earlier method, and it won't return exactly 1% of the results. It will return roughly 1%, but the value will change every time it is run. For example, running against the same test database, it returned 11,504, 13,441 and 11,427 rows when executing the query three times in a row.

Inserting data

Querying databases may be the most common use case, but you will usually need to put some data in there in the first place. One of the most commonly used features when inserting records into a relational DB is the identity column. This is an auto-incrementing ID that is generated by the database, and doesn't need to be supplied when adding data.

For example, in our `BlogPost` table from earlier, the `BlogPostId` column is created as `INT IDENTITY(1,1)`. This means that it's an integer value starting at one and increasing by one for every new row. You `INSERT` into this table, without specifying `BlogPostId`, like so:

```
INSERT INTO BlogPost (Title, Content)
VALUES ('My Awesome Post', 'Write something witty here...')
```

Identities can be very useful, but you will usually want to know the ID of your newly created record. It is typical to want to store a row, then immediately retrieve it so that the ID can be used for future editing operations. You can do this in one shot with the `OUTPUT` clause, like so;

```
INSERT INTO BlogPost (Title, Content)
OUTPUT INSERTED.BlogPostId
VALUES ('My Awesome Post', 'Write something witty here...')
```

In addition to inserting the row, the ID will be returned.

 You may see `SCOPE_IDENTITY()` (or even `@@IDENTITY`) advocated as ways of retrieving the identity, but these are outdated. The recommended way of doing this, on modern versions of SQL Server, is to use `OUTPUT`.

`OUTPUT` works on the `INSERT`, `UPDATE`, `DELETE`, and `MERGE` commands. It even works when operating on multiple rows at a time, as in this example of bulk inserting two blog posts:

```
INSERT INTO BlogPost (Title, Content)
OUTPUT INSERTED.BlogPostId
VALUES ('My Awesome Post', 'Write something witty here...'),
       ('My Second Awesome Post', 'Try harder this time...')
```

The preceding query will return a result set of two identities, for example, 3003 and 3004. In order to execute these inserts with Dapper, you can use the following method for a single record. First, let us create a blog post object, which we'll hard code here, but which would normally come from user input:

```
var post = new BlogPost
{
    Title = "My Awesome Post",
    Content = "Write something witty here..."
};
```

To insert this one post, and set the ID, you can use the following code. This will execute the insert statement, and return a single integer value.

```
post.BlogPostId = await connection.ExecuteScalarAsync<int>(@"
    INSERT INTO BlogPost (Title, Content)
    OUTPUT INSERTED.BlogPostId
    VALUES (@Title, @Content)",
    post);
```

You can then assign the returned ID to the post, and return that object to the user for editing. There is no need to select the record again, assuming the insert succeeds and no exceptions are thrown.

You can insert multiple records at once with the same SQL by using the execute method. However, the SQL will be executed multiple times, which may be inefficient, and you only get back the number of inserted rows, not their IDs. The following code supplies an array of posts to the same SQL used in the previous example:

```
var numberOfRows = await connection.ExecuteAsync(@"
    INSERT INTO BlogPost (Title, Content)
    OUTPUT INSERTED.BlogPostId
    VALUES (@Title, @Content)",
    new[] { post, post, post });
```

If you want multiple IDs returned, then you will need to use the query method to return a collection of values, as we have done previously. However, it is difficult to make this work for a variable number of records, without dynamically building SQL. The following code performs a bulk insert, using multiple separate parameters for the query:

```
var ids = await connection.QueryAsync<int>(@"
    INSERT INTO BlogPost (Title, Content)
    OUTPUT INSERTED.BlogPostId
    VALUES (@Title1, @Content1),
           (@Title2, @Content2)", new
    {
        Title1 = post.Title,
        Content1 = post.Content,
        Title2 = post.Title,
        Content2 = post.Content
    });
```

This will perform all the work in a single command, and return an enumerable collection of the identities. However, this code is not very scalable (or even elegant).

There are many helper methods in the `Dapper.Contrib` package which can assist you with inserting records and other operations. However, they suffer from the same limitations as the examples here, and you can only return a single identity or the number of rows inserted.

GUIDs

Integer identities can be useful to a database internally, but perhaps you shouldn't be using an identifying key externally, especially if you have multiple web servers or expose the IDs to users. An alternative is to use a **Globally Unique Identifier** (**GUID**), referred to as `UNIQUEIDENTIFIER` in SQL Server. We have already touched on these, as they are generated by the `NEWID()` function used in the suboptimal sampling example.

GUIDs are used ubiquitously, and are 16 bytes long—four times bigger than an integer. The size of GUIDs means that you are unlikely to get a **unique constraint** conflict when inserting a random GUID into an already populated table.

People sometimes worry about GUID collisions, but the numbers involved are so staggeringly huge that collisions are incredibly unlikely. The GUIDs generated by .NET (using a `COM` function on Windows) are, specifically, **Universally Unique Identifiers** (**UUIDs**) version 4. These have 122 bits of randomness, so you would need to generate nearly three billion GUIDs before having even half a chance of a collision.

At one new record per second, that would take over 90 billion years. Even at two million GUIDs per second (what an average computer today could produce), it would still take over 45 thousand years (more time than human civilization has been around). If you think that this will be an issue for your software, then you should probably be future-proofing it by using five-digit years, such as 02016, to avoid the *Y10K* (or *YAK* in hexadecimal) problem.

This uniqueness property allows you to generate a GUID in your application code and store it in a distributed database, without worrying about merging data later. It also allows you to expose IDs to users, without caring if someone will enumerate them or try and guess a value. Integer IDs often expose how many records there are in a table, which could be sensitive information depending on your use case.

One thing you have to watch out for with random GUIDs is using them as keys, as opposed to IDs. The difference between these two terms is subtle, and they are often one and the same. The key (**primary** or **clustered**) is what the DB uses to address a record, whereas the ID is what you would use to retrieve one. These can be the same value but they don't have to be. Using a random GUID as a key can cause performance issues with indexing. The randomness may cause fragmentation, which will slow down queries.

You can use sequential GUIDs, for example `NEWSEQUENTIALID()` can be the `DEFAULT` value for a column, but then you lose most of the beneficial qualities of GUIDs that mainly come from the randomness. You now effectively just have a really big integer, and if you're only concerned with the maximum number of rows in a table, and require more than two billion, then a `big int` (twice an `int`, but half a GUID) should suffice.

A good compromise is to have an `int` identity as the primary key, but to use a GUID as the ID (and enforce this with a unique constraint on the column). It's best if you generate the GUID in application code with `Guid.NewGuid()`, as using a default column value in the DB means you have to retrieve the ID after an insert, as shown previously.

A table using this strategy may partially look something like the following image. This is a screen capture of part of a table from the **MembershipReboot** user management and authentication library:

Advanced DB topics

There are many other database performance enhancing techniques that we could cover here, but don't have space for. We'll briefly mention some additional topics in case you want to look into them further.

A common requirement when saving data is to insert a record if it doesn't yet exist, or to update an existing record if there is already a row containing that ID. This is sometimes referred to as an **upsert**, which is a portmanteau word combining update and insert.

You can use the MERGE command, to do this in one operation and not worry about choosing between UPDATE or INSERT (wrapped in a **transaction** inside a **stored procedure**). However, MERGE does not perform as well as UPDATE or INSERT, so always test the effects for your use case, and use it sparingly.

Stored procedures, transactions, and **locking** are all big subjects on their own. They are important to understand, and not only from a performance perspective. We can't fit all of these in here, but we will touch upon maintaining stored procedures later in the book.

Some other techniques you could look into are **cross-database joins**, which can save you from querying multiple DBs. There is also the practice of **denormalizing** your data, which involves flattening your relational records ahead of time to provide a single row rather than needing to join across many tables for a query. We briefly mentioned this in relation to data warehouses earlier.

 You can find lots of useful SQL documentation and information on MSDN (msdn.microsoft.com) and TechNet (technet.microsoft.com). Additionally, there are many good books on advanced SQL techniques.

Finally, a note on housekeeping. It's important to have a plan for managing the size of a database. You can't simply keep inserting data into a table, and hope it will continue to perform well forever. At some point, it will get so large that even deleting records from it will cause your DB to grind to a crawl. You should know ahead of time how you will remove or archive rows, and it is better to do this regularly in small batches.

Simulation and testing

To wrap up this chapter, let's reiterate the importance of being able to test your application on realistic infrastructure. Your test environments should be as live-like as possible. If you don't test on equivalent DBs and networks, then you may get a nasty surprise come deployment time.

When using a cloud hosting provider (and if you automate your server builds), then this is easy: you can simply Spin-up a staging system that matches production. You don't have to provision it to the exact same scale as long as all the parts are there and in the same place. To reduce costs further, you only need to keep it around for as long as your test.

Alternatively, you could create a new live environment, deploy and test it, then switch over, and destroy or reuse the old live environment. This swapping technique is known as **blue-green deployment**. Another option is to deploy new code behind a **feature switch**, which allows you to toggle the feature at runtime, and only for some users. Not only does this allow you to functionally verify features with test users, you can also gradually roll out a new feature, and monitor the performance impact as you do so. We will cover both of these techniques in `Chapter 9`, *Monitoring Performance Regressions*.

Summary

We've covered a lot in this chapter, and it should hopefully be clear that being a high performance developer requires more than simply being a capable programmer. There are many externalities to consider around your code.

You now understand the basics of I/O, and the physical causes of the intrinsic limitations present. You can analyze and diagnose how a network logically fits together. We have covered how to make better use of the network to reduce overall latency, which is important as more I/O operations now happen over a network. You have also seen how to make better use of a database, and how to do more with fewer operations.

In the next chapter, we will dig into code execution in detail, and show you how to speed up your C#. We'll see how .NET Core and ASP.NET Core perform so much better than the previous versions, and how you can take advantage of these improvements.

6
Understanding Code Execution and Asynchronous Operations

This chapter covers solving performance problems in the execution of your code, which is not normally the first location that speed issues occur, but can be a good additional optimization. We'll discuss the areas where performance is needed, and where it is okay (or even required) to be slow. The merits of various data structures will be compared from the standard built-in generic collections to the more exotic. We will demonstrate how to compute operations in parallel, and how to take advantage of extra instruction sets that your CPU may provide. We'll dive into the internals of ASP.NET Core and .NET Core to highlight the improvements that you should be aware of.

The topics covered in this chapter include the following:

- .NET Core and the native tool chain
- **Common Language Runtime** (**CLR**) services such as GC, JIT, and NGen
- ASP.NET Core and the Kestrel web server
- Generic collections and Bloom filters
- Serialization and data representation formats
- Relative performance of hashing functions
- Parallelization (SIMD, TPL, and PLINQ)
- Poorly performing practices to avoid

You will learn how to compute results in parallel and combine the outputs at the end. This includes how to avoid incorrect ways of doing this, which can make things worse. You'll also learn how to reduce server utilization, and to choose the most appropriate data structures in order to process information efficiently for your specific situation.

Getting started with the core projects

There are many benefits of using .NET Core and ASP.NET Core over the old full versions of the frameworks. The main enhancements are the open source development and cross platform support, but there are also significant performance improvements. Open development is important and the source code is not only available, the development work happens in the open on GitHub. The community is encouraged to make contributions and these may be merged in upstream if they pass a code review; the flow isn't just one way. This has led to increased performance and additional platform support coming from outside of Microsoft. If you find a bug in a framework, you can now fix it rather than work around the problem and hope for a patch.

The multiple projects that make up the frameworks are split across two organizations on GitHub. One of the driving principles has been to split the frameworks up into modules, so you can just take what you need rather than the whole monolithic installation. The lower level framework, .NET Core, can be found, along with other projects, under `github.com/dotnet`. The higher level web application framework, ASP.NET Core, can be found under `github.com/aspnet`. The reason for this split is that .NET Core is managed by the *.NET Foundation* which is an independent organization, although most of the members are Microsoft staff. ASP.NET Core is managed directly by Microsoft.

Let's have a quick look at some of the various .NET Core repositories and how they fit together.

.NET Core

There are a couple of projects that form the main parts of .NET Core and these are CoreCLR and **CoreFX**. CoreCLR contains the .NET Core CLR and the base core library, `mscorlib`. The CLR is the virtual machine that runs the .NET code. CoreCLR contains a **just-in-time (JIT)** compiler, **Garbage Collector** (GC), and also base types and classes in `mscorlib`. CoreFX includes the foundational libraries and sits on top of CoreCLR. This includes most built-in components that aren't simple types.

 You may be familiar with the `<gcServer>` element used to set a GC mode, more suitable for server use, with shorter pauses. You can read more about the original version at `msdn.microsoft.com/en-us/library/ms229357`. In .NET Core you can set the `COMplus_gcServer` environment variable to 1 or set `System.GC.Server` to `true` as a runtime option in a JSON runtime configuration file.

It's worth highlighting another project called **CoreRT**, which is a runtime that allows **ahead-of-time** (**AOT**) compilation, instead of the JIT of CoreCLR. This means that you can compile your C# code to native machine code, and run it without any dependencies. You end up with a single (statically linked) binary and don't need .NET installed, which is very similar to how **Go** operates. With the Roslyn compiler, you no longer always need to compile to **Common Intermediate Language** (**CIL**) bytecode then have the CLR JIT compile to native instructions at runtime with **RyuJIT**.

This native tool chain allows for performance improvements, as the compilation does not have to happen quickly, in real time, and can be further optimized. For example, a build can be tuned for execution speed at the expense of compilation speed. It's conceptually similar to the **Native Image Generator** (**NGen**) tool, which has been in the full .NET Framework since its inception.

ASP.NET Core

ASP.NET Core runs on top of .NET Core, although it can also run on the full .NET Framework. We will only cover running on .NET Core, as this performs better and ensures enhanced platform support. There are many projects that make up ASP.NET Core and it's worth briefly mentioning some of them.

> It's useful to not include any framework references to .NET 4.5/4.6 in your project, so that you can be sure you're only using .NET Core and don't accidentally reference any dependencies that are not yet supported.

ASP.NET Core includes **Model View Controller** (**MVC**), **Web API,** and **Web Pages** (a way to make simple pages with **Razor**, similar to PHP, and the spiritual successor to classic ASP). These features are all merged together, so you don't need to think of MVC and Web API as separate frameworks anymore. There are many other projects and repositories, including **EF Core**, but the one we will highlight here is the Kestrel HTTP server.

Kestrel

Kestrel is a new web server for ASP.NET Core and it performs brilliantly. It's based on **libuv**, which is an asynchronous I/O abstraction and support library that also runs below Node.js. Kestrel is blazingly fast, and the benchmarks are very impressive. However, it is pretty basic, and for production hosting, you should put it behind a reverse proxy, so that you can use caching and other features to service a greater number of users. You can use many HTTP or proxy servers for this purpose such as IIS, NGINX, Apache, or HAProxy.

You should be careful with your configuration if using NGINX as a reverse proxy, as by default, it will retry POST requests if the response from your web server times out. This could result in duplicate operations being performed, especially if used as a load balancer across multiple backend HTTP servers.

Data structures

Data structures are objects that you can use to store the information you're working on. Choosing the best implementation for how your data is used can have dramatic effects on the speed of execution. Here, we'll discuss some common and some more interesting data structures that you might like to make use of.

As this is a book about web application programming and not one on complex algorithm implementation or micro-optimization, we won't be going into a huge amount of detail on data structures and algorithms. As briefly mentioned in the introduction, other factors can dwarf the execution speed in a web context, and we assume you're not writing a game engine. However, good algorithms can help speed up applications, so, if you are working in an area where execution performance is important, you should read more about them.

We're more interested in the performance of the system as a whole, not necessarily the speed the code runs at. It is often more important to consider what your code expresses (and how this affects other systems) than how it executes. Nevertheless, it is still important to choose the right tool for the job, and you don't want to have unnecessarily slow code. Just be careful of over-optimizing when it already executes fast enough, and above all, try to keep it readable.

Lists

A .NET List<T> is a staple of programming in C#. It's type safe, so you don't have to bother with casting or boxing. You specify your generic type and can be sure that only objects of that class (or primitive) can be in your list. Lists implement the standard list and enumerable interfaces (IList and IEnumerable), although you get more methods on the concrete list implementation, for example, adding a range. You can also use **Language-Integrated Query** (**LINQ**) expressions to easily query them, which is trivial when using **fluent lambda functions**. However, although LINQ is often an elegant solution to a problem, it can lead to performance issues, as it is not always optimized.

A list is really just an enhanced, one-dimensional, array. In fact, it uses an array internally to store the data. In some cases, it may be better to directly use an array for performance. Arrays can occasionally be a better choice, if you know exactly how much data there will be, and you need to iterate through it inside a tight loop. They can also be useful if you need more dimensions, or plan to consume all of the data in the array.

You should be careful with arrays; use them sparingly and only if benchmarking shows a performance problem when iterating over a list. Although they can be faster, they also make parallel programming and distributed architecture more difficult, which is where significant performance improvements can be made.

Modern high performance means scaling out to many cores and multiple machines. This is easier with an **immutable** state that doesn't change, which is easier to enforce with higher level abstractions than with arrays. For example, you can help enforce a read-only list with an interface.

If you are inserting or removing a lot of items in the middle of a large list, then it may be better to use the `LinkedList<T>` class. This has different performance characteristics to a list, as it isn't really a list—it's more of a chain. It may perform better than a list for some specialized cases, but, in most common cases, it will be slower. For example, access by index is quick with a list (as it is array backed), but slow with a linked list (as you will have to walk the chain).

It is normally best to initially focus on the what and why of your code rather than the how. LINQ is very good for this, as you simply declare your intentions, and don't need to worry about the implementation details and loops. It is a bad idea to optimize prematurely, so do this only if testing shows a performance problem. In most common cases, a list is the correct choice unless you need to select only a few values from a large set, in which case, dictionaries can perform better.

Dictionaries

Dictionaries are similar to lists, but excel at quickly retrieving a specific value with a key. Internally, they are implemented with a hash table. There's the legacy `Hashtable` class (in the `System.Collections.NonGeneric` package) but this is not type safe, whereas `Dictionary<T>` is a generic type, so you probably shouldn't use `Hashtable` unless you're porting old code to .NET Core. The same applies to `ArrayList`, which is the legacy, non-generic version of `List`.

A dictionary can look up a value with a key very quickly, whereas a list would need to go through all the values until the key was found. You can, however, still enumerate a dictionary as it is ordered, although this isn't really how it is intended to be used. If you don't need ordering, then you can use a `HashSet`. There are sorted versions of all of these data structures, and you can again use read-only interfaces to make them difficult to mutate.

Collection benchmarks

Accurate benchmarking is hard and there are lots of things which can skew your results. Compilers are very clever and will optimize, which can make trivial benchmarks less valuable. The compiler may output very similar code for different implementations.

What you put in your data structures will also have a large effect on their performance. It's usually best to test or profile your actual application and not optimize prematurely. Readability of code is very valuable and shouldn't be sacrificed for runtime efficiency unless there is a significant performance problem (or if it's already unreadable).

There are benchmarking frameworks that you can use to help with your testing, such as BenchmarkDotNet which is available at `github.com/PerfDotNet/BenchmarkDotNet`. However, these can be an overkill, and are sometimes tricky to set up, especially on .NET Core. Other options include **Simple Speed Tester** (which you can read more about at `theburningmonk.github.io/SimpleSpeedTester`) and **MiniBench** (available from `github.com/minibench`).

We'll perform some simple benchmarks to show how you might go about this. However, don't assume that the conclusions drawn here will always hold true, so test for your situation. First, we will define a simple function to run our tests:

```
private static long RunTest(Func<double> func, int runs = 1000)
{
    var s = Stopwatch.StartNew();
    for (int j = 0; j < runs; j++)
    {
        func();
    }
    s.Stop();
    return s.ElapsedMilliseconds;
}
```

We use `Stopwatch` here as using `DateTime` can cause problems, even when using UTC, as the time could change during the test and the resolution isn't high enough. We also need to perform many runs to get an accurate result. We then define our data structures to test and prepopulate them with random data.

```
var rng = new Random();
var elements = 100000;
var randomDic = new Dictionary<int, double>();
for (int i = 0; i < elements; i++)
{
    randomDic.Add(i, rng.NextDouble());
}
var randomList = randomDic.ToList();
var randomArray = randomList.ToArray();
```

We now have an array, list, and dictionary containing the same set of 100,000 key/value pairs. Next, we can perform some tests on them to see what structure performs best in various situations.

```
var afems = RunTest(() =>
{
    var sum = 0d;
    foreach (var element in randomArray)
    {
        sum += element.Value;
    }
    return sum;
}, runs);
```

The preceding code times how long it takes to iterate over an array in a `foreach` loop and sums up the double precision floating point values. We can then compare this to other structures and the different ways of accessing them. For example, iterating a dictionary in a `for` loop is done as follows:

```
var dfms = RunTest(() =>
{
    var sum = 0d;
    for (int i = 0; i < randomDic.Count; i++)
    {
        sum += randomDic[i];
    }
    return sum;
}, runs);
```

This performs very badly, as it is not how dictionaries are supposed to be used. Dictionaries excel at extracting a record by its key very quickly. So quickly in fact that you will need to run the test many more times to get a realistic value.

```
var lastKey = randomList.Last().Key;
var dsms = RunTest(() =>
{
    double result;
    if (randomDic.TryGetValue(lastKey, out result))
    {
        return result;
    }
    return 0d;
}, runs * 10000);
Console.WriteLine($"Dict select {(double)dsms / 10000} ms");
```

Getting a value from a dictionary with `TryGetValue` is extremely quick. You need to pass the variable to be set into the method as an `out` parameter. You can see if this was successful and if the item was in the dictionary by testing the Boolean value returned by the method.

Conversely, adding items to a dictionary one by one can be slow, so it all depends on what you're optimizing for. The following image shows the output of a very simple console application that tests various combinatorial permutations of data structures and their uses:

These results, shown in the preceding image, are informative, but you should be skeptical, as many things can skew the output, for example, the ordering of the tests. If the gap is small, then there is probably not much to choose between two variants, but you can clearly see the big differences.

> To get more realistic results, be sure to compile in release mode and run without debugging. The absolute results will depend on your machine and architecture, but the relative measures should be useful for comparisons. You may get higher performance if compiling to a single executable binary with the .NET native tool chain or with a different release of the .NET Core framework.

The main lesson here is to measure for your specific application and choose the most appropriate data structure for the work that you are performing. The collections in the standard library should serve you well for most purposes, and there are others that are not covered here, which can sometimes be useful, such as a `Queue` or `Stack`.

You can find more information about the built-in collections and data structures on MSDN (`msdn.microsoft.com/en-us/library/system.collections.generic`). You can also read about them on the .NET Core documentation site on the GitHub pages (`dotnet.github.io/docs/essentials/collections/Collections-and-Data-Structures.html`).

However, there are some rarer data structures, not in the standard collection, that you may occasionally wish to use. We'll show an example of one of these now.

Bloom filters

Bloom filters are an interesting data structure that can increase performance for certain use cases. They use multiple overlaid hashing functions and can quickly tell you if an item definitely does not exist in a set. However, they can't say with certainty if an item exists, only that it is likely to. They are useful as a pre-filter, so that you can avoid performing a lookup, because you know for sure that the item won't be there.

The following image shows how a Bloom filter works. **A**, **B**, and **C** have been hashed and inserted into the filter. **D** is hashed to check if it is in the filter but, as it maps to a zero bit, we know that it is not in there.

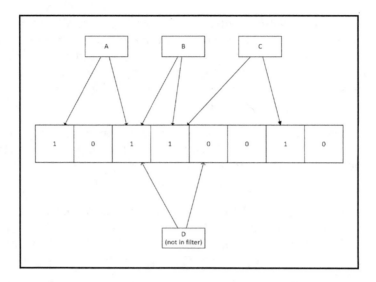

Bloom filters are much smaller than holding all the data or even a list of hashes for each item in the set. They can also be much quicker, as the lookup time is constant for any size of set. This constant time can be lower than the time to look up an item in a large list or dictionary, especially if it is on the file system or in a remote database.

An example application for a Bloom filter could be a local DNS server, which has a list of domains to override, but forwards most requests to an upstream server. If the list of custom domains is large, then it may be advantageous to create a Bloom filter from the entries and hold this in memory.

When a request comes in, it is checked against the filter, and if it doesn't exist, then the request is forwarded to the upstream server. If the entry does exist in the filter, then the local hosts file is consulted; if the entry is there, its value is used. There is a small chance that the entry will not be in the list, even if the filter thinks it is. In this case, when it isn't found, the request is forwarded, but this approach still avoids the need to consult the list for every request.

Another example of using a Bloom filter is in a caching node, perhaps as part of a proxy or CDN. You wouldn't want to cache resources that are only requested once, but how can you tell when the second request occurs if you haven't cached it? If you add the request to a Bloom filter, you can easily tell when the second request occurs and then cache the resource.

They are also used in some databases to avoid expensive disk operations and in **Cache Digests**, which allow an agent to declare the contents of its cache. HTTP/2 may support Cache Digests in the future, but this will probably use **Golomb-coded sets (GCS)**, which are similar to Bloom filters, but smaller, at the expense of slower queries.

There is an open source implementation of a Bloom filter in .NET available at `bloomfilter.codeplex.com` among others. You should test the performance for yourself to make sure they offer an improvement.

Hashing and checksums

Hashing is an important concept, which is often used to ensure data integrity or lookup values quickly and so it is optimized to be fast. This is why general hashing functions should not be used on their own to securely store passwords. If the algorithm is quick, then the password can be guessed in a reasonably short amount of time. Hashing algorithms vary in their complexity, speed of execution, output length, and collision rate.

A very basic error detection algorithm is called a **parity check**. This adds a single bit to a block of data and is rarely used directly in programming. It is, however, extensively used at the hardware level, as it is very quick. Yet, it may miss many errors where there are an even number of corruptions.

A **Cyclic Redundancy Check (CRC)** is a slightly more complex error detecting algorithm. The **CRC-32** (also written **CRC32**) version is commonly used in software, particularly in compression formats, as a **checksum**.

> You may be familiar with the built-in support for hash codes in .NET (with the `GetHashCode` method on all objects), but you should be very careful with this. The only function of this method is to assist with picking buckets in data structures that use hash tables internally, such as a dictionary, and also in some LINQ operations. It is not suitable as a checksum or key, because it is not cryptographically secure and it varies across frameworks, processes, and time.

You may have used the **Message Digest 5 (MD5)** algorithm in the past, but today its use is strongly discouraged. The security of MD5 is heavily compromised and collisions can be produced easily. Since it is very quick, it may have some non-secure uses, such as non-malicious error checking but there are better algorithms that are fast enough.

If you need a strong but quick hashing function, then the **Secure Hash Algorithm** (**SHA**) family is a good choice. However, **SHA-1** is not considered future proof, so for a new code, **SHA-256** is generally a better choice.

When signing messages, you should use a dedicated **Message Authentication Code** (**MAC**), such as a **Hash-based MAC** (**HMAC**), which avoids vulnerabilities in a single pass of the hashing function. A good option is the HMACSHA256 class built into .NET. Various APIs, such as some of the AWS REST APIs, use **HMAC-SHA256** to authenticate requests. This ensures that, even if the request is performed over an unencrypted HTTP channel, the API key can't be intercepted and recovered.

As briefly mentioned in Chapter 1, *Why Performance Is a Feature*, password hashing is a special case and general purpose hashing algorithms are not suitable for it—they are too fast. A good choice is **Password-Based Key Derivation Function 2** (**PBKDF2**), which we used as an example in Chapter 2, *Measuring Performance Bottlenecks*. PBKDF2 is a particularly popular choice for .NET, as it is built into the framework, and so, the implementation is more likely to be correct. It has been built against an RFC and reviewed by Microsoft, which you can't say for any random piece of code found online. For example, you could download an implementation of **bcrypt** for .NET, but you have to trust that it was coded correctly or verify it yourself.

Hashing benchmarks

Let's do some simple benchmarking of various hash functions to see how they compare performance wise. In the following code snippet, we define a method for running our tests, similar to the one for the previous collection benchmarks, but taking an Action parameter, rather than a Func<double>, as we don't want to return a value:

```
private static long RunTest(Action func, int runs = 1000)
{
    var s = Stopwatch.StartNew();
    for (int j = 0; j < runs; j++)
    {
        func();
    }
    s.Stop();
    return s.ElapsedMilliseconds;
}
```

We include the following using statement:

```
using System.Security.Cryptography;
```

Next, we define a short private constant string (`hashingData`) to hash in the class and get the bytes for it in an 8-bit Unicode (`UTF8`) format.

```
var smallBytes = Encoding.UTF8.GetBytes(hashingData);
```

We also want to get a larger block of bytes to hash to see how it compares performance wise. For this, we use a cryptographically secure random number generator.

```
var largeBytes = new byte[smallBytes.Length * 100];
var rng = RandomNumberGenerator.Create();
rng.GetBytes(largeBytes);
```

We need a `key` for some of our functions, so we use the same technique to generate this.

```
var key = new byte[256];
var rng = RandomNumberGenerator.Create();
rng.GetBytes(key);
```

Next, we create a sorted list of the algorithms to test and execute the tests for each one:

```
var algos = new SortedList<string, HashAlgorithm>
{
    {"1.          MD5", MD5.Create()},
    {"2.        SHA-1", SHA1.Create()},
    {"3.      SHA-256", SHA256.Create()},
    {"4.   HMAC SHA-1", new HMACSHA1(key)},
    {"5. HMAC SHA-256", new HMACSHA256(key)},
};
foreach (var algo in algos)
{
    HashAlgorithmTest(algo);
}
```

Our test method runs the following tests on each algorithm. They all inherit from `HashAlgorithm`, so we can run the `ComputeHash` method on each of them for the small and large byte arrays.

```
var smallTimeMs = RunTest(() =>
{
    algo.Value.ComputeHash(smallBytes);
}, runs);
var largeTimeMs = RunTest(() =>
{
    algo.Value.ComputeHash(largeBytes);
}, runs);
```

We then calculate the average (mean) time for both sizes. We cast the long integer to a double precision floating point number so that we can represent small values between one and zero.

```
var avgSmallTimeMs = (double)smallTimeMs / runs;
var avgLargeTimeMS = (double)largeTimeMs / runs;
```

The preceding method then outputs these mean times to the console. We need to test PBKDF2 separately, as it doesn't inherit from `HashAlgorithm`.

```
var slowRuns = 10;
var pbkdf2 = new Rfc2898DeriveBytes(hashingData, key, 10000);
var pbkdf2Ms = RunTest(() =>
{
    pbkdf2.GetBytes(256);
}, slowRuns);
```

PBKDF2 is so slow that it would take a considerable amount of time to perform 100,000 runs (this is the point of using it). Internally, this RFC2898 implementation of the key-stretching algorithm runs HMAC SHA-1 10,000 times. The default is 1,000, but due to the computing power available today, it is recommended to set this to at least an order of magnitude higher. For example, **Wi-Fi Protected Access II (WPA2)** uses 4,096 rounds of iterations to produce a 256-bit key with the **Service Set Identifier (SSID)** as the **salt**.

The output will look something like the following:

```
C:\Windows\system32\cmd.exe                                    _ □ ×

Over 100000 runs:
1.          MD5 average time 42B 0.00072 ms 4200B 0.01245 ms
2.        SHA-1 average time 42B 0.00080 ms 4200B 0.01310 ms
3.      SHA-256 average time 42B 0.00096 ms 4200B 0.03125 ms
4.   HMAC SHA-1 average time 42B 0.00096 ms 4200B 0.01339 ms
5. HMAC SHA-256 average time 42B 0.00162 ms 4200B 0.03201 ms
6.       PBKDF2 average time 125 ms (over 10 runs)

Press any key...
```

From the preceding output, you can see that the time taken for one hash varies from about 720 nanoseconds for a small MD5 to 32 microseconds for a large HMAC SHA-256 and **125** milliseconds for a small PBKDF2 with typical parameters.

Benchmarking results can vary dramatically, so you shouldn't read too much into absolute values. For example, the output from the BenchmarkDotNet tool comparing MD5 and SHA-256 on the same machine looks like this:

```
// ***** BenchmarkRunner: Finish *****

// * Export *
  Algo_Md5VsSha256-report.csv
  Algo_Md5VsSha256-report-stackoverflow.md
  Algo_Md5VsSha256-report-default.md
  Algo_Md5VsSha256-report-github.md
  Algo_Md5VsSha256-report.txt
  Algo_Md5VsSha256-measurements.csv
  BuildPlots.R
  Algo_Md5VsSha256-report.html

// * Detailed results *
Algo_Md5VsSha256_Md5
Mean = 31.2803 us, StdError = 0.0880 us (0.28%); N = 20, StdDev = 0.3936 us
Min = 30.5574 us, Q1 = 31.0145 us, Median = 31.2130 us, Q3 = 31.6598 us, Max = 31.9157 us
IQR = 0.6453 us, LowerFence = 30.0466 us, UpperFence = 32.6277 us
ConfidenceInterval = [31.1078 us; 31.4528 us] (CI 95%)


Algo_Md5VsSha256_Sha256
Mean = 201.0418 us, StdError = 1.5320 us (0.76%); N = 33, StdDev = 8.8008 us
Min = 186.5222 us, Q1 = 193.0558 us, Median = 199.2981 us, Q3 = 208.7261 us, Max = 221.1175 us
IQR = 15.6703 us, LowerFence = 169.5503 us, UpperFence = 232.2315 us
ConfidenceInterval = [198.0391 us; 204.0446 us] (CI 95%)


Total time: 00:00:31 (31.33 sec)

// * Summary *
BenchmarkDotNet-Dev=v0.9.3.0+
OS=Microsoft Windows NT 6.2.9200.0
Processor=Intel(R) Core(TM) i5-3317U CPU @ 1.70GHz, ProcessorCount=4
Frequency=1656392 ticks, Resolution=603.7218 ns
HostCLR=MS.NET 4.0.30319.42000, Arch=64-bit DEBUG

Type=Algo_Md5VsSha256  Mode=Throughput

 Method :     Median :    StdDev :
--------------------------------------
    Md5 :  31.2130 us :  0.3936 us :
 Sha256 : 199.2981 us :  8.8008 us :

// * Warnings *
Benchmark was built in DEBUG configuration. Please, build it in RELEASE.

// ***** BenchmarkRunner: End *****

Global total time: 00:00:32 (32 sec)
```

You can see in the last image that the results are different to our homemade benchmark. However, this uses the full .NET Framework, calculates median rather than mean for the average time, and runs in debug mode (which it helpfully warns us of) among other things.

A faster machine will have a higher throughput (as can be seen in the BenchmarkDotNet README.md on GitHub). Dedicated hardware such as **Graphics Processing Units (GPUs)**, **Field-Programmable Gate Arrays (FPGAs)**, and **Application-Specific Integrated Circuits (ASICs)** can be much faster. These tend to be used in the mining of bitcoin (and other crypto currencies), as these are based on hashing as a proof-of-work. Bitcoin uses SHA-256, but other currencies use different hashing algorithms.

The same algorithms form the basis of TLS, so faster hardware can handle a greater number of secure connections. As another example, Google built a custom ASIC called a **Tensor Processing Unit** (**TPU**) to accelerate their machine learning cloud services.

Other benchmarking samples are available in BenchmarkDotNet, and when you first run it, you will be presented with the following menu:

```
Available Benchmarks:
 #0  Algo_BitCount
 #1  Algo_Md5VsSha256
 #2  Algo_MostSignificantBit
 #3  Cpu_Atomics
 #4  Cpu_BranchPerdictor
 #5  Cpu_Ilp_Inc
 #6  Cpu_Ilp_Max
 #7  Cpu_Ilp_RyuJit
 #8  Cpu_Ilp_VsBce
 #9  Cpu_MatrixMultiplication
#10  Framework_DateTime
#11  Framework_DictionaryVsIDictionary
#12  Framework_SelectVsConvertAll
#13  Framework_StackFrameVsStackTrace
#14  Framework_Stopwatch
#15  Framework_StringConcatVsStringBuilder
#16  IL_Loops
#17  IL_ReadonlyFields
#18  IL_Switch
#19  IntroBaseline
#20  IntroBasic
#21  IntroColumns
#22  IntroCommandStyle
#23  IntroConfigSource
#24  IntroConfigUnion
#25  IntroDefaultToolchain
#26  IntroJobsFull
#27  IntroMultipleRuntimes
#28  IntroParams
#29  IntroTags
#30  Jit_ArraySumLoopUnrolling
#31  Jit_AsVsCast
#32  Jit_Bce
#33  Jit_BoolToInt
#34  Jit_GenericsMethod
#35  Jit_Inlining
#36  Jit_InterfaceMethod
#37  Jit_LoopUnrolling
#38  Jit_RegistersVsStack
#39  Jit_RotateBits
#40  Array_AccessNormalRefUnsafe
#41  Array_HeapAllocVsStackAlloc
#42  Math_DoubleSqrt
#43  Math_DoubleSqrtAvx
#44  Os_Sleep
```

The previous benchmark was the second option, (number #1 **Algo_Md5VsSha256**).

Benchmarking is hard, so it's a good idea to use a library such as BenchmarkDotNet if you can. The only conclusion we can draw from our benchmarks is that SHA-256 is slower than MD5. However, SHA-256 should be fast enough for most applications and it's more secure for integrity checking. However, it is still not suitable for password storage.

SHA-256 can be used to provide signatures for verifying downloaded files, which must be retrieved over HTTPS to be safe, and for signing certificates. When used as part of an HMAC, it can also be used to securely authenticate messages—API requests, for example. You will only connect successfully if you know the correct API key to hash with.

Serialization

Serialization is the process of turning objects into data suitable for transmission over a network or for storage. We also include deserialization, which is the reverse, under this umbrella. Serialization can have significant performance implications, not only on the network transmission speed but also on computation, as it can make up most of the expensive processing on a web server. You can read more about serialization on MSDN (msdn.microsoft.com/en-us/library/mt656716).

Serialization formats can be text-based or binary. Some popular text-based formats are Extensible Markup Language (**XML**) and **JavaScript Object Notation** (**JSON**). A popular binary format is **Protocol Buffers**, which was developed at Google. There's another binary serialization format (BinaryFormatter) built into the full .NET, but this is not in .NET Core.

XML has fallen out of fashion with developers, and JSON is now generally preferred. This is partly due to the smaller size of equivalent JSON payloads, but it may also be due to the use of XML in the originally named **Simple Object Access Protocol** (**SOAP**). This is used in **Windows Communication Foundation** (**WCF**), but SOAP is no longer an acronym, as developers discovered it is far from simple.

JSON is popular due to being compact, human-readable, and because it can easily be consumed by JavaScript, particularly in web browsers. There are many different JSON serializers for .NET, with different performance characteristics. However, because JSON is not as rigidly defined as XML, there can be differences in implementations, which make them incompatible, especially when dealing with complex types such as dates. For example, the very popular **Json.NET** represents dates in the **International Organization for Standardization** (**ISO**) format, whereas the JSON serializer used in old versions of ASP.NET MVC represented dates as the number of milliseconds since the Unix **epoch**, wrapped in a JavaScript date constructor.

The .NET developer community has converged on Json.NET, and compatibility is always preferable to performance. ASP.NET Web API has used Json.NET as the default for a while now, and ASP.NET Core also uses Json.NET. There is a serializer that's part of the **ServiceStack** framework called **ServiceStack.Text**, which claims to be faster, but you should probably value compatibility and documentation over speed. The same applies to other JSON libraries such as Jil (github.com/kevin-montrose/Jil) and **NetJSON** (github.com/rpgmaker/NetJSON), which can be even faster than ServiceStack in benchmarks.

If you are after pure performance, and you control all of the endpoints, then you probably would want to use a binary protocol. However, this may limit future interoperability with third-party endpoints which you don't control. Therefore, it's best to only use these internally.

It would be a bad idea to build your own custom message protocol on top of UDP. So, if you want to use binary serialization, you should look at something like **protobuf-net**, which is a Protocol Buffers implementation for .NET. You may also wish to consider Microsoft's Bond framework (`github.com/Microsoft/bond`) or Amazon's Ion (`amznlabs.github.io/ion-docs`). You may need to tune these tools for best performance, for example, by changing the default buffer size.

SIMD CPU instructions

Single Instruction Multiple Data (**SIMD**) is a technique that is available on many modern processors and can speed up execution by parallelizing calculations even in a single thread on one core. SIMD takes advantage of additional instructions available on CPUs to operate on sets of values (vectors) rather than just single values (scalars).

The most common instruction set for this is called **Streaming SIMD Extensions 2** (**SSE2**) and it has been around for over 15 years since its debut with the Pentium 4. A newer instruction set called **Advanced Vector Extensions** (**AVX**) offers superior performance over SSE2 and has been around for over five years. So, if you're using a reasonably recent x86-64 CPU, then you should have access to these extra instructions.

 Some ARM CPUs (such as those in the Raspberry Pi 2 and 3) contain a similar technology called **NEON**, officially known as **Advanced SIMD**. This is not currently supported in .NET, but may be in the future. An official open source library project in C is hosted at `projectne10.org`.

You can use the following Boolean property to test if SIMD is supported:

```
Vector.IsHardwareAccelerated
```

This property is JIT intrinsic, and the value is set by RyuJIT at runtime.

You can instantiate a generic typed `Vector` or use one of the two/three/four dimensional convenience classes. For example, to create a single precision floating point vector, you could use the following generic code:

```
var vectorf = new Vector<float>(11f);
```

To create a single precision floating point 3D vector instead, you could use this code:

```
var vector3d = new Vector3(0f, 1f, 2f);
```

A two dimensional double precision floating point vector can be a good substitute for a `Complex` structure. It will give higher performance on hardware accelerated systems. `Vector2` only supports single precision floating point numbers, but you can use the generic type to specify the real and imaginary components of the complex number as a double. `Complex` only supports double precision floating point numbers, but, if you don't need high precision, you could still use the `Vector2` convenience class. Unfortunately, this means that it's not simply a drop in replacement, but the math is different anyway.

You can now use standard vector mathematics, but modifying your algorithms to take advantage of vectors can be complex and isn't something you should typically be doing in a web application. It can be useful for desktop applications, but, if a process takes a long time in a web request, it's often best to run it in the background and then it doesn't need to be as quick.

We will cover this distributed architecture approach in the next chapter. For this reason, we won't be going into any more detail on SIMD, but you can read more on it if you wish, now that you have a taste of it. You can read some background information at `wikipedia.org/wiki/SIMD` and you can find the documentation for the .NET implementation on MSDN at `msdn.microsoft.com/en-us/library/dn858218`. You could also take a look at the example console application, which is available for download along with this book, as a simple starter for ten.

Parallel programming

While SIMD is good at increasing the performance of a single thread running on one core, it doesn't work across multiple cores or processors and its applications are limited. Modern scaling means adding more CPUs, not simply making a single thread faster. We don't just want to parallelize our data as SIMD does; we should actually focus more on parallelizing our processing, as this can scale better.

There are various .NET technologies available to help with parallel processing so that you don't have to write your own threading code. Two such parallel extensions are **Parallel LINQ (PLINQ)**, which extends the LINQ operations you're familiar with, and the **Task Parallel Library (TPL)**.

Task Parallel Library

One of the main features of the TPL is to extend loops to run in parallel. However, you need to be careful with parallel processing, as it can actually make your software slower while doing simple tasks. The overheads involved with marshalling the multiple tasks can dwarf the execution of the workload for trivial operations.

For example, take the following simple `for` loop:

```
for (int i = 0; i < array.Length; i++)
{
    sum += array[i];
}
```

The array in the preceding `for` loop contains 100,000 integers, but adding integers is one of the easiest things a CPU can do and using a `for` loop on an array is a very quick way of enumerating. This accumulation will complete in under a tenth of a millisecond on a reasonably modern machine.

You may think that you would be able to speed this up by parallelizing the operation. Perhaps you could split the array, run the summation on two cores in parallel and add the results.

You might use the following code to attempt this:

```
Parallel.For(0, array.Length, i =>
{
    Interlocked.Add(ref sum, array[i]);
});
```

 You must use an interlocked add or you will get an incorrect summation result. If you don't, the threads will interfere with each other, corrupting the data when writing to the same location in memory.

However, this code actually runs over 42 times slower than the first example. The extra overhead, complexity of running many threads, and locking the variable so that only one thread can write to it at a time is just not worth it in this case.

Parallelization can be useful for more complex processes, especially if the body of the loop performs some slow operation such as accessing the file system. However, blocking I/O operations may be better dealt with by using asynchronous access. Parallel access can cause contention, because access may eventually have to be performed in series at some point, for example, at the hardware level.

If we want to perform a more processor-intensive operation, such as hashing multiple passwords, then running the tasks in parallel can be beneficial. The following code performs a PBKDF2 hash on each password in a list and then calculates the Base64 representation of the result:

```
foreach (var password in passwords)
{
    var pbkdf2 = new Rfc2898DeriveBytes(password, 256, 10000);
    Convert.ToBase64String(pbkdf2.GetBytes(256));
}
```

We're not using the output in this example, but you may be doing this to upgrade the security of the passwords in your database by migrating them to a more resilient key-stretching algorithm. The input may be plaintext passwords or the output of a legacy one-way hash function, for example MD5 or an unsalted SHA.

We can improve the speed of this on a multicore system by using the `Parallel.ForEach` loop, using code such as the following:

```
Parallel.ForEach(passwords, password =>
{
    var pbkdf2 = new Rfc2898DeriveBytes(password, 256, 10000);
    Convert.ToBase64String(pbkdf2.GetBytes(256));
});
```

This will speed up the process, but by how much will depend on many factors, such as the number of passwords in the list, the number of logical processors and the number of CPU cores. For example, on a Core i5 CPU with two cores, but four logical processors, having only two passwords in the list does not result in a massive improvement (only 1.5 times quicker). With four passwords (or more) in the list, the improvement is better (about 1.9 times quicker). There is still some overhead, so you can't get double the speed with twice the CPU cores.

We can see the reason for this difference by looking at the CPU utilization in the task manager during benchmarking. With only two passwords to hash, the CPU graph looks like the following:

In the preceding graph, we can see that initially, when hashing in series, the CPU is running at about 25%, fully using one logical CPU. When hashing two passwords in parallel, it uses 50%, running on two logical processors. This doesn't translate into a twofold increase in speed due to the intrinsic overheads and the nature of **hyper-threading**.

 Hyper-threading is a technology that typically exposes two logical processors to the OS for each physical core. However, the two logical CPUs still share the execution resources of their single core.

Although there are two cores on the CPU die, hyper-threading exposes four logical CPUs to the OS. As we only have two threads, because we are hashing two passwords, we can only use two processors. If the threads are executed on different cores, then the speed increase can be good. But if they are executed on processors sharing the same core, then performance won't be as impressive. It is still better than single-threaded hashing due to scheduling improvements, which is what hyper-threading is designed for.

When we hash four passwords at the same time, the CPU graph looks like the following:

We can see that now the initial 25% usage jumps to almost full utilization and we are making use of most of the processor. This translates to just under a doubling of the performance as compared to hashing in sequence. There are still significant overheads involved, but, as the main operation is now so much quicker, the tradeoff is worth it.

Parallel LINQ

There are other ways to take advantage of parallel programming, such as LINQ expressions. We could rewrite the previous example as a LINQ expression and it may look something like the following:

```
passwords.AsParallel().ForAll(p =>
{
    var pbkdf2 = new Rfc2898DeriveBytes(p, 256, 10000);
    Convert.ToBase64String(pbkdf2.GetBytes(256));
});
```

You can enable these features with the `AsParallel()` method. The `ForAll()` method has the same purpose as the loops in previous examples and is useful if the order is unimportant. If ordering is important, then there is an `AsOrdered()` method, which can help solve this. However, this can reduce the performance gains due to the extra processing involved.

This example performs similarly to the previous one that used a parallel loop, which is unsurprising. We can also limit the number of operations that can occur in parallel, using the `WithDegreeOfParallelism()` method as follows:

```
passwords.AsParallel().WithDegreeOfParallelism(2).ForAll(p =>
{
    var pbkdf2 = new Rfc2898DeriveBytes(p, 256, 10000);
    Convert.ToBase64String(pbkdf2.GetBytes(256));
});
```

This preceding example limits the hashes to two at a time and performs similarly to when we only had two passwords in the list, which is to be expected. This can be useful if you don't want to max out the CPU, because there are other important processes running on it.

You can achieve the same effect with the TPL by setting the `MaxDegreeOfParallelism` property on an instance of the `ParallelOptions` class. This object can then be passed into overloaded versions of the loop methods as a parameter, along with the main body.

> It's important, when you're using parallel LINQ to query datasets, that you don't lose sight of the best place for the query to be performed. You may speed up a query in the application with parallelization, but the best place for the query to occur may still be in the database, which can be even faster. To read more on this topic, refer back to `Chapter 5`, *Optimizing I/O Performance*, and `Chapter 3`, *Fixing Common Performance Problems*.

Parallel benchmarking

Let's have a look at the output of a simple .NET Core console application, which benchmarks the techniques that we have just discussed. It shows one situation where parallelization doesn't help and actually makes things worse. It then shows another situation where it does help.

When calculating a sum, by accumulating 100,000 random integers between zero and ten, the quickest way is to use an array in a simple `foreach` loop. Using parallelization here makes the process much slower, and if used naïvely, without locking, will give an incorrect result, which is much worse.

When performing a more computationally intensive workload, such as a PBKDF2 hashing function on multiple passwords, parallelization can help significantly. The time is almost halved, as it is running across two cores. The final operation, which limits the number of threads, can take a varying amount of time on different runs. This is likely due to the threads sometimes sharing a core and sometimes running on different cores. It can be almost as quick as using all logical cores, depending on the work.

The CPU graph for the benchmark looks like the following:

The initial parallel summations max out the CPU and are very inefficient. Next, the single-threaded hashing uses only one logical processor (25%), but the other, later hashes make almost full use of both the cores. The final hashing, limited to two passwords at a time, only makes use of half the CPU power.

Parallel programming limitations

Performance problems with web applications don't typically mean increasing speed for a single user on the system in isolation. It's easy to make a web app perform when there's only one user, but the challenge lies in maintaining that single user performance as the number of users scales up and you have wall-to-wall requests.

The parallel programming techniques discussed in this section have limited use in scaling web applications. You already have a parallelized system, as each user request will be allocated its own resources. You can simply add more instances, agents, or machines to meet demand. The problem then is in distributing work efficiently between them and avoiding bottlenecks for shared resources. We'll cover this more in the next chapter, but first let's look at some things that you should be avoiding.

Practices to avoid

We've shown some ways of speeding up software, but it's often better to illustrate what not to do and how things can go wrong. Web applications generally perform well if no bad practices have been followed and here we'll highlight a few things you should watch out for.

Reflection

Reflection is the process of programmatically inspecting your code with other code, and digging into its internals at runtime. For example, you could inspect an assembly when it is loaded to see what classes and interfaces it implements so that you can call them. It is generally discouraged and should be avoided if possible. There are usually other ways to achieve the same result that don't require reflection, although it is occasionally useful.

Reflection is often bad for performance, and this is well-documented, but, as usual, it depends on what you're using it for. What is new is that there are significant changes to reflection for .NET Core. The API has changed and it is now optional. So, if you don't use reflection, you don't have to pay the performance penalty. This allows the native tool chain to optimize compilation better, as reflection adds restrictions to what can be done with static linking.

There is an extra method on the reflection API now, so, whereas previously you would have called something like `myObject.GetType().GetMembers()`, you now need to call it as `myObject.GetType().GetTypeInfo().GetMembers()` by inserting the new `GetTypeInfo()` method, which is in the `System.Reflection` namespace.

If you must use reflection, then it is best not to perform it repeatedly or in a tight loop. However, it would be fine to use it once during the startup of your application. Yet, if you can avoid using it entirely, you can benefit from some of the new improvements in .NET Core, for example, native compilation and the performance boost that it brings.

Regular expressions

A **regular expression (regex)** can be very useful, but can perform badly and is typically misused in situations where another solution would be better. For example, a regex is often used for e-mail validation when there are much more reliable ways to do this.

If reusing a regex repeatedly, you may be better off compiling it for performance by specifying the `RegexOptions.Compiled` option in the constructor. This only helps if you're using the regex a lot and involves an initial performance penalty. So, ensure that you check if there is actually an improvement and it isn't now slower.

The `RegexOptions.IgnoreCase` option can also affect performance, but it may in fact slow things down, so always test for your inputs. Compiling has an effect on this too and you may want to use `RegexOptions.CultureInvariant` in addition, to avoid comparison issues.

Be wary of trusting user input to a regex. It is possible to get them to perform a large amount of backtracking and use excessive resources. You shouldn't allow unconstrained input to a regex, as they can be made to run for hours.

Regexes are often used for e-mail address validation, but this is usually a bad idea. The only way to fully validate an e-mail address is to send an e-mail to it. You can then have the user click a link in the e-mail to indicate that they have access to that mailbox and have received it. E-mail addresses can vary a lot from the common ones that people are regularly exposed to, and this is even truer with the new top-level domains being added.

Many of the regexes for e-mail address validation found online will reject perfectly valid e-mail addresses. If you want to assist the user, and perform some basic e-mail address validation on a form, then all you can sensibly do is check that there is an @ symbol in it (and a . after that) so that the e-mail is in the form `x@y.z`. You can do this with a simple string test and avoid the performance penalty and security risk of a regular expression.

String concatenation in tight loops

As strings are immutable and can't change, when you concatenate a string, a new object is created. This can cause performance problems and issues with memory use if you do it a lot inside a tight loop.

You may find it better to use a string builder or another approach. However, don't fret too much about this, as it only applies at a large scale. Always test to see if it is genuinely a problem and don't micro-optimize where you don't need to.

It's good general advice to work out where your code is spending most of its time, and focus your optimization there. It's obviously much better to optimize code executed millions of times inside a loop than code that only runs occasionally.

Dynamic typing

C# is a statically typed language and variable types are checked at compile time, but it does have some dynamic features. You can use the `dynamic` type and objects such as `ExpandoObject` to get some of the features of a dynamically typed language. The `var` type is not in fact dynamic, and is simply inferred at compile time.

Dynamic typing has a performance and safety penalty, so it is best avoided if you can find another way to solve your problem. For example, the `ViewBag` in ASP.NET MVC is dynamic, so it is best not to use `ViewBag`, and use a well-defined view model instead. This has many other benefits apart from performance, such as safety and convenience.

Synchronous operations

Synchronous methods block execution, and should be avoided if possible, especially if they are slow or access I/O. We've covered asynchronous (async for short) operations in previous chapters. Understanding how to use async is important for modern high performance programming, and new language features make it more accessible than ever. If an async method is available, then it should generally be used in preference to the synchronous blocking version.

The `async` and `await` keywords make asynchronous programming much easier than it used to be, but, as covered in `Chapter 3`, *Fixing Common Performance Problems*, the effects on web applications are not always visible for a lone user. These convenient features allow you to serve more users simultaneously by returning threads to the pool during downtime, while waiting for operations to complete. The threads can then be used to service other users' requests, which allows you to handle more users with less servers than otherwise.

Async methods can be useful, but the big gains come not from writing asynchronous code, but from having an asynchronous architecture. We will cover distributed architecture in the next chapter, when we discuss message queuing.

Exceptions

Exceptions should, as the name suggests, be reserved for exceptional circumstances. Exceptions are slow and expensive and shouldn't be used as flow control in business logic if you know that an event is likely to occur.

This isn't to say that you shouldn't use exception handling—you should. However, it should be reserved for events that are genuinely unexpected and rare. If you can predict ahead of time that a condition may occur then you should handle it explicitly.

For example, the disk becoming full and your code not being able to write a file because there is no space is an exceptional situation. You would not expect this to normally happen, and you can just `try` the file operation and `catch` any exceptions. However, if you are trying to parse a date string or access a dictionary, then you should probably use the special `TryParse()` and `TryGetValue()` methods and check for null values rather than just relying on exception handling.

Summary

In this chapter, we discussed some techniques that can improve the performance of code execution and dug into the projects that make up .NET Core and ASP.NET Core. We explored data structures, serialization, hashing, and parallel programming and how to benchmark for measuring relative performance.

Linear performance characteristics are easier to scale and code that does not exhibit this behavior can be slow when the load increases. Code that has an exponential performance characteristic or has erratic outliers (which are rare but very slow when they occur) can cause performance headaches. It is often better to aim for code, that while being slightly slower in normal cases is more predictable and performs consistently over a large range of loads.

The main lesson here is to not blindly apply parallel programming and other potentially performance-enhancing techniques. Always test to make sure that they make a positive impact, as they can easily make things worse. We aim for the situation where everything is awesome, but, if we're not careful, we can make everything awful by mistake.

In the next chapter, you'll learn about caching and message queuing—two advanced techniques that can significantly improve the performance of a system.

7
Learning Caching and Message Queuing

Caching is incredibly useful and can be applied to almost all layers of an application stack. However, it's hard to always get caching working correctly, so, in this chapter, we will cover caching at the web, application, and database levels. We will show you how to use a reverse proxy server to store the results of your rendered web pages and other assets. We'll also cover caching at lower levels, using an in-memory data store to speed up access. You will learn how to ensure that you can always flush (or bust) your cache if you need to force the propagation of updates.

This chapter also covers asynchronous architecture design using message queuing and abstractions that encapsulate various messaging patterns. You will learn how to perform a long running operation (such as video encoding) in the background, while keeping the user informed of its progress.

You will learn how to apply caching and message queuing software design patterns to slow operations so that they don't have to be performed in real time. You'll also learn about the complexity that these patterns can add, and understand the tradeoffs involved. We'll see how to combat these complexities and mitigate the downsides, in Chapter 8, *The Downsides of Performance-Enhancing Tools*.

The topics covered in this chapter include the following:

- Web caching background
- JavaScript service workers
- Varnish proxy and IIS web servers
- Redis and Memcached in-memory application caching

- Message Queuing and messaging patterns
- RabbitMQ and its various client libraries

Why caching is hard

Caching is hard, but it's not hard because it's difficult to cache something. Caching indefinitely is easy, the hard part is invalidating the cache when you want to make an update. There's a well-used quote from the late Phil Karlton of Netscape that goes:

> *"There are only two hard things in Computer Science: cache invalidation and naming things."*

There are also many humorous variants on it, as used previously throughout this book. This sentiment may be a slight exaggeration, but it highlights how complex removing your "done-computer-stuff ^{TM}" from your "quick-things-box 2.0 ^{TM}" is perceived to be. Naming things is genuinely very hard though.

Caching is the process of storing a temporary snapshot of some data. This temporary cache can then be used instead of regenerating the original data (or retrieving it from the canonical source) every time it is required. Doing this has obvious performance benefits, but it makes your system more complicated and harder to conceptualize. When you have many caches interacting, the results can appear almost random unless you are disciplined in your approach.

When you are reasoning about caching (and message queuing), it is helpful to dispel the idea that data only exists in a single consistent state. It is easier if you embrace the concept that data has a freshness, and is always stale by some amount. This is in fact always the case, but the short timeframes involved in a small system mean that you can typically ignore it in order to simplify your thinking. However, when it comes to caching, the timescales are longer and so, freshness is more important. A system at scale can only be eventually consistent, and various parts of it will have a different temporal view of the data. You need to accept that data can be in motion, otherwise you're just not thinking four-dimensionally!

As a trivial example, consider a traditional static website. A visitor loads a page in their browser, but this page is now instantly out-of-date. The page on the server could have been updated just after the visitor retrieved it, but they will not know, as the old version will remain in their browser until they refresh the page.

If we extend this example to a database-backed web application, such as an ASP.NET or WordPress website, then the same principle applies. A user retrieves a web page generated from data in the database, but it could be out-of-date as soon as it is loaded. The underlying data could have changed, but the page containing the old data remains in the browser.

By default, web apps typically regenerate HTML from the DB for every page load, but this is incredibly inefficient if the data has not changed. It is only done like this so that when a change is made, it shows up immediately as soon as the page is refreshed.

However, a user may have an old page in their browser, and you have limited control over this. So you may as well cache this page on the server as well and only remove it when the underlying data in the database changes. Caching the rendered HTML like this is often essential for maintaining performance at a scale beyond simply a small number of users.

Web caching

The first category of caching that we'll discuss is at the web level. This involves storing the final output of your web stack as it would be sent to users so that, when requested again, it's ready to go and doesn't need to be regenerated. Caching at this stage removes the need for expensive database lookups and CPU-intensive rendering at the application layer. This reduces latency and decreases the workload on your servers, allowing you to handle more users and serve each user rapidly.

Web caching typically occurs on your web servers or on reverse proxy servers, which you have put in front of your web servers to shield them from excessive load. You might also choose to hand this task over to a third party, such as a CDN. Here we will cover two pieces of web server and proxy server software, IIS and Varnish. However, many more web caching and load balancing technologies are available, for example, NGINX or HAProxy.

Caching at the web layer works best for static assets and resources such as JavaScript, CSS, and images. Yet it can also work for anonymous HTML that is rarely updated but regularly accessed, such as a homepage or landing page, which is unauthenticated and not customized for a user.

We touched upon proxy servers in Chapter 3, *Fixing Common Performance Problems*, and covered web layer caching a little in Chapter 4, *Addressing Network Performance*. However, in this chapter, we'll go into more detail on web caching.

Caching background

Before we delve into the implementation details, it helps to understand a little about how caching works on the web. If you take the time to study the mechanisms at work, then caching will be less confusing and less frustrating than if you just dived straight in.

It is helpful to read and understand the relevant HTTP specifications. However, don't assume that software always strictly adheres to these web standards even if it claims to.

First, let's look at a typical network setup which you may be traversing with your HTTP traffic. The following diagram illustrates an example of a common configuration for a web application:

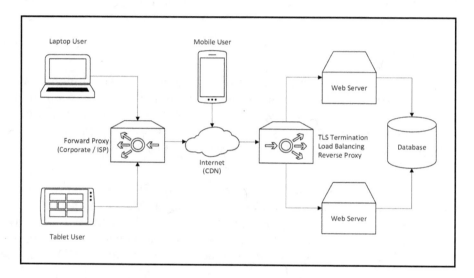

As seen in the preceding diagram, the laptop and tablet users are connecting through a caching forward proxy server (which may be on a corporate network or at an ISP). The mobile user is connecting directly over the internet. However, all users are going through a CDN before reaching your infrastructure.

After your firewall (not shown), there is an appliance which terminates the TLS connections, balances the load between web servers, and acts as a caching reverse proxy. These functions are often performed by separate devices, but we've kept things simple here.

Copies of your resources will be kept on your web servers, your reverse proxy, your CDN, any forward proxies, and in the browsers on all user devices. The simplest way to control the caching behavior of these resources is to use in-band signaling and add HTTP headers to your content, declaring cache control metadata only in a single place.

It's good practice to apply the same standard HTTP caching techniques to your own web servers and proxies even though you could customize them and flush their caches at will. This not only cuts down on the amount of configuration that you have to do, and avoids duplicated work, but it also ensures that any caches that you don't control should behave correctly too. Even when using HTTPS, the browser will still perform caching and there may also be transparent corporate proxies or meddling ISP captive portals in the way.

HTTP headers

HTTP caching involves setting cache control headers in your responses. There are many of these headers, which have been added over the years from different standards and various versions of the protocol. You should know how these are used, but you should also understand how the uniqueness of a cacheable resource is determined—for example, by varying the URL or by altering only a part of it, such as query string parameters.

Many of these headers can be categorized by function and the version of HTTP that they were introduced with. Some headers have multiple functions and some are non-standard, yet are almost universally used. We won't cover all of these headers, but we will pick out some of the most important ones.

There are broadly two types of caching header categories. The first defines an absolute time during which the cache can be reused, without checking with the server. The second defines rules which the client can use to test with the server if the cache is still valid.

Most instructional headers (those that issue caching commands) fit into one of these two header categories. In addition to these, there are many purely informational headers, which provide details about the original connection and client, which may otherwise be obscured by a cache (for example, the original client IP address).

Some headers, such as `Cache-Control`, are part of the latest standard, but others, such as `Expires`, are typically used only for backwards compatibility, in case there is an ancient browser or an old proxy server in the way. However, this practice is becoming increasingly unnecessary as infrastructure and software is upgraded.

The latest caching standard in this case is HTTP/1.1 as HTTP/2 uses the same caching directives (RFC 7234). Some headers date from HTTP/1.0, which is considered a legacy protocol. Very old software may only support HTTP/1.0.

Standards may not be implemented correctly in all applications. It is a sensible idea to test that any observed behavior is as expected.

The `Age` header is used to indicate how long (in seconds) a resource has been in a cache. On the other hand, the `ETag` header is used to specify an identifier for an individual object or a particular unique version of that object.

The `Cache-Control` header tells caches if the resource may be cached. It can have many values including a `max-age` (in seconds) or `no-cache` and `no-store` directives. The confusing, yet subtle, difference between `no-cache` and `no-store` is that `no-cache` indicates that the client should check with the server before using the resource, whereas `no-store` indicates that the resource shouldn't be cached at all. To prevent caching, you should generally use `no-store`.

The ASP.NET Core `ResponseCache` action attribute sets the `Cache-Control` header and is covered in `Chapter 4`, *Addressing Network Performance*. However, this header may be ignored by some older caches. `Pragma` and `Expires` are older headers used for backward compatibility and they perform some of the same functions that the `Cache-Control` header now handles.

The `X-Forwarded-*` headers are used to provide more information about the original connection to the proxy or load balancer. These are non-standard, but widely-used, and are standardized as the combined `Forwarded` header (**RFC 7239**). The `Via` header also provides some proxy information, and `Front-End-Https` is a non-standard Microsoft header, which is similar to `X-Forwarded-Proto`. These protocol headers are useful for telling you if the original connection used HTTPS when this is stripped at the load balancer.

If you are terminating the TLS connections at a load balancer or proxy server, and are also redirecting users to HTTPS at the application level, then it is important to check the `Forwarded` headers. You can get stuck in an infinite redirection loop if your web servers desire HTTPS but only receive HTTP from the load balancer. Ideally, you should check all varieties of the headers, but, if you control the proxy, you can decide what headers to use.

There are lots of different HTTP headers that are involved in caching. The following list includes some of the ones that we haven't covered here. The large quantity of headers should give you an idea of just how complicated caching can be.

- If-Match
- If-Modified-Since
- If-None-Match
- If-Range
- If-Unmodified-Since
- Last-Modified
- Max-Forwards
- Proxy-Authorization
- Vary

Cache busting

Cache busting (also known as cache bursting, cache flushing, or cache invalidation) is the hard part of caching. It is easy to put an item in a cache, but, if you don't have a strategy ahead of time to manage the inevitable change, then you may come unstuck.

Getting cache busting correct is usually more important with web-level caching. This is because, with server side caching (which we'll discuss later in this chapter), you are in full control and can reset if you get it wrong. A mistake on the web can persist and be difficult to remedy.

In addition to setting the correct headers, it is helpful to vary the URL of resources when their content changes. This can be done by adding a timestamp, but often a convenient solution is to use a hash of the resource content and append this as a parameter. Many frameworks, including ASP.NET Core, use this approach. For example, consider the following JavaScript tag in a web page:

```
<script src="js/site.js"></script>
```

If you make a change to site.js, then the browser (or proxy) won't know that it has altered and may use a previous version. However, it will re-request it if the output is changed to something like the following:

```
<script src="js/site.js?v=EWaMeWsJBYWmL2g_KkgXZQ5nPe-a3IchpOLEgzXczKo">
</script>
```

Here the v (version) parameter is the **Base64 URL encoded**, SHA-256 hashed content of the site.js file. Making a small change to the file will radically alter the hash due to the **avalanche effect**.

Base64 URL encoding is a variant on standard Base64 encoding. It uses different non-alphanumeric characters (+ becomes – while / changes to _) and percent encodes the = character (which is also made optional). Using this safe alphabet (from RFC 4648) makes the output suitable for use in URLs and filenames.

In ASP.NET Core, you can easily use this feature by adding the `asp-append-version` attribute with a value of `true` in your Razor views like so:

```
<script src="~/js/site.js" asp-append-version="true"></script>
```

Service workers

If you are writing a client-side web app, rather than a simple dynamic website, then you may wish to exert more control over caching using new browser features. You can do this by writing your cache control instructions in JavaScript (technically **ECMAScript 6 (ES6)**). This gives you many more options when it comes to a visitor using your web app offline.

A **service worker** gives you greater control than the previous AppCache API. It also opens the door to features such as mobile web app install banners (which prompt a user to add your web app to their home screen). However, it is still a relatively new technology.

Service workers are a new experimental technology, and as such, are currently only supported in some recent browsers (partially in Chrome, Firefox, and Opera). You may prefer to use the previous deprecated AppCache method (which is almost universally supported) until adoption is more widespread.

Information on current browser support is available at `caniuse.com/#feat=serviceworkers` and `caniuse.com/#feat=offline-apps` (for AppCache).

A more detailed service worker breakdown is available at `jakearchibald.github.io/isserviceworkerready`.

A service worker can do many useful things (such as background synchronization and push notifications), but the interesting parts, from our point of view, are the scriptable caches, which enable offline use. It effectively acts as an in-browser proxy server and can be used to improve the performance of a web application in addition to allowing interaction without an internet connection (after initial installation, of course).

There are other types of **web workers** apart from service workers (for example, audio workers, dedicated workers, and shared workers), but we won't go into these here. All web workers allow you to offload work to a background task so that you don't make the browser unresponsive (by blocking the main UI thread with your work).

Service workers are asynchronous and rely heavily on JavaScript **promises**, which we'll assume you are familiar with. If you're not, then you should read up on them, as they're useful in many other contexts involving asynchronous and parallel scripting.

Service workers require the use of HTTPS (yet another good reason to use TLS on your entire site). However, there is an exception for localhost, so you can still develop locally.

Service worker example

To install a service worker, first create a file for it (which is served over HTTPS). In the following example, this file is called service-worker.js. Then inside a <script> tag on your HTML page (also served over HTTPS), add the following JavaScript code:

```
if ('serviceWorker' in navigator) {
    navigator.serviceWorker.register('service-worker.js', {
        scope: '/'
    });
}
```

The preceding code snippet first checks to see if service workers are supported, and if they are, registers your worker. You can now fetch resources and add them to the cache. An interesting performance enhancing use case for this is prefetching resources (that the user may need) ahead of time and putting them in the cache. Scope is an optional parameter and isn't strictly necessary in this case, as the file is in the root of the domain. We've shown it only to demonstrate usage, but it may be useful to specify this if the file was in a subfolder.

Before going any further, you should check that your worker has been installed correctly. In Chrome, you can open the special URL chrome://inspect/#service-workers to see any active service workers. For example, after opening instabail.uk in one tab, you can open the service worker inspector in another; you should see something like the following screenshot:

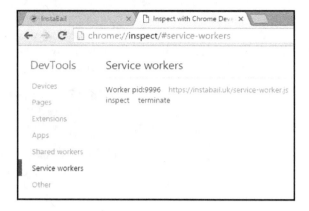

You can also visit `chrome://serviceworker-internals` in Chrome to see the status of all service workers that have been registered, even if the sites aren't still open. For example, even after closing `instabail.uk` you should continue to see something like the following screenshot:

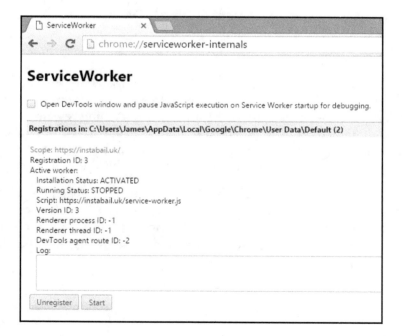

You can remove service workers by clicking the **Unregister** button. If the service is running, you will have **Stop** and **Inspect** buttons in place of **Start**. This page may be removed or merged into the inspector in a future version of Chrome.

If you are using an older version of Chrome (earlier than 50), you may see an error (`net::ERR_FILE_EXISTS`) against your service worker file in the console; but this is fine, so don't worry. It's simply a bug in Chrome as it tries to update your service worker, but finds that there aren't any changes.

Now you can start adding content to your service worker JavaScript file. We first need to install the worker and cache some files, which is done with an event listener, as shown in the following code:

```
self.addEventListener('install', function (event) {
    event.waitUntil(
        caches.open('cache-v01').then(function (cache) {
            return cache.addAll([
                '/',
                '/Content/bootstrap.min.css'
            ]);
        })
    );
});
```

We have named our cache `cache-v01`, and provided an array of resources to cache. You would probably have more entries here and define the array outside of the function, but we have kept things simple here for clarity.

Don't cache your homepage if it dynamically renders live content. You may also want to use cache busting parameters for resources, as mentioned previously.

We can then add a `fetch` event listener to perform the magic of caching and fetching resources.

```
self.addEventListener('fetch', function (event) {
    event.respondWith(
        caches.match(event.request)
            .then(function (response) {
                if (response) return response;
                var myReq = event.request.clone();
                return fetch(myReq).then(
                    function (response) {
                        var myResp = response.clone();
```

```
caches.open('cache-v01')
    .then(function (cache) {
        cache.put(event.request, myResp);
    });
return response;
}
);
}
)
);
});
```

First we check if the requested resource is in the cache and if it is, we return this. With promises, you can chain the `then` functions together and fall through them. If there is a cache miss due to the resource not being in the cache, we perform a `fetch` to our server to get the resource and return this. We then add the resource to the others by putting it in the same cache. We clone the request and response, because they are streams and can only be consumed once.

 The `fetch` function is the modern version of an `XMLHttpRequest` (XHR) and is used to retrieve data over the network. You can't use a synchronous XHR inside of a service worker, as they're designed to be asynchronous.

You can inspect your service worker and the caches in more detail by using the browser developer tools (*F12*). On the **Resources** tab, select **Service Workers** and you will see something like the following screenshot:

If you select **Cache Storage,** you will see the contents of the cache, which will look something like the following:

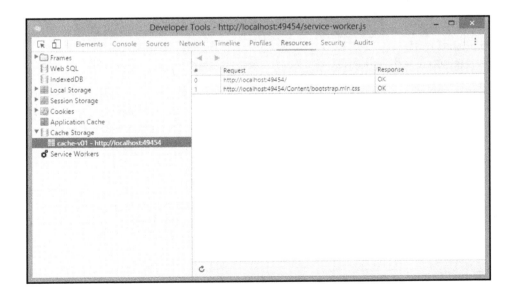

You can refresh the cache and delete items by right clicking. The **Application Cache**, above **Cache Storage**, would show the deprecated AppCache resources. As you navigate around, your site pages will be added to the cache (these pages should be suitable for caching, as they won't be requested from the server after this if using our demo code). After this, once you refresh the cache view, you should see more entries listed, which may look something like the following screenshot:

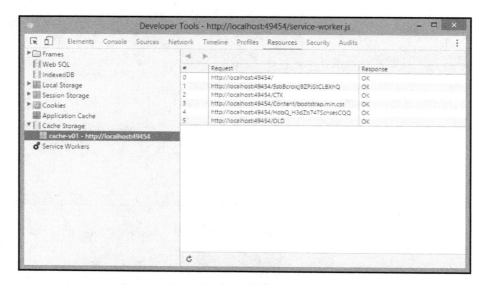

You can see that the cache entries are listed alphabetically and not in the order in which they were added to the cache. These pages will now be a snapshot, fixed at the point in time that they were retrieved. This may not be the functionality that you want!

For simplicity, the service worker that we've built here is a trivial example and you would likely want to expand it to at least handle the case where the network `fetch` fails by adding a `catch` statement. For example, you could serve a previously cached offline fallback page in its place. You should also check that you're not caching error pages from the server, so test the response status code.

You also need to carefully consider your cache invalidation strategy. Service workers give you the tools to build this, as they don't make as many assumptions as the HTML5 AppCache did. For example, you can now programmatically delete entries from the cache.

We'll leave it here for client-side script controlled caching, but you may want to look into this in more detail, especially once the specification has stabilized and browser support is more widespread. There are many other new features now available in JavaScript, which make async programing like this easier than it used to be. For example, arrow functions, which are similar to LINQ lambda expressions in C#.

Web and proxy servers

Caching from a server's point of view is intimately linked to client-side caching in the browser. In addition to storing resources on the server, the headers that you set will be used to control caches everywhere.

The HTTP headers that you set are used by both proxy servers and browsers, including not only standard browsing, but also fetching from a service worker. For example, if the `Cache-Control` header specifies `no-store`, then you won't be able to add the resource to a cache from your worker.

IIS

Internet Information Services (**IIS**) is Microsoft's web server. It can be used to serve content from your ASP.NET application or as a proxy server along with many other things such as FTP. Although IIS does support output caching, the `OutputCache` action attribute is not available in ASP.NET Core. Yet, you can use `ResponseCache` to set the correct headers instead, as covered in `Chapter 4`, *Addressing Network Performance*.

IIS can also be used as a proxy, for example, in front of the Kestrel web server on a single machine. However, when caching for multiple web servers, you may be better off using dedicated proxy server software such as Varnish.

Varnish

Varnish is a free reverse proxy server that runs on Unix-like operating systems such as **Linux** and **FreeBSD**. You can install it with your package manager (for example, **apt** or **yum**) or provision a proxy server with DevOps software such as **Chef** or **Puppet**. To configure Varnish, you use a **domain-specific language** (**DSL**) called **Varnish Configuration Language** (**VCL**).

You can read more about Varnish at `varnish-cache.org`.

You shouldn't need to configure Varnish too much if you are using HTTP caching headers correctly. You can also use the custom HTTP PURGE method to remove entries from the cache, which works with the Squid proxy software too. You may occasionally see a cryptic **guru meditation** error if Varnish is not properly configured, but you should be able to track down the issue in the Varnish logs. It could indicate that no healthy web servers are available.

Varnish configuration is beyond the scope of this book, but it's very well documented on the Varnish website. If you don't want to run your own proxy server, then you could use a CDN. You may still want your own proxy in addition to using a CDN, as large CDNs, with many **points of presence** (**PoP**), might request the same resource via each PoP, and not share assets across them. This can be an issue if you pay a lot for bandwidth, although some CDNs have a feature (often called origin shielding) that can help with this.

Working with a content delivery network

A content delivery network is commonly used in two ways—as a proxy for offloading your content or as a hosting provider for common third party libraries and frameworks. You can use a dynamic CDN service, such as CloudFlare or Akamai, for the first use case, but the second situation (using a static CDN from Google or Microsoft) is more common and that's what we'll cover here.

Although using a CDN for your libraries, such as jQuery and Twitter bootstrap, is becoming less useful with the adoption of HTTP/2, it can still be helpful for reducing your hosting costs. If you use a popular CDN and library, then the user may also already have a copy. For example, if the user has been to another site that uses jQuery from Google's CDN, then it will already be in their browser cache.

It is essential to have a fallback copy of whatever files you require from a CDN. This is easier than ever with the Razor view engine support built into ASP.NET Core.

The following code shows how jQuery is included in the default MVC Razor layout, for non-development environments. Both the CDN and local versions are specified along with a test.

```
<script
  src="https://ajax.aspnetcdn.com/ajax/jquery/jquery-2.1.4.min.js"
  asp-fallback-src="~/lib/jquery/dist/jquery.min.js"
  asp-fallback-test="window.jQuery">
</script>
```

The preceding code snippet not only renders the standard `<script>` tag for the Microsoft CDN, but also adds the following inline JavaScript afterwards, which includes the local version if the CDN load fails:

```
(window.jQuery || document.write(
"<script src="\/lib\/jquery\/dist\/jquery.min.js"><\/script>"));
```

Previously, you would have to do this manually, usually in a hurry when your CDN went down. This new helper also works for other scripts and CSS files. For more examples, take a look at `_Layout.cshtml` in the default template.

> It's important to use a secure HTTPS connection to CDN resources in order to avoid mixed content warnings or script loading errors in browsers; most popular CDNs now support HTTPS. For additional information on CDNs, see `Chapter 4`, *Addressing Network Performance*.

When not to cache

There are certain situations when you shouldn't cache pages or at least you need to be very careful in how you go about it. As a general rule of thumb, caching the rendered output of an authorized page is a bad idea. In other words, if a user has logged into your site, and you are serving them customized content (which could easily be sensitive), then you need to consider caching very carefully.

If you accidentally serve one user's cached content to another, then at best, it will be annoying, as the personalization will be incorrect. At worst, you could expose private information to the wrong person and potentially get into legal trouble.

> This is similar to the general rule of not universally enabling CORS if you serve authenticated content. It can be done successfully, but you need to understand the mechanisms in order to configure it to work safely.

For caching, you would need a unique identifier in the URL that can't be guessed. Some dynamic cache control systems, used by network appliances and CDNs, can make use of cookies for this, but it's beyond normal HTTP-based cache control. It is similar to how you might need sticky sessions on a load balancer, because your application was not designed to be stateless.

For authenticated caching, it may be better to not cache at the web level and instead cache at the application level and below. This allows you to cache smaller discrete chunks rather than a whole page, which can enhance reusability.

Application layer caching

Application level (or layer) caching means storing reusable data temporarily inside your infrastructure, but not in the main database. This can be in the memory of your application or web servers, but with multiple servers, this tends to be in a distributed in-memory store such as Memcached or Redis.

You can, of course, use both in-memory stores on your web servers and a centralized cache. However, if you have multiple web servers, then you will need a way to synchronize the caches. You can use **publish-subscribe (pub/sub)** messaging for this, which we will cover later in this chapter.

The following diagram shows a simple centralized caching setup. In a real situation, you would probably have multiple clustered cache servers.

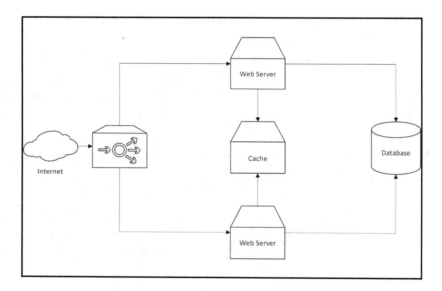

The web servers can now ask the cache if the data they need is in there, before going to the database. This reduces load on the DB and is often quicker, as the data will be in memory if present. If there is a cache miss and the database does need to be queried, then the result can be written to the cache for other servers to use.

Redis

Redis is a popular in-memory store that can also persist data to disk for permanent storage. It runs best on Linux, but a version is available on Windows for development purposes. Redis additionally supports pub/sub messaging, which can be useful for cache invalidation. You can read more about Redis at `redis.io`.

You may wish to use the Windows version of Redis for local development work, but still deploy to the supported version on Linux. You can get the Windows version at `github.com/MSOpenTech/redis` or you could run the Linux version in a virtual machine, perhaps using **Docker** or **Vagrant**.

Redis cache is provided as a service on both Azure and AWS (**ElastiCache** offers both Memcached and Redis). You don't need to manage your own server, but because the technology is not cloud-specific, you won't get locked in if you want to migrate in the future.

As Redis keeps the entire dataset in memory, but, is also able to persist to disk, it can be suitable as a primary data store unlike Memcached. However, it is more commonly used only as a cache, especially if a cloud service is used and it's paired with a cloud database such as **Azure SQL Database** or AWS **Relational Database Service** (**RDS**).

There are two recommended .NET C# clients for Redis—ServiceStack.Redis and StackExchange.Redis. The Stack Exchange client is used heavily on sites such as Stack Overflow and is easier to use correctly than the the ServiceStack one. You can read more about it at `github.com/StackExchange/StackExchange.Redis` and install it via NuGet.

If using caching at the application layer, then you will probably need to write a significant amount of custom code. You will also need to work out what format to serialize your data into for storage in the cache. If serving directly to browsers, then JSON could be useful. But if is to be used internally, then you may prefer a binary format such as MS Bond or Protocol Buffers.

See `Chapter 6`, *Understanding Code Execution and Asynchronous Operations*, for more on serialization formats and libraries.

Database result set caching

Caching at the database level is similar to application level caching, and it uses similar infrastructure, but requires less custom code. You can use the caching features built into an O/RM, which may make it easier to retrofit.

 When we talk about database caching here, we are not referring to caching within the database engine itself. DBs use extensive performance enhancing techniques, such as query caching, and hold lots of their data in memory. However, this is abstracted away from the developer, and the caching we mention here refers to storing the output of a query in an application cache. This is similar to, but subtly different from, the previous section, where you would be storing custom objects.

In the context of O/RMs (such as NHibernate and Entity Framework), this is known as second-level caching. First level caching generally already happens per session, by default, and is used to help avoid things like Select N+1 problems. Second-level caching operates at a level higher than individual transactions and allows you to share cached data across multiple database sessions over your entire application.

Message queuing

A **message queue** (**MQ**) is an asynchronous and reliable way of moving data around your system. It is useful for offloading work from your web application to a background service, but can also be used to update multiple parts of your system concurrently. For example, distributing cache invalidation data to all of your web servers.

MQs add complexity and we will cover managing this in Chapter 8, *The Downsides of Performance-Enhancing Tools*. However, they can also assist in implementing a **microservices architecture** where you break up your monolith into smaller parts, interfaced against contracts. This can make things easier to reason about within large organizations, where different teams manage the various parts of the application. We will discuss this in more detail in the next chapter, as queues aren't the only way of implementing this style of architecture. For example, HTTP APIs can also be used to do this.

Coffee shop analogy

If using MQs, then you may need to implement extra reconciliation logic for errors occurring in the background. This is best explained with a coffee shop analogy.

If you purchase a takeaway coffee, perhaps in a branch of a popular multinational chain of franchised caffeinated beverage outlets (that dislikes paying tax), then your drink is prepared asynchronously to the payment processing. Typically, you place your order and a barista will start to prepare your coffee, before you have paid for it. Additionally, you will normally pay before receiving your drink. There are many things that could go wrong here, but they are rare enough for the extra cost to be worth it, as it speeds up the ordinary workflow.

For example, you may find that you are unable to pay after placing your order, but the coffee creation process has already begun. This would result in wasted stock, unless there is another customer waiting whom it could be used for. Or perhaps, after you have paid, the barista discovers that a key ingredient for your order is missing. They could either offer you a refund, or negotiate a different drink.

Although more complex, this process is clearly superior to performing the actions in series. If you had to demonstrate that you had the means to pay, your drink was made, and then you completed paying, only one customer could be served at a time. Assuming there are enough staff, payment processing and drink preparation can be performed in parallel, which avoids a long queue of customers.

Running a coffee shop in this way makes intuitive sense and yet, in a web application, it is common to have a relatively long running transaction complete before informing the user of the result. In some situations, it may be better to assume the action will succeed, inform the user of this immediately and have a process in place in case it goes wrong.

For example, payment processing gateways can be slow and unreliable, so it may be better to charge a user's credit card after accepting an order. However, this means that you can no longer handle a failure by showing the user an error message. You will have to use other methods of communication.

When you order items on Amazon, they take payment details immediately, but they process the payment in the background and send you e-mails with the results. If the payment failed, they would need to cancel the order fulfilment and notify you. This requires extra logic, but is quicker than processing the payment transaction and checking stock before confirming the order.

Message queuing styles

There are, broadly, two styles of message queuing—with and without a central broker. With a broker, all messages go through a hub, which manages the communication. Examples of this style include **RabbitMQ**, **ActiveMQ,** and MS **BizTalk**.

There are also brokerless styles (that don't use a broker), where communication between nodes is direct. An example of this style includes ZeroMQ (**ØMQ**), which has a native C# port called **NetMQ**.

Cloud queuing services, including **Azure Service Bus**, Azure Queue storage, and AWS **Simple Queue Service** (**SQS**), are also available. However, as with all non-generic cloud services, you should be wary of getting locked in. There are cloud providers of standard RabbitMQ hosting, which makes migration to your own infrastructure easier down the line if you don't initially want to run your own server. For example, CloudAMQP offers RabbitMQ hosting on multiple cloud platforms.

RabbitMQ implements the **Advanced Message Queuing Protocol** (**AMQP**), which helps to ensure interoperability between different MQ brokers, for example, to allow communication with the **Java Message Service** (**JMS**). Azure Service Bus also supports AMQP, but a big benefit of RabbitMQ is that you can install it on your development machine for local use, without an internet connection.

There is also **Microsoft Message Queuing** (**MSMQ**), which is built into Windows. While this is useful for communication between processes on a single machine, it can be tricky to get it working reliably between multiple servers.

Common messaging patterns

There are two types of common messaging patterns: point-to-point unicast and publish-subscribe. These send messages to a single recipient and many recipients respectively.

Unicast

Unicast is the standard message queuing approach. A message is sent from one service process or software agent to another. The queuing framework will ensure that this happens reliably and will provide certain guarantees about delivery.

This approach is dependable, but doesn't scale well as a system grows, because each node would need to know about all its recipients. It would be better to loosely couple system components together so that they don't need to have knowledge about any of the others.

This is often achieved by using a broker, which has three main advantages:

- By using a broker, you can decouple processes from each other so that they aren't required to know about the system architecture or be alive at the same time. They only care about the message types and the broker takes care of routing the message to the correct destination.

- Broker queues enable an easy distribution of work pattern, especially when combining multiple producers. You can have multiple processes consuming the same queue and the broker will allocate messages to them in a round-robin fashion. This is a simple way of building a parallel system, without having to do any asynchronous programming or worrying about threads. You can just run multiple copies of your code, perhaps on separate machines if constrained by hardware and they will run simultaneously.

- You can easily broadcast or multicast a particular type of message, perhaps to indicate that an event has occurred. Other processes that care about this event can listen to the messages without the publisher knowing about them. This is known as the pub/sub pattern.

Pub/sub

Pub/sub, as the name suggests, is where a software agent publishes a message onto a queue, and other agents can subscribe to that type of message to receive it. When a message is published, all subscribers receive it, but crucially the publisher does not require any knowledge of the subscribers or even need to know how many there are (or even if there are any at all).

Pub/sub is best done with the broker style of message queuing architecture. It can be done without a broker, but it is not particularly reliable. If your use case can tolerate message loss, then you may be able to get away without a broker. But, if you require guaranteed delivery, then you should use one. Using the RabbitMQ broker also allows you to take advantage of exchanges which can perform complex routing of messages.

If you don't want to lose messages, then you need to carefully design your pub/sub system (even if using a broker). A published message that has no subscribers may simply disappear into the ether without a trace and this might not be what you want.

The following diagram shows the differences between simple message forwarding, work distribution, and pub/sub:

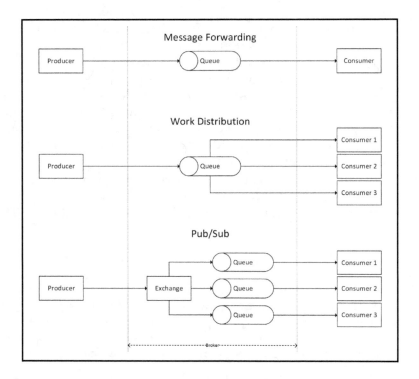

Clearly, if you require a reliable broker, then it needs to be highly available. Typically, you would cluster multiple brokers together to provide redundancy. Using a broker also allows you to write custom rules to define which subscribers receive what messages. For example, your payment system may only care about orders, but your logging server may want to get all messages from all systems.

You will want to monitor not only your broker servers but also the length of the queues. In other words, the number of messages in each queue should always be steady and close to zero. If the number of messages in a queue is steadily growing, this might indicate a problem which your operations team will need to resolve. It may be that your consumers can't process messages faster than your producers are sending them and you need to add more consumers. This could be automated and your monitoring software could Spin-up an extra instance to scale your system, meeting a temporary spike in demand.

RabbitMQ

RabbitMQ is a free and open source message queuing server. It's written in Erlang, which is the same robust language that WhatsApp uses for its messaging backend.

RabbitMQ is currently maintained by Pivotal (whose labs also make the Pivotal Tracker agile project management tool), but it was originally made by LShift. It was then acquired by VMware before being spun out as a joint venture. It's distributed under the **Mozilla Public License** (**MPL**) v1.1, an older version of the license that the Firefox web browser uses.

The messaging server can be used from many different languages and frameworks such as Java, Ruby, and .NET. This can make it helpful for linking diverse applications together, for example, a Rails app that you want to interface with an ASP.NET Core app or C# service.

 You can read more about RabbitMQ and download builds from
`rabbitmq.com`.

RabbitMQ is more modern than systems such as MSMQ and includes features such as an HTTP API and a web admin management interface. Along with HTTP and AMQP, it also supports **Simple Text Orientated Messaging Protocol** (**STOMP**) and **MQTT**, which is useful for lightweight **Internet of Things** (**IoT**) hardware applications. All of these protocols improve interoperability with other messaging systems and they can normally be secured using standard TLS.

The web management interface shows you how many messages are flowing through your queues, and how they are configured. It also allows you to administer your queues (tasks such as purging or deleting messages) and looks something like the following screenshot:

Queuing frameworks and libraries

You will typically want to use a prebuilt client library or framework to interact with your message queues. There are official libraries in many different languages for the various queuing systems, which offer low-level access. For example, RabbitMQ has an official .NET/C# client library.

However, there are also other opinionated clients and frameworks, which offer a higher level of abstraction for common messaging tasks. For example, **NServiceBus** (**NSB**), which supports RabbitMQ, MSMQ, SQL Server, and Azure, is a commercial offering.

A free alternative to NSB is **MassTransit** (`masstransit-project.com`), which is a lightweight service bus and distributed application framework. It has also spun out the super convenient **Topshelf** framework (`topshelf-project.com`), which makes creating Windows services really easy. Neither yet runs on .NET Core, but support for both of these projects is in progress.

One interesting feature of MassTransit (and NSB) is support for sagas. A saga is a complex state machine that allows you to model the story of an entire workflow. Rather than defining individual messages and documenting how they all fit together, you can implicitly capture the golden path and error flows within a saga.

There is also the excellent open source library **EasyNetQ**, which makes implementing pub/sub on RabbitMQ trivial. You can read about it at EasyNetQ.com. Unfortunately, neither the official RabbitMQ client nor EasyNetQ support .NET Core at the time of writing. However, work is in progress for the official client and EasyNetQ has the issue logged.

The RabbitMQ team is working on a new, asynchronous official .NET client, which will only target .NET Core and the **Task Parallel Library** (**TPL**). We covered the TPL, which is part of the parallel extensions that also include PLINQ, in Chapter 6, *Understanding Code Execution and Asynchronous Operations*.

Hopefully, by the time you read this, things will have stabilized and you will be able to use RabbitMQ with .NET Core. Otherwise, you can use the traditional .NET Framework, which may currently be more suitable for the enterprise style applications that normally require message queuing.

However, you could look into using **RestBus**, which is a RabbitMQ library that supports ASP.NET Core. You can read more about it at restbus.org; it also supports both Web API and ServiceStack.

 Library and framework support for .NET Core and ASP.NET Core can change rapidly, so check ANCLAFS.com for the latest information. Feel free to help out and contribute to this list or to any of the open source projects that need porting.

Summary

In this chapter, we have investigated the various tools and methods used for caching and message queuing. These two techniques offer different ways of improving the performance of your system by moving data to other locations and not having one massive monolith do everything.

These are both advanced topics and difficult to cover in such a small space. Hopefully, you have been introduced to some fresh ideas that can help you with solving problems in original ways. If you have discovered a new technology that you think will assist, you're encouraged to read the documentation and specifications for all of the implementation details.

However, before you dive in, you should understand that advanced techniques are complex and have downsides, which can reduce your development speed. In the next chapter, we'll learn about these downsides and discover approaches for managing complexity such as microservices.

8
The Downsides of Performance-Enhancing Tools

A lot of the topics that we covered in this book improve performance at a cost. Your application will become more complicated and harder to understand or reason about. This chapter discusses these trade-offs and how to mitigate their impact.

You should implement many of the approaches that you learned so far in this book only if you require them and not just because they are interesting or challenging. It's often preferable to keep things simple if the existing performance is good enough.

You will learn how to make pragmatic choices about what technologies and techniques you should use. You'll also see how to manage the complexities if you choose to use advanced methods.

Topics covered in this chapter include the following:

- Managing complexity with frameworks and architecture
- Building a healthy culture to deliver high performance
- Distributed debugging and performance logging
- Understanding statistics and stale data

Many books and guides only focus on the positives of new tools and frameworks. However, nothing comes for free, and there is always a penalty, which may not be immediately obvious.

You may not feel the effects of the choices that you make, particularly in technical architecture, for a long time. You might not discover that a decision was bad until you try to build on it, perhaps years later.

Managing complexity

One of the main problems with performance-enhancing techniques is that they typically make a system more complicated. This can make a system harder to modify and it may also reduce your productivity. Therefore, although your system runs faster, your development is now slower.

We commonly find this complexity problem in enterprise software, although usually for different reasons. Typically, many unnecessary layers of abstraction are used, supposedly to keep the software flexible. Ironically, this actually makes it slower to add new features. This may seem counterintuitive, until you realize that simplicity makes change easier.

 There's a satirical enterprise edition of the popular programmer interview coding test *FizzBuzz*, which is available at `fizzbuzz.enterprises`. It's good inspiration for how not to do things.

If you don't need a feature yet, then it's often best to leave it out rather than building it just in case you might need it in the future. The more code you write, the more bugs it will have, and the harder it will be to understand. Over-engineering is a common negative psychological trait that is easy to fall victim to if you aren't aware of it, and marketers often exploit this.

For a non-software example, four-wheel drive SUVs are sold to people who will never need their off-road capabilities on the false premise that it may potentially come in useful someday. Yet the financial, safety, environmental, and parking convenience costs outweigh this supposed benefit because it's never used.

We often term this development advice from the **extreme programming** (**XP**) philosophy, **You Aren't Going to Need It** (**YAGNI**). Although we sometimes use slightly different words, the meaning is the same. YAGNI advocates keeping things simple and only building what you immediately need.

This doesn't mean that you should make your software hard to modify. It's still important to stay flexible, just don't add features before you need them. For example, adding an abstraction interface when there is only a single implementation may be overkill. You could easily add it along with the second implementation if and when you build it.

It's difficult to move fast yet not break things when doing so. How you achieve high reliability in addition to a consistently good development speed will depend on many things that are specific to your situation, such as your team size, organizational structure, and company culture.

One method is to embrace change and develop a system where you can refactor your code in confidence. Using a statically-compiled language, such as C#, is a good start, but you should also have a comprehensive test suite to avoid regressions.

You should design a system so that it is loosely coupled, which means that you can change parts in isolation without a lot of knock-on effects. This also makes it easier to unit test and unit tests are invaluable to refactor in confidence and prevent functional regressions.

We will cover testing and automation with a **Continuous Integration** (**CI**) workflow in the next chapter. In this chapter, we will talk more about various architectural styles that can help you maintain your application.

Understanding complexity

When learning about new ways of doing things, you should avoid doing them without understanding the reasons. You should know the benefits and downsides and then measure the changes to prove that they are what you expect. Don't just blindly implement something and assume it improves the situation. Try to avoid **cargo cult programming** and always objectively evaluate a new approach.

Cargo cult programming is the practice of emulating something successful but failing to understand the reasons why it works. Its name comes from the cargo cults of the Pacific who built false airstrips after the Second World War to encourage cargo delivery. We use it to describe many things where correlation has been confused with causation.
One example is a company encouraging long hours to deliver a project because they have heard of successful projects where employees worked long hours. However, they fail to understand that the successful project and long hours are both independent byproducts of a highly motivated and competent workforce, and they are not directly related.

It's important to keep code readable, not just for others on your team or new members but also for yourself in the future (when you will forget how something works and why you wrote it in this way). This doesn't simply mean writing helpful explanatory comments in the code, although this is a very good practice. It also applies to source control comments and keeping documentation up to date.

Readability also involves keeping things simple by only making them as complex as they need to be and not hiding functionality in unnecessary layers of abstraction. For example, not using clever programming techniques to reduce the file line-count when a standard structure (for example, a loop or `if` statement) would be more readable and only slightly longer.

It helps to have a standard way of doing things in your team to avoid surprises. Using the same method everywhere can be more valuable than finding a better way of doing it, and then having lots of different ways. If there is consensus, then you can go back and retrofit the better method everywhere where you need it.

Complexity reduction

There are various solutions to manage the complexity that performance-enhancing techniques can add. These usually work by reducing the amount of logic that you need to think about at any one time by hiding the complications.

One option is to use frameworks that standardize how you write your application, which can make it easier to reason about. Another approach is to use an architecture that allows you to only think about small parts of your code base in isolation. By breaking up a complex app into manageable chunks, it becomes easier to work with.

 This idea of modularity is related to the **Single Responsibility Principle** (**SRP**), which is the first of the **SOLID** principles (the others are Open/Closed, Liskov substitution, Interface segregation, and Dependency inversion). It is also similar to the higher level **Separation of Concerns** (**SoC**) and to the simplicity of the Unix philosophy. It is better to have many tools that each do one thing well, rather than one tool that does many things badly.

Frameworks

Frontend frameworks, such as **React** (created at Facebook), are designed to reliably build web application views in JavaScript. These help large teams work on a project by simplifying the data flow and standardizing the approach.

 React can be integrated with ASP.NET Core using the **ReactJS.NET** project (`reactjs.net`). We can use **React Native** to build cross-platform apps that share code across iOS, Android, and the **Universal Windows Platform** (**UWP**), targeting phone, desktop, and Xbox (`github.com/ReactWindows`). There's also **CodePush** to let you live update your JavaScript apps (including Cordova), without going through an app store (`microsoft.github.io/code-push`).
If you prefer coding in C#, then you can build your cross-platform mobile apps with **Xamarin** (which is now free after Microsoft acquired it). However, we won't go further into any of these technologies in this book.

On the backend, we have the server-side frameworks of .NET Core and ASP.NET Core. Along with C# features, these provide convenient ways of simplifying historically-complicated features. For example, the `async` and `await` keywords hide a lot of the complicated logic associated with asynchronous programming, and lambda functions concisely express intent.

We covered many of these features earlier in this book, so we won't go over them again here. We also highlighted libraries that can make your life easier by hiding boilerplate code for complex operations, for example, `EasyNetQ` and `RestBus`.

 Hiding a complex process is never perfect, and you will occasionally come across abstractions that leak some of their implementation detail. For example, when handling exceptions, you may find that the issue you're interested in is now wrapped in an aggregate exception. If you're not careful, then your error logs may no longer contain the detail that you desire.

What we have yet to talk about in detail is the architecture of a web application. Splitting a monolithic system up into discrete parts can not only improve performance, but if done right, it can also make it easier to maintain.

Architecture

In the previous chapter, when discussing message queuing, we briefly covered the microservices architecture. This style is a more modern reimagining of the traditional **Service Oriented Architecture** (**SOA**), and although using reliable MQ communication is preferred, we can also perform this with **representational state transfer** (**REST**ful) HTTP APIs.

Typically, we build a traditional web app as a single application or monolith. This is common if the app has grown organically over an extended period of time, and this is a perfectly acceptable practice. It's a poor decision to over-engineer too early before there is any need, which may never materialize.

Excessive popularity is a nice problem to have, but don't optimize for this prematurely. This isn't an excuse to make things unnecessarily slow, so be sure to understand the tradeoffs involved.

Using a monolithic architecture is not an excuse to build something badly, and you should plan for expansion, even if you do not implement it immediately. You can keep things simple while still allowing for future growth.

Although the application is a single unit, you should split the code base into well-organized modules, which are linked together in a simple, logical, and easy-to-understand way. Refer to the SOLID principles, mentioned previously.

If a monolithic application can't easily scale to meet user demand and is performing poorly as a result, then you can split it up into smaller separate services. You may also wish to split an app up if it has become too cumbersome to iterate on quickly and development speed has slowed.

Monolith versus microservices

The following diagram shows some differences between a typical monolith and a microservices architecture:

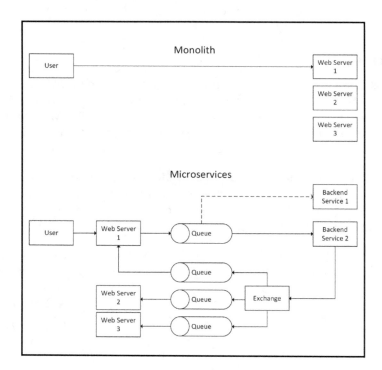

Here, the user makes a request to an application running on a web farm. We have omitted firewalls, load balancers, and databases for clarity, but multiple web servers are shown to illustrate that the same codebase runs on multiple machines.

In the initial monolith architecture, the user communicates directly with a single web server. This is ideally per request/response pair. However, if the application was poorly designed and holds state in memory, then **sticky sessions** may cause the load to pool on certain servers.

The second example in the diagram of a microservices architecture is obviously more complicated but also more flexible. The user again sends a request to a web server, but instead of doing all of the work, the server puts a message into a queue.

The work in this queue is distributed between multiple backend services of which the first one is busy, so a second service picks up the message. When the service completes, it sends a message to an exchange on the message broker, which uses a pub/sub broadcast to inform all of the web servers.

One added piece of complexity is that the architecture should have already sent the response to the user's original web request, so you need to consider the **user experience** (**UX**) more carefully. For example, you can display a progress indicator and update the status of this with an asynchronous WebSocket connection.

Architecture comparison

The monolith approach is simple, and you can just add more web servers to handle additional users. However, this approach can become cumbersome as an application (and development team) grows larger because the slightest change requires a full redeployment to each web server.

In addition, a monolith is easy to scale vertically (up) but hard to scale horizontally (out), which we covered previously. However, a monolith is easier to debug, so you need to be careful and have good monitoring and logging. You don't want any random outage investigation to turn into a murder mystery hunt because of unnecessarily implemented microservices.

Historically, Facebook had a deployment process that consisted of slowly compiling their PHP code base to a gigantic gigabyte-scale binary (for runtime performance reasons). They then needed to develop a modified version of BitTorrent to efficiently distribute this huge executable to all of their web servers. Although this was impressive infrastructure engineering, it didn't address the root cause of their **technical debt** problem, and they have since moved on to better solutions, such as the **HipHop Virtual Machine (HHVM)**, which is similar to the .NET CLR.

If you wish to practice continuous delivery and deploy multiple times a week (or even many times a day), then it's advantageous to break your web application up. You can then maintain and deploy each part separately, communicating with each other using messages against an agreed API.

This separation can also help you use agile development methodologies—for example, using many smaller teams—rather than big teams because smaller teams perform better.

Your instrument of control to scale a monolith is very crude, as all work is done in one place. You can't scale parts of your app independently to the other components. You can only scale the whole thing even if the high load is concentrated in a small part. This is analogous to a central bank only having control of a single interest rate as a lever, which affects many things at once. If your app is distributed, then you only need to scale the part that requires it, avoiding over provisioning and reducing costs.

A well-used (and often rephrased) quote from Abraham Maslow goes:

"I suppose it is tempting, if the only tool you have is a hammer, to treat everything as if it were a nail."

This is known as the law of the instrument and is related to the confirmation bias. If you only have one tool, then you are likely to use this tool for everything and only see things that support your existing ideas. This commonly applies to tools and frameworks, but it can also apply to scaling techniques.

The first step towards modularity may be to split a big web application into many smaller web apps so that you can deploy them separately. This strategy can have some benefits, but it also has many limitations. Some logic may be unsuitable to host in a web app, for example, long-running processes, such as those monitoring a filesystem or used to manipulate media.

You may also find that you need to duplicate code that was shared in the original monolith. If you adhere to the **Don't Repeat Yourself** (**DRY**) doctrine, then you might extract this functionality to a library. Yet, now you have dependencies and versioning to manage. You'll also need processes to build, package and host your library in a private repository, all of which can slow down development and reduce your agility.

 Sometimes, we also refer to DRY as **Duplication Is Evil** (**DIE**), and this is the sensible idea that an implementation should only occur in a unique location. If other code requires this functionality, then it should call the original function and not have copied code pasted in. This means that you only need to make a change in a single place to apply it everywhere.

A more advanced approach is to extract functionality into a separate service, which can handle many different web applications. If designed correctly, then this service won't need to have any knowledge of these apps and will simply respond to messages. This allows you to add a new web app without making changes to the code of other applications or services.

Refactoring

Refactoring a monolith into services can be tricky if the application has become a tightly-coupled big-ball-of-mud, but if it's been well-built (with plenty of test coverage and loosely-coupled code), then it shouldn't be too taxing. There's a big difference between a well-built monolith and a big-ball-of-mud made with little thought.

It's worth expanding on test coverage, as unit tests are essential for successful refactoring without introducing regressions or new bugs. Unit tests allow you to refactor and tidy up in confidence, and they prevent the creation of code that is fragile, which developers are afraid to touch. We will cover testing in greater detail, including automation, in Chapter 9, *Monitoring Performance Regressions*.

Both of these design patterns may appear superficially similar, but internally, it's a different story. The following diagram illustrates the differences between a well-architected monolith and a messy big-ball-of-mud:

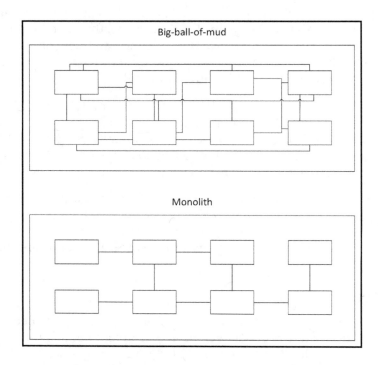

The large boxes represent the code running on each web server (the **Web Server N** boxes from the monolith example in the earlier diagram). From the outside, they look the same, but the difference is in the internal coupling of the code.

The big-ball-of-mud is a tangled mess with code referencing other functions throughout the application. The monolith is well-structured with a clear separation of concerns between different modules.

Changes to code in the big-ball-of-mud can have unexpected side effects because other parts of it may rely on the implementation details of what you are modifying. This makes it brittle, difficult to alter, and developers may be afraid of touching it.

The well-built monolith is easy to refactor and split out into separate services because the code is neatly-organized. It uses abstract interfaces to communicate between modules, and code doesn't reach into another class's concrete implementation details. It also has excellent unit test coverage, which runs automatically.

Although both are a single code base, the quality of the monolith is much higher because it is well-distributed internally. Good design is important for future-proofing, as we build in and allow for expansion. The monolith hasn't been split up too early (before scaling was required), but the design makes this easy to do later. In contrast, the big-ball-of-mud has accumulated a large amount of technical debt, which it needs to pay off before we can make any further progress.

Technical debt (or tech debt for short) is the concept of not finishing a job or cutting corners, which could lead to more difficulties until it is paid back. For example, failing to properly document a system will make altering it later more difficult.

Tech debt is not necessarily a bad thing if it is deliberately taken on in full knowledge, logged, and paid back later. For example, waiting to write documentation until after a release can speed up delivery. However, tech debt that is not paid back or is accumulated without knowledge (simply due to sloppy coding), will get worse over time and cause bigger issues later.

The best way to deliver a high-quality and flexible application (that's easy to refactor) is to have a competent and conscientious development team. However, these attributes can often be more about culture, communication, and motivation than simply skill or raw talent. Although this isn't a book about team management, having a healthy culture is very important, so we'll cover a little of this here. Everyone in an operations and software development department can help create a positive and friendly culture, even if you usually need buy-in from higher up as well.

Tools are also very useful in refactoring and testing. We covered the Visual Studio IDE and ReSharper plugin previously, but there are many more tools for testing. We will cover more testing tools, including automation, in Chapter 9, *Monitoring Performance Regressions*.

A culture of high performance

If you want to achieve high performance, then it's important to foster a company culture that encourages this and recognizes performance as vital. Culture can't just come from the bottom up only involving engineers, it also needs to come from the top-down and management must buy in to the performance prerogative.

This section is not very technical, so feel free to skip it if you don't care about management or the human side of software development.

A blameless culture

The most important attributes of a high-performance culture are that it should be open and blameless. Everyone needs to be focused on achieving the best possible outcomes through measuring and learning. Attributing fault to individuals is toxic to delivering great software, and this is not only the case when it comes to performance.

If something goes wrong, then it is a process problem and the focus should be on improving it and preventing repeat mistakes in the future, for example, by automating it. This is similar to how safety-critical industries, such as air travel, behave because they recognize that blaming people discourages them from raising issues early before a disaster occurs.

A related philosophy is the Japanese process of Kaizen, which encourages continuous improvement by everyone. The car manufacturer Toyota pioneered Kaizen practices to improve the efficiency of their production line, and most automotive companies and many other different industries have since adopted them.

Some industries also have processes to encourage whistle-blowing that protect the individuals raising concerns. However, if this is required in web application development, then it's a sure sign that the culture needs work. Developers should feel that they are able to directly raise concerns bypassing their line manager without consequence. If everyone's opinion is respected, then this shouldn't even be necessary.

Intellectual dishonesty

If team members get defensive when ideas are challenged, then this is a sign that things may not be working well. Everybody makes mistakes and has gaps in their knowledge, a truth the best engineers embrace. You should strive for a culture where everyone is open to new ideas and is always asking questions.

If people are unable to accept constructive criticism and have their ideas challenged, then they may lack confidence and be covering up a lack of competence. Experienced developers know that you never stop learning, they admit their ignorance and are always open to offers of improvements.

Being closed to suggestions alters the behavior of others, and they will stop raising small issues early. This results in open secrets about poor quality, and the first that is known about a problem is at release time, at which point everything is much worse (or on fire).

This is not an excuse to be nasty to people, so always try to be nice and gently explain the reasons behind your criticism. It's easy to find fault in anything, so always propose an alternative approach. If you are patient, then a reasonable person will be grateful for the learning opportunity and appreciate gaining experience.

A good rule to follow is "don't be a jerk" and treat others as you would like to be treated, so be kind and think about how you would feel if the situation was reversed. Just remember that being nice is not always compatible with doing the right thing.

A little self-deprecation can go a long way to making you more approachable, rather than simply dictating the one-true-way. However, you should make it clear when something is a joke or tongue in cheek, especially when dealing with cultures that are more direct or when communicating textually.

For example, North Americans are often less subtle than and not as sarcastic as the British (who also spell some word differently, and some would say more correctly). Obviously, use your own judgment because this may be terrible advice and could cause offense or, even worse, a full-on diplomatic incident. Hopefully, it is self-evident that this whole paragraph is tongue in cheek.

People who have integrity and confidence in their ideas can afford to be modest and self-deprecating, but internal company culture can influence this too. A particularly bad practice is to conduct performance reviews by *laddering* (also known as stack ranking), which involves putting everyone in order, relative to everybody else. This is toxic because it rewards people who focus more on marketing themselves than those who recognize the deficiencies in their technical skills and try to improve them. In the pathological case, all of the best people are forced out, and you end up with a company full of sociopathic sharp suits, who are technically illiterate or even morally bankrupt.

Slow down to go faster

Sometimes, the company must allow the development team to slow down on feature delivery in order to focus on performance and resolving technical debt. They should be given time to be thoughtful about design decisions so that they can cogitate avoiding premature generalization or careless optimization.

Performance is a significant selling point of software, and it is much easier to build quality throughout the development process than in a polishing phase at the end. There is a significant body of evidence that suggests that good performance improves **Return on Investment** (**RoI**) and creates customers. This is especially true on the web, where poor performance decreases conversion rate and search engine ranking.

Having a healthy culture is not only important for the runtime performance of your software but also for the speed at which you can develop it. The team should be encouraged to behave rigorously and write precise, but also concise, code.

You get what you measure, and if you only measure the rate of feature delivery, or even worse simply **Lines of Code** (**LoC**) written, then quality will suffer. This will hurt you in the long run and is a false economy.

False economies are when you make short term cost saving measures that actually lose you more money in the long term. Examples of this are skimping on hardware for developers or interrupting someone in the middle of coding with something trivial, which could easily wait until later, and forcing them to switch contexts.

Another nonsoftware example is a shortsighted government making cuts to investment in research by sacrificing long-term growth for short-term gain, possibly due to the lack of any long-term economic plan.

 Hardware is significantly cheaper than developer time. Therefore, if everyone on your team doesn't have a beefy box and multiple massive monitors, then productivity is being needlessly diminished. Even over a decade ago, Facebook's software developer job adverts listed dual 24-inch widescreen monitors as a perk.

From the ground up

In a healthy and progressive culture, it can be tempting to rewrite poor quality software from scratch, perhaps in the latest trendy framework, but this is usually a mistake. Released software is battle-hardened (no matter how badly it was built), and if you rewrite it, then you will probably make the same mistakes again, for example, re-implementing bugs that you already patched. This is especially true if the software was not built with good unit test coverage, which can help prevent regressions.

The only case where you could reasonably rewrite an application from the ground up is if you had deliberately made a prototype to explore the problem space with the sole intention of throwing it away. However, you should be very careful because if you've actually built a **Minimum Viable Product** (**MVP**) instead, then these have a habit of sticking around for a long time and forming the foundations of larger applications.

A better approach to a full rewrite is to add tests to the application (if it doesn't already have them) and gradually refactor it to improve the quality and performance. If you built an application in such a way as to make it difficult to unit test, then you can start with **User Interface** (**UI**) tests, perhaps using a headless web browser. We will cover testing more, including performance testing, in the next chapter.

Shared values

Culture is really just a set of shared values—things such as openness, sustainability, inclusivity, diversity, and ethical behavior. It can help having these values formally documented so that everyone knows what you stand for.

You may have a progressive open salary policy so that others can't use secret earning information as a tool to pay people less. However, this would need to apply universally, as it's unhealthy to have multiple conflicting cultures because this can precipitate an us-versus-them attitude.

There's plenty more to say about culture, but, as you can see, there are many competing concerns to balance. The most important idea is to make intentional and thoughtful tradeoffs. There isn't one correct choice, but you should always be conscious of the consequences and appreciate how tiny actions can alter team performance.

The price of performance

Developers should have an idea of the available budget for performance and understand the cost of the code that they write, not just in execution throughput but in readability, maintainability, and power efficiency. Throwing more cores at a unit of work is not nearly as good as refactoring it to be simpler.

Efficiency has become increasingly important, especially with the rise of mobile devices and cloud computing time-based usage billing. Parallelizing an inefficient algorithm may solve a performance problem in the time domain, but it's a crude brute-force approach and altering the underlying implementation may be better.

Less is often more and sometimes doing nothing is the best approach. Software engineering is not only about knowing what to build but what not to build. Keeping things simple helps others on your team use your work. You should aim to avoid surprising anyone with nonobvious behavior. For example, consider that you build an API and then give it conventional defaults; if this could potentially take a long time, then make the methods asynchronous to indicate this fact.

You should aim to make it easy to succeed and hard to fail when building on your code. Make it difficult to do the wrong thing, for example, if a method is unsafe, name it to document this fact. Being a competent programmer is only a small part of being a good developer, you also need to be helpful and proficient at communicating clearly.

In fact, being an expert programmer can be a downside if you don't deliberately keep things simple to aid the understanding of others on your team. You should always balance performance improvements against the side effects, and you shouldn't make them at the expense of future development efficiency without good reason.

Distributed debugging

Distributed systems can make it difficult to debug problems, and you need to plan for this in advance by integrating technology that can help with visibility. You should know what metrics you want to measure and what parameters are important to record.

As you run a web application, it isn't a case of deploy and forget as it might be with mobile apps or desktop software. You will need to keep a constant automated eye on your application to ensure that it is always available. If you monitor the correct performance metrics, then you can get early warning signs of problems and can take preventative action. If you only measure uptime or responsiveness, then the first that you may know of a problem is an outage notification, probably at an unsociable hour.

You may outsource your infrastructure to a cloud-hosting company so that you don't have to worry about hardware or platform failures. However, this doesn't completely absolve you of responsibility and your software will still need continuous monitoring. You may need to architect your application differently to work in harmony with your hosting platform and scale or self-heal when issues arise.

If you design your system correctly, then your web application will run itself, and you'll rarely get notified of actions that require your attention. If you can successfully automate all of the things, rather than babysitting a live deployment, then that's more time you can use to build the future.

In a distributed architecture, you can't simply attach a debugger to the live web server, not that this is a good idea even when possible. There is no live server anymore, there are now many live servers and even more processes. To get a holistic picture of the system, you will need to simultaneously examine the state of multiple modules.

There are many tools that you can use to help with centralizing your debug information. You can retrofit some of them. However, to get the most out of them, you should decide what to measure upfront and build telemetry capabilities into your software from the start.

Logging

Logging is vital to a high-performance application, so while it is true that logging adds some overhead and can slow down execution, omitting it would be short-sighted and a false economy. Without logging, you won't know what is slow and requires improvement. You will also have other concerns, such as reliability, for which logging is essential.

Error logging

You may have used (or at least be familiar with) the excellent ASP.NET package called **Error Logging Modules and Handlers (ELMAH)** to catch unhandled exceptions (`elmah.github.io`). ELMAH is great for already existing applications, as you can drop it into a live running web app. However, it's preferable to have error logging built into your software from the start.

Unfortunately, ASP.NET Core does not support ELMAH, but there is a similar package called **Error Logging Middleware (ELM)**. Adding this to your web application is just as simple as installing Glimpse, but it is really just a prototype and doesn't have all the features of ELMAH. First, add the `Microsoft.AspNetCore.Diagnostics.Elm` NuGet package to your project, as shown in the following image:

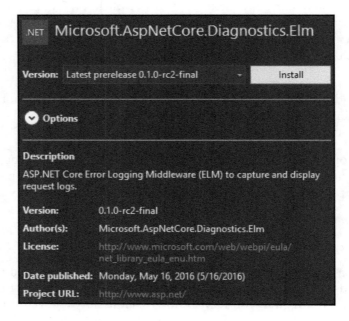

Then, in the `ConfigureServices` method of the `Startup` class, add the following line of code:

```
services.AddElm();
```

You also need to add the following lines to the `Configure` method of the same class:

```
app.UseElmPage();
app.UseElmCapture();
```

 To start with, you may want to put these in the `env.IsDevelopment()` `if` statement so that they are only active on your workstation. If you use ELM on production, then these logs will definitely need securing.

You can now visit the `/Elm` path of your web application in your browser to see the logs, as shown in the following image. Use the search box to filter results, click on **v** at the end of each line (not shown) to expand the entry's details, and click on **^** to collapse it again:

Path	Method	Host	Status Code
RequestId:0HKS4EMQJE8H4 RequestPath:/Elm			
Non-scope Log			
Non-scope Log			
Non-scope Log			
Non-scope Log			
/images/banner3.svg	GET	localhost:53820	200
Non-scope Log			
/lib/bootstrap/dist/fonts/glyphicons-halflings-regular.woff2	GET	localhost:53820	200
Non-scope Log			
/images/banner4.svg	GET	localhost:53820	200
Non-scope Log			
/images/banner2.svg	GET	localhost:53820	200
/images/banner1.svg	GET	localhost:53820	200
Non-scope Log			
Non-scope Log			
Non-scope Log			
/js/site.js	GET	localhost:53820	200
/lib/bootstrap/dist/js/bootstrap.js	GET	localhost:53820	200

 When using ELM, ELMAH, or even the default error pages, you should be careful to not show detailed exceptions or stack traces to real users. This isn't simply because they're unfriendly and unhelpful, they are a genuine security concern. Error logs and stack traces can reveal the internal workings of your application, which malicious actors can exploit.

ELM is fairly basic, but it can still be useful. However, there are better solutions already built into the default templates—things, such as the integrated support for logging and **Application Insights**.

Application Insights

Application Insights allows you to monitor the performance of your application and view requests or exceptions. You can use it with Azure, but it will also work locally without needing an Azure account. You can easily enable Application Insights by keeping the relevant checkbox ticked, as shown in the following image, when you create a new ASP.NET Core web application project in Visual Studio, and you don't need to sign in to Azure to do this:

The Application Insights template option is only available under the **Web** templates not the **.NET Core** templates.

Build and run the new project, then open the **Application Insights Search** window to see the output. Navigate around the web app in your browser, and you will see records start to appear, which should look something like the following:

If you don't see any records in the output, then you may need to update the NuGet package (`Microsoft.ApplicationInsights.AspNetCore`) or click on the Search icon.

You can filter by event type, for example, requests or exceptions, and there are more detailed filters to refine your search. You can select an individual record to see more details, which will look something like the following:

Although you can access this information locally without Azure, you can choose to select **Configure Application Insights** and set up logging of data to your Azure account.

If you know what you're doing, then you can use **Advanced Mode** and enter your **Subscription ID** and **Instrumentation Key** manually:

 Secret configuration information, such as this, is now stored outside of the source tree to help prevent it leaking. You can now define secrets as environment variables or in a secrets store held in your user profile.

Once you set up Azure, then you can view the telemetry results online and aggregate information from many diverse systems. We don't have space to cover this in more detail here, but you can find more information online at `azure.microsoft.com/en-us/documentation/services/application-insights`.

Integrated logging

Logging is now built into ASP.NET Core (in the `Microsoft.Extensions.Logging` package) as well as **Dependency Injection (DI)**, and both are included in the default templates. This reduces the barrier to entry, and it's now trivial to use these helpful technologies in even the smallest of projects.

Previously, you would have to add logging and DI libraries before you started, which could put many people off using them. If you didn't already have a standard choice for both, then you would need to wade through the plethora of projects and research the merits of each.

 You can still use your preferred libraries if you are already acquainted with them. It's just that there are now sensible defaults, which you can override.

Logging is configured in the `Startup` class, and if you use the standard web application template, then this will already be included for you. The logger factory reads settings from the `appsettings.json` file. In here, you can configure the logging level, and by default, the relevant section looks like the following:

```
"Logging": {
  "IncludeScopes": false,
  "LogLevel": {
    "Default": "Debug",
    "System": "Information",
    "Microsoft": "Information"
  }
}
```

This sets a very chatty log level, which is useful for development, but you will probably want to only log warnings, and errors when you run this in production.

 Along with Application Insights and logging, useful debugging tools included by default in the `Startup` class include a developer exception page, which is like an advanced version of the old **Yellow Screen Of Death (YSOD)** ASP.NET error page. Also included is a database error page, which can helpfully apply EF migrations and mitigates a common pitfall of previous EF code-first migration deployments.

To add the logger to your MVC home controller via constructor injection, you can use the following code (after adding `using Microsoft.Extensions.Logging;` to your `using` statements at the top of the file):

```
private readonly ILogger Logger;
```

```
public HomeController(ILoggerFactory loggerFactory)
{
    Logger = loggerFactory.CreateLogger<HomeController>();
}
```

After this, you can use `Logger` to log events inside action methods, as follows:

```
Logger.LogDebug("Home page loaded");
```

There are many more logging levels available and overloaded methods so that you can log additional information, for example, exceptions. We won't go into any more detail here, but you don't simply have to log text events, you can also record execution times (perhaps with a stopwatch) or increment counters to see how often certain events occur. Next, we'll see how to view these numbers centrally and read them correctly.

 For more examples of how to use logging, you can examine the default account controller (if you included individual user accounts authentication in the template). For more information, you can read the documentation at `docs.asp.net/en/latest/fundamentals/logging.html`.

Centralized logging

Logging is great. However, in a distributed system, you will want to feed all of your logs and exceptions into a single location, where you can easily analyze them and generate alerts. One potential option for this is Logstash (`elastic.co/products/logstash`), which we fleetingly mentioned in `Chapter 2`, *Measuring Performance Bottlenecks*.

If you prefer a more modular approach and want to record performance counters and metrics, then there is **StatsD**, which listens for UDP packets and pushes to Graphite for storage and graphing. You can get it at `github.com/etsy/statsd` and there are a few .NET clients listed on the wiki, along with example C# code in the main repository.

You may wish to use message queuing for logging so that you can quickly put a logged event into a queue and forget about it, rather than directly hitting a logging server. If you directly call an API (and aren't using UDP), then make sure that it's asynchronous and nonblocking. You don't want to slow down your application by logging inefficiently.

There are also cloud options available, although the usual caveats about lock-in apply. AWS has **CloudWatch**, which you can read more about at `aws.amazon.com/cloudwatch`. Azure Diagnostics is similar, and you can integrate it with Application Insights, read more at `azure.microsoft.com/en-us/documentation/articles/azure-diagnostics`.

There are other cross-platform cloud services available, such as New Relic or Stackify, but these can be quite expensive, and you may wish to keep your logging within your own infrastructure. You could shoehorn the data into analytics software, such as **Google Analytics** or the privacy-focused Piwik (which is open source and can be self-hosted), but these are less suitable because they're designed for a slightly different purpose.

Statistics

When interpreting your collected metrics, it helps to know some basic statistics in order to read them correctly. Taking a simple *mean* average can mislead you and may not be as important as some other characteristics.

When instrumenting your code to collect metadata, you should have a rough idea of how often particular logging statements will be called. This doesn't have to be exact, and a rough order of magnitude approximation (or **Fermi estimate**) will usually suffice.

The question you should try to answer is how much of the data should be collected, all of it or a random sample? If you need to perform sampling, then you should calculate how big the sample size should be. We covered sampling in relation to SQL in Chapter 5, *Optimizing I/O Performance*, and the idea is similar here. Performance statistics require the same level of rigor as benchmarking does, and you can easily be misled or draw incorrect conclusions.

StatsD includes built-in support for sampling, but there are many other approaches available if you want to investigate them. For example, online streaming algorithms and reservoirs are two options. The important thing to keep in mind for performance is to use a fast **random number generator** (RNG). As, for sampling, this doesn't need to be cryptographically secure, a **pseudorandom number generator** (PRNG) is fine. In .NET, you can use new Random() for a PRNG, rather than the more secure option of RandomNumberGenerator.Create(). See Chapter 6, *Understanding Code Execution and Asynchronous Operations*, for more examples of how to use both of these.

When looking at your results, the outliers may be more interesting than the average. Although the median is more valuable than the mean, in this case, you should really look at the percentiles, for example, the 90th, 95th, and 99th percentiles. These data points can represent only a small fraction of your data, but at scale, they can occur frequently. You want to optimize for these worst case scenarios because if your users experience pages loads taking over five seconds ten percent of the time (even though the average looks fast), then they may go elsewhere.

There's much more to say on statistics, but beyond the basics, there are diminishing returns. If your math is rusty, then it is probably wise to have a refresher (Wikipedia is great for this). Then, you can explore some more advanced techniques, for example, the high-performance HyperLogLog (**HLL**) algorithm, which can estimate the size of a large set of elements using very little memory. Redis supports the HLL data structure (with the `PFADD`, `PFCOUNT`, and `PFMERGE` commands). For more on different data structures, refer to `Chapter 6`, *Understanding Code Execution and Asynchronous* Operations.

This is only a brief introduction to performance logging, but there is much more for you to explore. For example, if you want to standardize your approach, then you can look into APDEX (`apdex.org`), which sets a standard method to record the performance of applications and compute scores.

Managing stale caches

It's worth providing a quick reminder to still consider simple issues after all of this complexity. It is far too easy to get lost in the details of a complicated bug or performance tweak and miss the obvious.

A good technique to help with this is *rubber duck debugging*, which gets its name from the process of explaining your problem to a rubber duck on your desk. Most of us have experienced solving a problem after asking for help, even though the other person hasn't said anything. The process of explaining the problem to someone (or something) else clarifies it, and the solution becomes obvious.

If something appears to not be working after a fix, then check simple things first. See whether the patch has actually been delivered and deployed. You may be seeing stale code from a cache instead of your new version.

When managing caches, versioning is a useful tool to help you identify stale assets. You can alter filenames or add comments to include a unique version string. This can be **Sematic Versioning** (**SemVer**), an ISO date and timestamp, or a hash of the contents. For more on cache busting, refer to `Chapter 7`, *Learning Caching and Message Queuing*.

SemVer, is a great way to version your code because it implicitly captures information on compatibility and breaking changes. You can read more about SemVer at `semver.org`.

Summary

In this chapter, we saw how there are always downsides to every decision and every choice has a cost attached because nothing comes for free. There are always tradeoffs involved, and you need to be aware of the consequences of your actions, which may be small and subtle.

The key lesson is to take a thoughtful and rigorous approach to adding any performance-enhancing technique. Measurement is crucial to achieving this, but you also need to know how data can mislead you if you collect or interpret it incorrectly.

In the next chapter, we will continue with the measurement theme and learn how to use tests to monitor for performance regressions. You will see how to use testing (including unit testing), automation, and continuous integration to ensure that once you solve a performance problem, it stays this way.

9
Monitoring Performance Regressions

This chapter will cover writing automated tests to monitor performance along with adding these to a **Continuous Integration** (**CI**) and deployment system. By constantly checking for regressions, you'll avoid accidentally building a slow application. We'll also cover how to safely load test a system without forcing it offline and how to ensure that tests mimic real life usage as far as possible.

Topics covered in this chapter include the following:

- Profiling
- Load testing
- Automated testing
- Performance monitoring
- Continuous integration and deployment
- Realistic environments and production-like data
- UI testing with selenium and phantom headless browsers
- A/B testing for conversion optimization
- Cloud services and hosting
- DevOps

You will see how to automate performance monitoring and testing so that you don't need to remember to keep doing it manually. You'll learn how to catch regressions early before they cause trouble and how to safely back them out for rework.

Profiling and measurement

We started this book by highlighting the importance of measurement and profiling by covering some simple techniques in `Chapter 2`, *Measuring Performance Bottlenecks*. We continued this theme throughout, and we'll end the book on it as well because it's impossible to overstate how important measuring and analyzing reliable evidence is.

Previously, we covered using Glimpse to provide insights into the running of your web application. We also demonstrated the Visual Studio diagnostics tools and the Application Insights **Software Development Kit** (**SDK**). There's another tool that's worth mentioning and that's the Prefix profiler, which you can get at `prefix.io`.

Prefix is a free web-based ASP.NET profiler that supports ASP.NET Core. However, it doesn't support .NET Core yet (although this is planned), so you'll need to run ASP.NET Core on .NET Framework 4.6 for now. There's a live demo on their website (at `demo.prefix.io`) if you want to quickly check it out and it looks like the following:

ASP.NET Core can run on top of either .NET Core or the existing stable framework. For a refresher on how everything fits together, refer back to `Chapter 1`, *Why Performance Is a Feature*, or for more details, refer to `Chapter 6`, *Understanding Code Execution and Asynchronous Operations*.

You may also want to look at the **PerfView** performance analysis tool from Microsoft, which is used in the development of .NET Core. You can download PerfView from `microsoft.com/download/details.aspx?id=28567` as a ZIP file that you can just extract and run. It is useful to analyze the memory of .NET applications among other things, and it looks like this when you launch it:

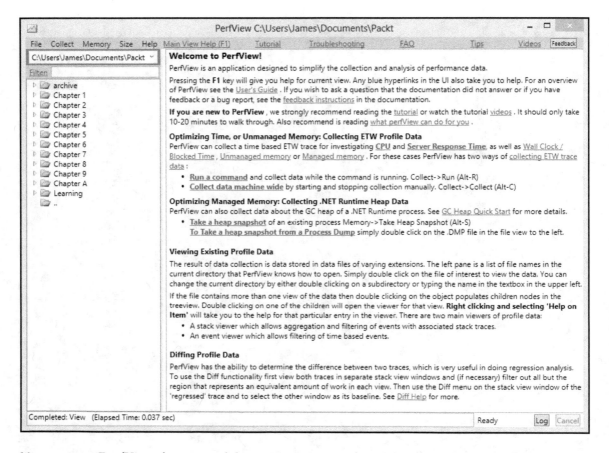

You can use PerfView for many debugging activities, for example, to take a snapshot of the heap or force GC runs. We don't have space for a detailed walkthrough here, but the included instructions are good, and there are blogs on MSDN with guides and many video tutorials on *Channel 9* at `channel9.msdn.com/Series/PerfView-Tutorial` if you need more information.

 Sysinternals tools (`technet.microsoft.com/sysinternals`) can also be helpful, but as they do not focus much on .NET, they are less useful in this context.

While tools such as these are great, what would be even better is to build performance monitoring into your development workflow. Automate everything that you can, and this makes performance checks transparent, routine, and run by default.

Manual processes are bad because you can skip steps, and you can easily make errors. You wouldn't dream of developing software by e-mailing files around or editing code directly on a production server, so why not automate your performance tests too.

Change control processes exist to ensure consistency and reduce errors. This is why using a **Source Control Management (SCM)** system, such as Git or **Team Foundation Server (TFS)** is essential. It's also extremely useful to have a build server and perform CI or even fully-automated deployments.

 Source control allows multiple people to work on a file simultaneously and merge the changes later. It's like Word's track changes feature, but actually usable. We assume that we're preaching to the converted and you already use source control. If not, stop reading right now and go install an SCM system.

If the code deployed in production differs from what you have on your local workstation, then you have very little chance of success. This is one of the reasons why SQL **Stored Procedures (SPs/sprocs)** are difficult to work with, at least without rigorous version control. It's far too easy to modify an old version of an SP on a development DB, accidentally revert a bug fix, and end up with a regression. If you must use SPs, then you will need a versioning system, such as ReadyRoll (which Redgate has now acquired).

As this isn't a book on **Continuous Delivery (CD)**, we will assume that you are already practicing CI and have a build server, such as JetBrains TeamCity, ThoughtWorks GoCD, CruiseControl.NET, or a cloud service, such as AppVeyor. Perhaps you're even automating your deployments using a tool, such as Octopus Deploy, and you have your own internal NuGet feeds, using software such as The Motley Fool's Klondike, or a cloud service, such as MyGet (which also supports npm, bower, and VSIX packages).

 NuGet packages are a great way of managing internal projects. In new versions of Visual Studio, you can see the source code of packages and debug into them. This means no more huge solutions containing a ludicrous number of projects.

Bypassing processes and doing things manually will cause problems, even if you are following a script. If it can be automated then it probably should be, and this includes testing.

Testing

Testing is essential to producing high-quality and well-performing software. The secret to productive testing is to make it easy, reliable, and routine. If testing is difficult or tests regularly fail because of issues unrelated to the software (for example, environmental problems), then tests will not be performed or the results will be ignored. This will cause you to miss genuine problems and ship bugs that you could have easily avoided.

There are many different varieties of testing, and you may be familiar with the more common cases used for functional verification. In this book, we will mainly focus on tests pertaining to performance. However, the advice here is applicable to many types of testing.

Automated testing

As previously mentioned, the key to improving almost everything is automation. Tests that are only run manually on developer workstations add very little value. Of course, it should be possible to run the tests on desktops, but this shouldn't be the official result because there's no guarantee that they will pass on a server (where the correct functioning matters more).

 Although automation usually occurs on servers, it can be useful to automate tests that run on developer workstations too. One way of doing this in Visual Studio is to use a plugin, such as **NCrunch**. This runs your tests as you work, which can be very useful if you practice **Test-Driven Development** (TDD) and write your tests before your implementations. You can read more about NCrunch and see the pricing at `ncrunch.net`, or there's a similar open source project at `continuoustests.com`.

One way of enforcing testing is to use gated check-ins in TFS, but this can be a little draconian, and if you use an SCM, such as Git, then it's easier to work on branches and simply block merges until all the tests pass. You want to encourage developers to check-in early and often because this makes merges easier. Therefore, it's a bad idea to have features in progress sitting on workstations for a long time (generally no longer than a day).

Continuous integration

CI systems automatically build and test all of your branches and feed this information back to your version control system. For example, using the GitHub API, you can block the merging of pull requests until the build server reports a successfully tested merge result.

Both **Bitbucket** and **GitLab** offer free CI systems, called pipelines, so you may not need any extra systems in addition to one for source control because everything is in one place. GitLab also offers an integrated Docker container registry, and there is an open source version that you can install locally. .NET Core and Visual Studio support Docker well, and we'll cover this again later in the chapter.

You can do something similar with **Visual Studio Team Services** for CI builds and unit testing. Visual Studio also has Git services built into it.

This process works well for unit testing because unit tests must be quick so that you get feedback early. Shortening the iteration cycle is a good way of increasing productivity, and you'll want the lag to be as small as possible.

However, running tests on each build isn't suitable for all types of testing because not all tests can be quick. In this case, you'll need an additional strategy so as not to slow down your feedback loop.

 There are many unit testing frameworks available for .NET, for example, NUnit, xUnit, and MSTest (Microsoft's unit test framework) along with multiple graphical ways of running tests locally, such as the Visual Studio Test Explorer and the ReSharper plugin. People have their favorites, but it doesn't really matter what you choose because most CI systems will support all of them.

Slow testing

Some tests are slow, but even if each test is fast, they can easily add up to a lengthy time if you have a lot of them. This is especially true if they can't be parallelized and need to be run in sequence, so you should always aim to have each test stand on its own without any dependencies on others.

It's good practice to divide your tests into rings of importance so that you can at least run a subset of the most crucial on every CI build. However, if you have a large test suite or some tests that are unavoidably slow, then you may choose to only run these once a day (perhaps overnight) or every week (maybe over the weekend).

Some testing is simply slow by nature and performance testing can often fall into this category, for example, load testing or **User Interface** (UI) testing. We usually class this as integration testing, rather than unit testing because they require your code to be deployed to an environment for testing and the tests can't simply exercise the binaries.

To make use of such automated testing, you will need to have an automated deployment system in addition to your CI system. If you have enough confidence in your test system, then you can even have live deployments happen automatically. This works well if you also use **feature switching** to control the rollout of new features.

We won't go into the implementation details of Continuous Integration or automated deployments in this book. However, we will cover feature switching, how to apply performance testing to CI processes, and what to do when you discover a regression.

Fixing performance regressions

If you discover a performance issue at the unit testing stage, then you can simply rework this feature, but it's more likely that these problems will surface in a later testing phase. This can make it more challenging to remedy the problem because the work may already have been built upon and have other commits on top of it.

The correct course of action is often to back-out regressions immediately or at least as soon as possible upon discovery. Delays will only make the issue harder to fix later, which is why it's important to get fast feedback and highlight problems quickly.

It's important to be disciplined and always remove regressions, even though it may be painful. If you let the occasional minor regression in, then you can easily become sloppy and let more serious ones in over time because of the precedent it sets.

Load testing

Load testing is the process of discovering how many concurrent users your web app can support. You generally perform it on a test environment with a tool that gradually ramps up a simulated load, for example, JMeter (`jmeter.apache.org`). Perhaps, you'd prefer using a JMeter compatible cloud service, such as BlazeMeter, or an alternative, such as **Loader.io**, if your test systems are web-facing.

Load testing can take a significant amount of time depending on the scale of your service because it can be configured to continue until the test environment gets unacceptably slow for users or falls over and becomes unresponsive. You need to be extremely careful with load testing and not only from the point of view of accidentally testing your live systems to destruction while they're in use.

You also need to be wary of getting false results, which may mislead you into concluding that your system can handle more load than it actually will. Balancing these two competing concerns of safety and realism can be difficult. It's important to get realistic results, but you need to balance this against not stressing your production environment and impacting the experience of real users.

Realism

Keeping it real is an important principle of performance testing. If you don't use a realistic environment and workload, then your results may be worse than having no data because they could mislead you into bad decisions. When you have no information, you at least know that you're in the dark and just guessing.

We'll cover workloads and feature switching shortly, including an example of how to implement your own simple version from scratch. First, let's look at how to make your test environments representative of production.

Realistic environments

Using a test environment that is as close to production (or as live-like) as possible is a good step toward ensuring reliable results. You can try and use a smaller set of servers and then scale your results up to get an estimate of live performance. However, this assumes that you have an intimate knowledge of how your application scales and what hardware constraints will be the bottlenecks.

A better option is to use your live environment or rather what will become your production stack. You first create a staging environment that is identical to live, then you deploy your code to it, and then you run your full test suite, including a comprehensive performance test, ensuring that it behaves correctly. Once you are happy, then you simply swap staging and production, perhaps using DNS or Azure **staging slots**.

The following diagram shows how you first release to staging and go live simply by making staging become production:

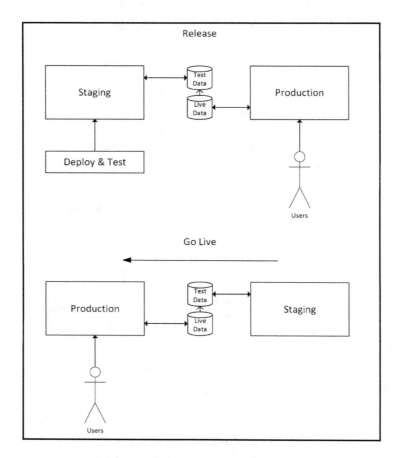

Your old live environment now either becomes your test environment or if you use immutable cloud instances, then you can simply terminate it and Spin-up a new staging system. This concept is known as *blue-green deployment*, but unfortunately specific implementation instructions are beyond the scope of this book.

You don't necessarily have to move all users across at once in a big bang, and you can move a few over first to test whether everything is correct. We'll cover this shortly in the section on feature switching.

Realistic workloads

Another important part of performing realistic testing is to use real data and real workloads. Synthetic data often won't exercise a system fully or find exotic edge cases. You can use **fuzzing** to generate random data, but if you have a production system, then you can simply use the data from this and parse your logs to generate a realistic workload to replay.

Obviously, don't replay actions onto a live system that could modify user data and be wary of data privacy concerns or any action that could generate an external event, for example, sending a mass e-mail or charging a credit card. You can use a dedicated test system, but you still need to be careful to stub out any external APIs that don't have a test version.

Another approach is to use dummy users for your testing if you don't mind your users discovering the fakes and possibly interacting with them. One case of this approach is Netflix's cult *Example Show*, which is a homemade video of an employee running around their office grounds with a laptop.

Feature switching

An alternative to fake users or test environments is to run performance tests on your real live environment using genuine users as they interact with your web application. You can use feature switching to gradually roll out a new feature to a small subset of your user base and monitor the system for excessive load. If everything seems normal, then you can continue the rollout; otherwise, you can rollback.

 You may hear similar ideas referred to by other names, such as **Feature Flags**, **Feature Toggles**, **Canary Releases**, or **Branch by Abstraction**. Some of these may have subtly different meanings but the general guiding principle of gradually releasing a change is much the same.

The following diagram shows how you could progressively migrate users to a new feature by deploying it but not initially enabling it. Your first users could be members of staff so that any issues are detected early:

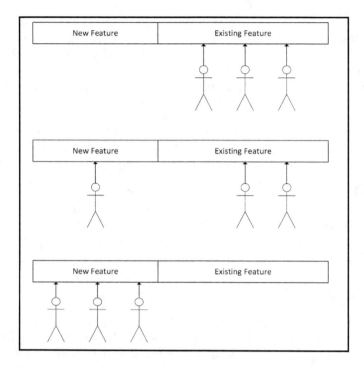

Once all users are consuming the new feature, then you can safely remove the old feature (and the feature switch itself). It's a good idea to regularly tidy up like this to avoid clutter and make later work easier.

If you discover that your system experiences excessive load as you slowly increase the percentage of users on the new feature, then you can halt the rollout and avoid your servers becoming overloaded and unresponsive. You then have time to investigate and either back out of the change or increase available resources.

One variation on this theme is when a new feature requires a data migration and this migration is computationally or networking-intensive, for example, migrating user-submitted videos to a new home and transcoding them in the process. In this case, the excessive load that you are monitoring will only be transient, and you don't need to back out of a feature. You only need to ensure that the rate of migration is low enough to not excessively tax your infrastructure.

Although the new feature is usually branched to in code, you can instead perform switching at the network level if you use blue-green deployment. This is known as a canary release and can be done at the DNS or load balancer level. However, specific implementation details are again beyond the remit of this book.

You can find many open source feature switching libraries online or you could write your own, which we will show you how to do later. A couple of .NET feature-switching libraries are github.com/mexx/FeatureSwitcher and github.com/Jason-roberts/FeatureToggle. Unfortunately, neither of these work on .NET Core yet, although support is planned for **FeatureToggle**. There are also paid cloud services available, which offer easy management interfaces, such as **LaunchDarkly**.

 Library and framework support for .NET Core and ASP.NET Core change rapidly, so check ANCLAFS.com for the latest information.

To illustrate feature switching, let's build our own extremely simple implementation for an ASP.NET Core web application. To start with, we take the default existing homepage view (Index.cshtml) and make a copy (IndexOld.cshtml). We then make our changes to Index.cshtml, but these aren't important for the purposes of this demo.

In HomeController.cs, we change the logic to return the new view a relatively small percentage of the time, and the old one otherwise. The original code was simply the following:

```
public IActionResult Index()
{
    return View();
}
```

We change this action to return the new view in a quarter of the cases, like the following:

```
public IActionResult Index()
{
    var rand = new Random();
    if (rand.Next(99) < 25)
    {
        return View();
    }
    return View("IndexOld");
}
```

This code picks a random number out of a hundred, and if it is less than 25, then it loads the new view. Clearly, you wouldn't hardcode values like this, and you would probably use a database to store configuration and control it with a web admin page.

If you load the page in a browser, then three out of four times you should get the original page, which looks like the following:

However, roughly one every four page loads, you will get the new page, which looks like the following:

We removed the carousel and cut the number of image loads in half. You can see the difference in the browser developer tools, for example, the Firefox performance analysis for the original looks like the following:

Whereas for the new version it looks like this.

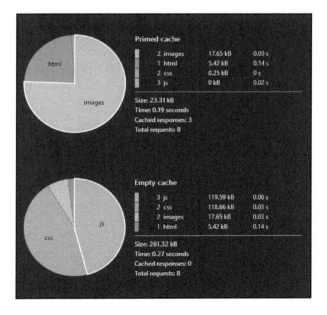

You can see that the number of **images** decreased, which has reduced the page size and the total number of requests required.

 These measurements were taken with the hosting environment set to `Production`. If you remain with the default of `Development`, then your results will differ. Refer to the following documentation page for how to change this: `docs.asp.net/en/latest/fundamentals/environments.html`.

Once the new view has been progressively rolled out to all users (with no performance problems), then the action method code can be reverted to the original state and the old view deleted. Obviously, this is a trivial example. Hopefully, you can now see how feature switching can be performed.

Using feature switching to rollout in this way works well for performance testing, but you need to be confident that your new code is functionally correct or at least safe to deploy. However, in certain circumstances you can also test functionality by extending this approach and performing experiments.

Experimenting for science

If you take the feature switching rollout to its logical conclusion, then you can switch on a new refactored version for a small percentage of users, but not actually expose the output. You will run the existing version in parallel as a control and show this to the user. However, you will collect the results of both versions, including performance data. You can then compare them to ensure that the new (hopefully higher performance) version is correct and consistent with the existing behavior.

GitHub have an open source Ruby library, called `Scientist`, which they used to successfully refactor their permissions and merging code. In the process, they discovered existing legacy bugs, found missing features, optimized database queries, and swapped a search system. Scientist not only displays the correctness of new code but also its performance relative to the old implementation.

 An important concern with `Scientist` (or any method using this experimentation approach) is to not change data. All operations should be read-only and have no side effects; otherwise, you will perform the modification more than once, which could have undesirable consequences.

There's a .NET port of `Scientist` by GitHub employee Phil Haack, called *Scientist.NET*, and you can get it at `github.com/Haacked/Scientist.net`. You could also install it via NuGet. However, it's currently a prerelease as it's still a work in progress, but it should support .NET Core. Check `ANCLAFS.com` for the latest information.

This idea of experimenting on users is similar to the marketing concept of **A/B testing**, which is used to discover conversion effectiveness. However, with `Scientist`, you don't typically show the users different outputs or even intend the output to change, you just record the new output for the subset of users that you have it enabled for.

A/B testing

A/B testing is similar to feature switching, but we usually use it to test the effectiveness of different web page designs and how they affect the *conversion funnel* analytics. We normally use it for digital marketing rather than for software development because it's less about what is correct and more about what customers prefer. However, the underlying technical principals are comparable to feature switching and experimenting.

In a simple example, you serve half of your visitors the old version of a page and the other half a new version designed to increase engagement. You then record how many visitors click through or perform some action on each variant. If the new version performs better, then you keep it and roll it out to everyone. However, if it converted worse, you roll back to the old version and try again.

You can see that this is very similar to how feature switching works, and you can use the same tools to do both. The only difference is what you are measuring, user analytics or the health of your infrastructure.

A/B testing is not normally used for backend features and is simply to assess UI alternatives. However, it is different to functionally testing your web interface, so let's cover the basics of UI testing now.

User interface testing

There's one area of an application that is traditionally difficult to test, and that's the UI. This is particularly the case for GUIs, as used in web applications. One reason for this is that users typically have a lot of flexibility in how they display their interface, and this is especially true for web browsers. A naïve pixel-based testing approach is going to be extremely fragile.

You need to design your application to be easily testable, and the UI is no exception. While it is possible to test the UI of a poorly-designed legacy application and this may even be the easiest testing approach, if you consider UI testing up front, then life will be a lot easier. For example, including sensible IDs on your HTML **Document Object Model** (**DOM**) elements makes testing much more straightforward and less fragile.

Checking your application from a web browser perspective can be a useful additional step on top of automated unit and integration testing. You can use it not only to test for functional correctness and regressions but also to measure client side performance, which is increasingly important. There are many UI testing tools available, most of which you can integrate into your CI pipeline to automate testing.

Web UI testing tools

One of the most popular web-testing tools is **Selenium**, which allows you to easily write tests and automate web browsers using **WebDriver**. Selenium is useful for many other tasks apart from testing, and you can read more about it at `docs.seleniumhq.org`.

 WebDriver is a protocol to remote control web browsers, and you can read about it at `w3c.github.io/webdriver/webdriver-spec.html`.

Selenium uses real browsers, the same versions your users will access your web application with. This makes it excellent to get representative results, but it can cause issues if it runs from the command line in an unattended fashion. For example, you may find your test server's memory full of dead browser processes which timed out.

You may find it easier to use a dedicated headless test browser, which, while not exactly the same as what your users will see, is more suitable for automation. Of course, the best approach is to use a combination of both, perhaps running headless tests first and then running the same tests on real browsers with WebDriver.

One of the most well-known headless test browsers is **PhantomJS**. This is based on the **WebKit** engine, so it should give you similar results to Chrome and Safari. PhantomJS is useful for many things apart from testing, such as capturing screenshots, and you can drive it with many different testing frameworks. As the name suggests, you can control PhantomJS with JavaScript, and you can read more about it at `phantomjs.org`.

WebKit is an open source engine for web browsers, which was originally part of the **KDE** Linux desktop environment. It is mainly used in Apple's Safari browser, but a fork called **Blink** is used in Google Chrome, Chromium, and Opera. You can read more at `webkit.org`.

Other automatable testing browsers, based on different engines, are available, but they have some limitations. For example, **SlimerJS** (`slimerjs.org`) is based on the **Gecko** engine used by Firefox, but is not fully headless.

You probably want to use a higher-level testing utility rather than scripting browser engines directly. One such utility that provides many useful abstractions is **CasperJS** (`casperjs.org`), which supports running on both PhantomJS and SlimerJS.

Another tool is **Capybara**, which allows you to easily simulate user interactions in Ruby. It supports Selenium, WebKit, **Rack**, and PhantomJS (via Poltergeist), although it's more suitable for Rails apps. You can read more at `jnicklas.github.io/capybara`.

There is also **TrifleJS** (`triflejs.org`), which uses the .NET `WebBrowser` class (the Internet Explorer **Trident** engine), but this is a work in progress. Additionally, there's **Watir** (`watir.com`), which is a set of Ruby libraries targeting Internet Explorer and WebDriver. However, neither have been updated in a while, and IE has changed a lot recently.

 Microsoft Edge (codenamed Spartan) is the new version of IE, and the Trident engine was forked to **EdgeHTML**. The JavaScript engine (Chakra) was open sourced as **ChakraCore** (`github.com/Microsoft/ChakraCore`).

It shouldn't matter too much what browser engine you use, and PhantomJS will work fine as a first pass for automated tests. You can always test with real browsers after using a headless one, perhaps with Selenium or with PhantomJS using WebDriver.

 When we refer to browser engines (WebKit/Blink, Gecko, or Trident/EdgeHTML), we generally mean only the rendering and layout engine, not the JavaScript engine (SFX/Nitro/FTL/B3, V8, SpiderMonkey, or Chakra/ChakraCore).

You'll probably still want to use a utility such as CasperJS to make writing tests easier, and you'll likely need a test framework, such as **Jasmine** (`jasmine.github.io`) or **QUnit** (`qunitjs.com`) too. You can also use a test runner that supports both Jasmine and QUnit, such as **Chutzpah** (`mmanela.github.io/chutzpah`).

You can integrate your automated tests with many different CI systems, for example, Jenkins or JetBrains TeamCity. If you prefer a cloud-hosted option, then there's Travis CI (`travis-ci.org`) and AppVeyor (`appveyor.com`), which is also suitable to build .NET apps.

You may prefer to run your integration and UI tests from your deployment system, for example, to verify a successful deployment in Octopus Deploy. There are also dedicated, cloud-based web-application UI testing services available, such as BrowserStack (`browserstack.com`).

Automating UI performance tests

Automated UI tests are clearly great to check for functional regressions, but they are also useful to test performance. You have programmatic access to the same information provided by the network inspector in the browser developer tools.

You can integrate the **YSlow** (`yslow.org`) performance analyzer with PhantomJS, enabling your CI system to check for common web-performance mistakes on every commit. YSlow came out of Yahoo!, and it provides rules used to identify bad practices, which can slow down web applications for users. It's a similar idea to Google's PageSpeed Insights service (which you can automate via its API).

However, YSlow is pretty old, and things have moved on in web development recently, for example, HTTP/2. A modern alternative is "the coach" from **sitespeed.io**, and you can read more at `github.com/sitespeedio/coach`. You should check out their other open source tools too, such as the dashboard at `dashboard.sitespeed.io`, which uses Graphite and Grafana.

You can also export the network results (in industry standard HAR format) and analyze them however you like, for example, visualizing them graphically in waterfall format, as you might do manually with your browser developer tools.

 The **HTTP Archive (HAR)** format is a standard way of representing the content of monitored network data to export it to other software. You can copy or save as HAR in some browser developer tools by right-clicking a network request.

Staying alert

Whenever you perform testing, particularly UI or performance testing, you will get noisy results. Reliability is not perfect, and there will always be failures that are not due to bugs in the code. You shouldn't let these false positives cause you to ignore failing tests, and although the easiest course of action may be disabling them, the correct thing to do to make them more reliable.

 The scientifically minded know that there is no such thing as a perfect filter in binary classification, and always look at the precision and recall of a system. Knowing the rate of false positives and negatives is important to get a good idea of the accuracy and tradeoffs involved.

To avoid testing fatigue, it can be helpful to engage developers and instill a responsibility to fix failing tests. You don't want everyone thinking that it's somebody else's problem. It should be pretty easy to see who broke a test by the commit in version control, and it's then their job to fix the broken test.

You can have a bit of fun with this and create something a bit more interesting than a wall mounted dashboard. Although having **information radiators** is useful if you don't get desensitized to them. There's plenty of cheap **Internet of Things (IoT)** hardware available today, which allows you to turn some interesting things into build or test failure alarms. For example, an **Arduino**-controlled traffic light, an **ESP8266**-operated foam-missile turret, or a Raspberry Pi-powered animatronic figure.

DevOps

When using automation and techniques such as feature switching, it is essential to have a good view of your environments so that you know the utilization of all the hardware. Good tooling is important to perform this monitoring, and you want to easily be able to see the vital statistics of every server. This will consist of at least the CPU, memory, and disk space consumption, but it may include more, and you will want alarms set up to alert you if any of these stray outside allowed bands.

The practice of **DevOps** is the culmination of all of the automation we covered previously with development, operations, and quality-assurance testing teams all collaborating. The only missing pieces left now are to provision and configure infrastructure and then monitor it while in use. Although DevOps is a culture, there is plenty of tooling that can help.

DevOps tooling

One of the primary themes of DevOps tooling is defining infrastructure as code. The idea is that you shouldn't manually perform a task, such as setting up a server, when you can create software to do it for you. You can then reuse these provisioning scripts, which will not only save you time but will also ensure that all of the machines are consistent and free of mistakes or missed steps.

Provisioning

There are many systems available to commission and configure new machines. Some popular configuration-management automation tools are **Ansible** (`ansible.com`), **Chef** (`chef.io`), and **Puppet** (`puppet.com`).

Not all of these tools work great on Windows servers, partly because Linux is easier to automate. However, you can run ASP.NET Core on Linux and still develop on Windows, using Visual Studio while testing in a VM. Developing for a VM is a great idea because it solves the problems in setting up environments and issues where it "works on my machine" but not in production.

Vagrant (`vagrantup.com`) is a great command line tool to manage developer VMs. It allows you to easily create, Spin-up, and share developer environments. The successor to Vagrant, **Otto** (`ottoproject.io`) takes this a step further and abstracts deployment too so that you can push to multiple cloud providers without worrying about the intricacies of **CloudFormation**, **OpsWorks**, or anything else.

If you create your infrastructure as code, then your scripts can be versioned and tested, just like your application code. We'll stop before we get too far off topic, but the point is that if you have reliable environments, which you can easily verify, instantiate, and perform testing on, then CI is a lot easier.

Monitoring

Monitoring is essential, especially for web applications, and there are many tools available to help with it. A popular open source infrastructure-monitoring system is **Nagios** (`nagios.org`). Another more modern open source alerting and metrics tool is **Prometheus** (`prometheus.io`).

If you use a cloud platform, then there will be monitoring built in, for example, AWS CloudWatch or Azure Diagnostics. There are also cloud services to directly monitor your website, such as **Pingdom** (`pingdom.com`), **UptimeRobot** (`uptimerobot.com`), **Datadog** (`datadoghq.com`), and **PagerDuty** (`pagerduty.com`).

You probably already have a system in place to measure availability, but you can also use the same systems to monitor performance. This is not only helpful to ensure a responsive user experience, but it can also provide early warning signs that a failure is imminent. If you are proactive and take preventative action, then you can save yourself a lot of trouble reactively fighting fires.

This isn't a book on operations, but it helps to consider application support requirements at design time. Development, testing, and operations aren't competing disciplines, and you will succeed more often if you work as one team rather than simply throwing an application over the fence and saying it "worked in test, ops problem now."

Hosting

It's well worth considering the implications of various hosting options because if developers can't easily access the environments they need, then this will reduce their agility. They may have to work around an availability problem and end up using insufficient or unsuitable hardware, which will hamper progress and cause future maintenance problems. Or their work will simply be blocked and delivery set back.

Unless you are a very large organization, hosting in-house is generally a bad idea for reliability, flexibility, and cost reasons. Unless you have some very sensitive data, then you should probably use a data center.

You can co-locate servers in a data center, but then you need staff to be on call to fix hardware problems. Or you can rent a physical server and run your application on "bare metal", but you may still need remote hands to perform resets or other tasks on the machine.

The most flexible situation is to rent self-service virtual machines, commonly known as cloud hosting. There are many hosting companies that offer this, but the big players are Amazon, Google, and Microsoft.

Microsoft's Azure is the obvious choice for a .NET shop and it has improved immensely since launch compared to its original offering. Its **Platform as a Service (PaaS)** to host .NET applications is the most polished and the easiest to get running on quickly. It also offers lots of extra services that go beyond simple VMs.

However, .NET Core and ASP.NET Core are new types of framework, which are not aimed solely at C# developers, who would usually pick the default option offered by Microsoft. The targeted market is developers who may be used to choosing alternative platforms and open source frameworks. Therefore, it makes sense to cover other options, which people new to .NET may be more familiar with.

The difference between PaaS and **Infrastructure as a Service (IaaS)** is that PaaS is higher level and provides a service to run applications, not computers. IaaS simply provides you with a VM. However, with PaaS, this is abstracted away, and you don't need to worry about setting up and updating an instance.

Amazon Web Services (AWS) is the most established cloud host, and it started by only offering IaaS, although they now offer PaaS options. For example, **Elastic Beanstalk** supports .NET. Even though Windows (and SQL Server) support has improved, it is still not first class, and Linux is clearly their main platform.

However, now that .NET Core and SQL Server 2016 run on Linux, this may be less of a problem. You will pay a premium for Windows server instances, but you're also charged more for some enterprise Linux distributions (**Redhat** and **SUSE**). However, you can run other Linux distributions, such as **Ubuntu** or **CentOS** without paying a premium.

Google Cloud Platform used to consist of **App Engine (GAE)**, which was quite a restrictive PaaS, but it is getting more flexible. They now offer a generic IaaS called **Compute Engine (GCE)**, and there's a new flexible version of GAE, which is more like GCE. These new offerings are useful, as you couldn't traditionally run .NET on GAE, and they also provide other products such as pre-emptible VMs and a cloud CDN (with HTTPS at no extra cost).

Azure may still be the best choice for you, and it integrates well with other Microsoft products, such as Visual Studio. However, it is worth having healthy competition because this keeps everyone innovating. It's definitely a good idea to frequently look at the pricing of all options, (which changes regularly) because you can save a lot of money depending on the workload that you run. You can avoid vendor lock-in by avoiding custom services.

If you are eligible for Microsoft's BizSpark program, then you can get three years of Azure credits (suitable to host a small application). You also get an MSDN subscription for free software licenses.

Whatever hosting provider you choose to use, it is sensible to avoid vendor lock-in and use services that are generic, which you can easily swap for an alternative. For example, using hosted open source software, such as PostgreSQL, Redis, or RabbitMQ, rather than an equivalent custom cloud provider product. You can also take a resilient multicloud approach to protect yourself from an outage of a single provider.

Docker is a great technology for this purpose because many different cloud services support it. For example, you can run the same container on Azure Container Service, Docker Cloud, AWS EC2 Container Service, and Google's **Kubernetes** Container Engine.

Docker also runs on Windows (using Hyper-V), and in the new version of Visual Studio you can deploy to and debug into a container. This can run ASP.NET Core on Linux, and when you are ready to deploy, you can just push to production and have confidence that it will work as it did on your machine. You can read more about this at `docker.com/Microsoft`, and there are some interesting videos on the Docker blog.

 When choosing a cloud (or even a region), it's important to not only consider the monetary cost. You should also factor in environmental concerns, such as the main fuel used for the power supply. For example, some regions can be cheaper, but this may be because they use dirty coal power, which contributes to climate change and our future security.

Summary

In this chapter, you saw how you might integrate automated testing into a CI system in order to monitor for performance regressions. You also learned some strategies to roll out changes and ensure that tests accurately reflect real life. We also briefly covered some options for DevOps practices and cloud-hosting providers, which together make continuous performance testing much easier.

In the next chapter, we'll wrap-up everything that we covered throughout this book and suggest some areas for further investigation. We'll reinforce our learnings so far, give you some interesting ideas to think about, contemplate possible futures for .NET, and consider the exciting direction the platform is taking.

10
The Way Ahead

This chapter sums up what you learned by reading this book. It refreshes the main tenets of performance and it reminds you that you should always remain pragmatic. We'll recap why you shouldn't optimize just for optimization's sake and why you should always measure the problems and results. This chapter also introduces more advanced and exotic techniques that you may wish to consider learning about if you need more speed or are a serious performance enthusiast.

Topics covered in this chapter include the following:

- A summary of previously-covered topics
- Platform invoke and native code
- Alternative architectures, such as ARM
- Advanced hardware (GPUs, FPGAs, ASICs, SSDs, and RAM SANs)
- Machine learning and AI
- Big data and MapReduce
- The Orleans virtual actor model
- Custom transport layers
- Advanced hashing functions
- Library and framework support
- The future of .NET Core

We'll reinforce how to assess and solve performance issues by refreshing your memory of the lessons in the previous chapters. You'll also gain an awareness of other advanced technology that's available to assist you with delivering high performance, which you may wish to investigate further. Finally, we'll highlight what libraries and frameworks support .NET Core and ASP.NET Core, and try to hypothesize possible future directions for these exciting new platforms.

Reviewing what we learned

Let's briefly recap what we covered earlier in this book to serve as an aide-mémoire.

In Chapter 1, *Why Performance Is a Feature*, we discussed the basic premise of this book and showed you why you need to care about the performance of your software. Then, in Chapter 2, *Measuring Performance Bottlenecks*, we showed you that the only way you can solve performance problems is to carefully measure your application.

In Chapter 3, *Fixing Common Performance Problems*, we looked at some of the most frequent performance mistakes and how to fix them. After this, we went a little deeper in Chapter 4, *Addressing Network Performance*, and dug into the networking layer that underpins all web applications. Then in Chapter 5, *Optimizing I/O Performance*, we focused on input/output and how this can negatively affect performance.

In Chapter 6, *Understanding Code Execution and Asynchronous Operations*, we jumped into the intricacies of C# code and looked at how its execution can alter performance. Then in Chapter 7, *Learning Caching and Message Queuing*, we initially looked at caching, which is widely regarded to be quite hard. Then, we investigated message queuing as a way to build a distributed and reliable system.

In Chapter 8, *The Downsides of Performance Enhancing Tools*, we concentrated on the negatives of the techniques that we previously covered, as nothing comes for free. Then in Chapter 9, *Monitoring Performance Regressions*, we looked at measuring performance again but, in this case, from an automation and **Continuous Integration (CI)** perspective.

Further reading

If you've read this far, then you will probably want some pointers for other things to research and read up on. For the rest of this chapter, we'll highlight some interesting topics that you may want to look into further, but we couldn't cover in more detail in this book.

Going native

One of the problems with the old ASP.NET is that it was really slow, which is why one of the main guiding principles of ASP.NET Core has been performance. Impressive progress has already been made, but there are plenty more opportunities for further enhancements.

One of the most promising areas is the native tool chain, which we briefly mentioned in Chapter 6, *Understanding Code Execution and Asynchronous Operations*. It's still in its early days but it looks like it could be very significant.

Previously, if you wanted to call unmanaged native code from managed .NET code, you needed to use Platform Invoke (**PInvoke**), but this had performance overheads and safety concerns. Even if your native code was faster, the overheads often meant it was not worth bothering about.

The native tool chain should give native levels of performance, but with the safety and convenience of a managed runtime. Ahead-of-time compilation is fascinating and very technical, but it can offer a performance boost along with simplified deployments if we know the architecture.

It's also possible to optimize for different processors that may offer special performance features and instructions. For example, targeting low-energy ARM chips instead of the usual Intel style processors.

Processor architecture

Typically, when writing desktop or server software, you will target an Intel-based architecture, such as x86 or x64. However, ARM-based chips are gaining popularity, and they can offer fantastic power efficiency. If software is specially optimized for them, then they can also offer excellent performance.

For example, the **Scratch** graphical programming language, used to teach computing, has been optimized for a Raspberry Pi 3 and it now runs roughly twice as quick as it does on an Intel Core i5. Other software has also been optimized for the ARM processor, for example, the Kodi open source media player.

ARM Holdings is simply an intellectual property company and they don't make any processors themselves. Other companies, such as Apple and Broadcom, license the designs or architecture and fabricate their **System on a Chip** (**SoC**) products.

This means that there are many different chips available, which run multiple different versions of the ARM architecture and instruction set. This fragmentation can make it harder to support unless you pick a specific platform.

Windows 10 IoT Core runs on the Raspberry Pi (version 2 and 3) and it can now be set up using the standard **New Out Of the Box Software** (**NOOBS**) installer. Windows 10 IoT Core is not a full desktop environment to run normal applications, but it does allow you to make hardware projects and program them with C# and .NET. However, for web applications, you would probably run .NET Core on Linux, such as Raspbian (based on **Debian**).

Hardware is hard

We previously mentioned additional hardware that can be used for computation in Chapter 6, *Understanding Code Execution and Asynchronous Operations*, including **Graphics Processing Units** (**GPUs**), **Field Programmable Gate Arrays** (**FPGAs**), and **Application Specific Integrated Circuits** (**ASICs**).

Not only can these devices be used for specific processing tasks, but their storage can be used as well. For example, you can borrow the RAM from a GPU if main memory is exhausted. However, this technique is not required as much as it used to be when memory was more limited.

You may have heard of RAM SANs, which were SANs using standard RAM for permanent storage (with a battery backup). However, these have become less relevant as SSDs (based on flash memory) improved in speed and increased in capacity to the point of replacing mechanical drives for many common tasks.

You can still purchase high performance SANs, but they will probably be based on flash memory rather than RAM. If you use RAM as your main storage (for example, with Redis), then it is important to use **error-correcting code memory** (**ECC**). ECC RAM is more expensive, but it is better suited for server use. However, some cloud instances don't use it or it's hard to find out whether it's even offered because it isn't listed in the specification.

One application of custom computation hardware is **Machine Learning** (**ML**), specifically the deep learning branch of ML, using multilevel neural networks. This technology saw impressive advances in recent years and this led to products, such as self-driving vehicles. ML applications can make very good use of non-CPU processing, particularly GPUs, and NVIDIA provides many tools and libraries to help with this.

Google also recently announced that they built a custom ASIC, called a **Tensor Processing Unit** (**TPU**), to accelerate their TensorFlow machine learning library and cloud services. You can read more at `tensorflow.org` and `cloud.google.com/ml`.

Machine learning

You don't only have to use **Artificial Intelligence** (**AI**) to replace drivers and other jobs, such as call center staff or even doctors. You can use some basic ML in your own web applications to provide product suggestions relevant to your customers or analyze marketing effectiveness, just like Amazon or Netflix do.

You don't even need to build your own ML systems, as you can use cloud services, such as **Azure ML**. This allows you to use a graphical drag and drop interface to build your ML systems, although you can also use Python and R.

You still need to know a little bit about data science, such as the elementary principles of binary classification and training data, but even so, it significantly reduces the barrier to entry. Yet, if you want to fully explore ML and big data possibilities, then you probably need a dedicated data scientist.

You can try out Azure ML at `studio.azureml.net` and you don't even need to register. The following screenshot shows an example of what it looks like:

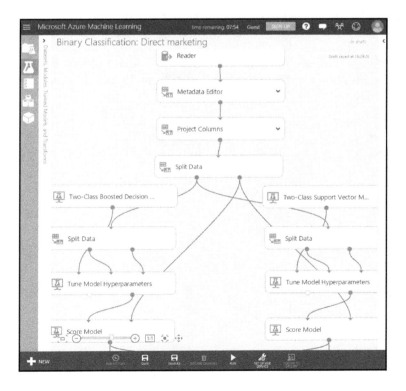

Big data and MapReduce

Big data is probably an overused term these days and what is sometimes described as big is usually more like medium data. Big data is when you have so much information that it is difficult to process, or even store, on a single machine. Traditional approaches often break down with big data, as they are not adequate for the huge automatically-acquired datasets that are common today. For example, the amount of data constantly collected by IoT sensors or by our interactions with online services can be vast.

One caveat of big data and ML is that, although they are good at finding correlations in large sets of data points, you cannot use them to find causations. You also need to be mindful of data privacy concerns and be very careful of not judging someone before they have acted, based only on a predicted predisposition.

 Anonymizing data is incredibly difficult and is not nearly as simple as removing personal contact details. There have been many cases of large "anonymized" datasets being released where individuals were later easily identified from the records.

One technology that is useful to analyze big data is **MapReduce**, which is a way of simplifying an operation so that it is suitable to run in parallel on a distributed infrastructure. A popular implementation of MapReduce is Apache Hadoop and you can use this in Azure with **HDInsight**, which also supports related tools, including Apache Spark and Apache **Storm**. Other options to handle large datasets include Google's Cloud Bigtable or **BigQuery**.

You can see the available options for Azure HDInsight in the portal, as shown in the following image. Some features are still in preview or have restrictions, but they may have moved to general availability by the time you read this.

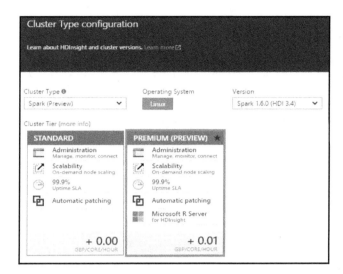

You can see from this image that Spark is in preview and is currently available only on Linux. Hadoop is more established and is also available on Windows, as shown in the following screenshot:

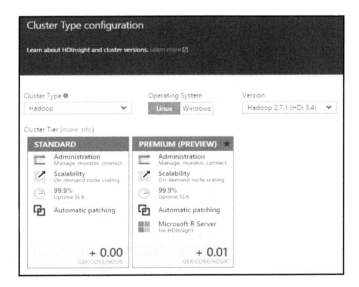

The next image shows that Storm is also available but not on the premium preview (including Microsoft R Server):

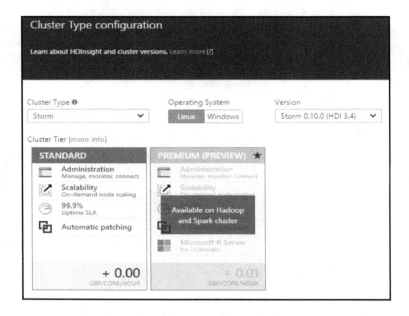

Orleans

Another interesting project is an open source framework from Microsoft called **Orleans**, which is a distributed virtual actor model that was used to power the cloud services of Halo Xbox games. What this means is that, if you build your system by separating your logic into separate actors, this allows it to easily scale, based on demand.

In Orleans, actors are known as grains and you can write them in C# by inheriting from an interface. These are then executed by an Orleans server, called a **silo**. Grains can be persisted to storage, such as SQL or **Azure Tables**, to save their state and to reactivate later. Orleans can also make use of the Bond serializer for greater efficiency.

Unfortunately, Orleans does not currently support .NET Core, but the porting work is in progress. Orleans allows you to write simple and scalable systems with low latency and you can read more at `dotnet.github.io/orleans`.

Custom transports

In Chapter 4, *Addressing Network Performance*, we started with an introduction to TCP/IP and briefly mentioned UDP. We also covered TLS encryption and how to minimize the impact of secure connections while still reaping performance benefits.

UDP is simpler and quicker than TCP, but you either need to not care about reliable delivery (multiplayer games and voice/video chat) or build your own layer to provide this. In Chapter 8, *The Downsides of Performance-Enhancing Tools*, we highlighted **StatsD**, which uses UDP to avoid blocking latency while logging to a remote central server.

There are alternatives to TLS if you aren't constrained to a browser, but if you're developing a web application, this will probably only apply inside of your server infrastructure. For example, the WhatsApp messaging app uses **Noise Pipes** and Curve25519 from the Noise Protocol Framework (noiseprotocol.org) between the smartphone app and their servers in addition to the Signal Protocol for end-to-end encryption.

Using Noise Pipes instead of TLS increases performance because fewer round trips are required to set up a connection. Another option with similar benefits is the **secure pipe daemon** (**spiped**), as used by and created for the secure Linux backup software, **Tarsnap**. However, you do need to preshare the keys, but you can read more about this at www.tarsnap.com/spiped.html.

Advanced hashing

We covered hashing functions a fair amount in this book, especially in Chapter 6, *Understanding Code Execution and Asynchronous Operations*. This area is constantly advancing and it is useful to keep an eye on the future to see what's coming. Although today it is reasonable to use a member of the SHA-2 family for quick hashing and PBKDF2 for slow (password) hashing, this is unlikely to always be the case.

For fast hashing, there is a new family of algorithms called **SHA-3**, which should not be confused with SHA-384 or SHA-512 (which are both in the SHA-2 family). SHA-3 is based on an algorithm called Keccak, which was the winner of a competition to find a suitable algorithm for the new standard. Other finalists included Skein (skein-hash.info) and BLAKE2 (blake2.net), which is faster than MD5, but actually secure.

An algorithm called Argon2 won a similar competition for password hashing (`password-hashing.net`). To see why this matters, you can visit `haveibeenpwned.com` (run by .NET security guru Troy Hunt) to see whether your details are in one of the large number of data breaches. For example, LinkedIn was breached and didn't use secure password hashing (only an unsalted SHA-1 hash). Consequently, most of the plain text passwords were cracked. Therefore, if a LinkedIn account password was reused on other sites, then these accounts can be taken over.

It's a very good idea to use a password manager and create strong unique passwords for every site. It is also beneficial to use two-factor authentication (sometimes also called two-step verification) if available. For example, you can do this by entering a code from a smartphone app in addition to a password. This is particularly useful for e-mail accounts, as they can normally be used to recover other accounts.

Library and framework support

There have been some significant changes to .NET Core and ASP.NET Core between RC1 and RC2, more than normal for release candidates. Sensibly, many popular libraries and frameworks were waiting for RC2, or later, before adding support.

Obviously, a book is a bad place to keep up with the changes, so the author has put together a website to display the latest compatibility information. You can find the *ASP.NET Core Library and Framework Support* list at `ANCLAFS.com`.

If you would like to update anything or add a library or framework, then please send a pull request. The repository is located at `github.com/jpsingleton/ANCLAFS` and it includes lots of useful tools, libraries, frameworks, and more. We mentioned many of these earlier in this book and the following sample is just a small selection of what is listed because package support will grow over time:

- Scientist.NET
- FeatureSwitcher
- FeatureToggle
- MiniProfiler
- Glimpse
- Prefix
- Dapper
- Simple.Data
- EF Core

- Hangfire
- ImageResizer
- DynamicImage
- ImageProcessorCore
- RestBus
- EasyNetQ
- RabbitMQ Client
- MassTransit
- Topshelf
- Nancy
- SignalR
- Orleans

The future

A quote often attributed to the physicist Niels Bohr goes, as follows:

> *"Prediction is very difficult, especially about the future."*

However, we'll have a go at this anyway, starting with the more straightforward bits. The official ASP.NET Core roadmap lists SignalR, Web Pages, and Visual Basic support shipping after the version 1.0 **Release To Manufacturing/Marketing (RTM)**.

After this, it is fairly safe to assume that features will be added to bring the Core line closer to the existing frameworks. This includes Entity Framework, which is currently missing some of the big features of the full EF, for example, lazy loading.

There is also the move towards the .NET Platform Standard, to enhance portability across .NET Core, the .NET Framework and Mono. For example, .NET Core 1.0 and .NET Framework 4.6.3 both implement .NET Platform Standard 1.6 (`netstandard1.6`). However, you probably don't need to worry about this unless you are writing a library. Refer to the documents at `dotnet.github.io/docs/core-concepts/libraries` if you are.

Microsoft has said it will listen to user feedback and use it to drive the direction of the platforms, so you have a voice. Even if you don't, then, as the code is all open source, you can help shape the future by adding the features that you want.

Further into the future is harder to predict, but there has been a steady stream of projects being open sourced by Microsoft from the early offerings of ASP.NET MVC to the Xamarin framework for cross-platform app development.

It's an exciting time to be working with C# and .NET, especially if you want to branch out from web development. The Unity game engine is now part of the .NET foundation, and there are some interesting recent developments in **Virtual Reality** (**VR**) or Augmented Reality (**AR**) hardware. For example, Microsoft Hololens, Oculus Rift, Samsung Gear VR, and HTC Vive are all unbelievably better than the basic VR that came out a couple of decades ago.

It's also a great time to be looking at IoT, which, while it may still be looking for its killer app, has so much more cheap and powerful hardware available. A Raspberry Pi Zero costs only $5 and it now supports an upgraded camera module. With a computer such as the Raspberry Pi 3, which offers almost desktop class performance for $35, anyone can now easily learn to code (perhaps in C# or .NET) and make things, especially children.

Following the wisdom of Alan Kay:

> *"The best way to predict the future is to invent it."*

So, get out there and make it! And make sure that you share what you've done.

Summary

We hope that you enjoyed this book and learned how to make your web applications high-performing and easy to maintain, particularly when you use C#, ASP.NET Core and .NET Core. We tried to keep as much advice as possible applicable to general web app development, while gently introducing you to the latest open source frameworks from Microsoft and others.

Clearly a topic such as this changes quite rapidly, so keep your eyes open online for updates. There is an announcements repository on GitHub that is worth watching at `github.com/aspnet/announcements`. Hopefully, a lot of the lessons in this book are generally good ideas and they will still be sensible for a long time to come.

Always keep in mind that optimizing for its own sake is pointless, unless it's just an academic exercise. You need to measure and weigh the benefits against the downsides; otherwise, you may end up making things worse. It is easy to make things more complex, harder to understand, difficult to maintain, or all of these.

It's important to instill these pragmatic performance ideas into team culture, or else teams won't always adhere to them. However, above all, remember to still have fun!

Index

IPv6 118

J

Java Message Service (JMS) 190
JavaScript Object Notation (JSON) 155
Jekyll
  about 63
JetBrains 35
Jil
  URL 155
JPEG Archive
  about 98
  URL 98
JPEG2000 98
JPEG
  about 68, 97
just-in-time (JIT) compiler 140

K

Kestrel 141
key stretching
  about 14
Kibana 41
Kodi 253

L

lag
  about 48
Language-Integrated Query (LINQ) 142
latency 13
  about 48
  disk latency 48
  example 49
  network latency 48
Lempel-Ziv-Markov chain Algorithm
    (LZMA/LZMA2) 93
LibGD
  URL 100
libuv 141
licensing costs
  about 19
Line of Business (LoB) applications 63
LINQ commands 58
lists

about 142, 143
Local Area Network (LAN)
  about 16
logging
  about 213
  Application Insights 216, 219
  centralized logging 221, 222
  error logging 213
  integrated logging 220
  URL 221
Logstash 41
  URL 221
lossless compression algorithms
  about 93, 94
Low Earth Orbit (LEO) 116

M

Machine Learning (ML)
  about 254, 255
Man in the Middle attack (MitM) 103
MapReduce 258
  about 256
MD5 14
Message Authentication Code (MAC) 150
Message Digest 5 (MD5) 149
message queue (MQ)
  about 188
  coffee shop analogy 189
  publish-subscribe 190
  styles 190
  unicast 190
message queues
  using 51
Message Queuing (MQ)
  about 49
microservices 122
microservices architecture
  versus monilith architecture 202, 203, 204,
    205
Microsoft Developer Network (MSDN) 19
Microsoft Message Analyzer
  about 39
Microsoft Message Queuing (MSMQ) 190
  about 20
Microsoft SQL Server (MS SQL) 128

T

Tabular Data Stream (TDS) 39, 129
Tarsnap
  about 259
  URL 259
Task Parallel Library (TPL)
  about 157, 158, 161
Team Foundation Server (TFS)
  about 20
TechNet
  URL 136
Telerik JustTrace 35
Tensor Processing Unit (TPU) 154, 254
TensorFlow
  URL 254
Test-Driven Development (TDD)
  about 44
testing 136, 137
thick client 64
thin client 64
thread 50
three-tier architecture 64
Time To First Byte (TTFB) 36
TLS handshake 79
tools
  about 19
  alternative tools 20
  for application profiling 29
  for customized performance measurement 41,
    44
  for monitoring HTTP 35
  network monitors 39
  SQL 25
  using 24
Top Level Domain (TLD)
  about 106
Tracert 113, 115
Traffic Manager 121
Transact-SQL (T-SQL) 128
Transmission Control Protocol/Internet Protocol
    (TCP/IP)
  about 72, 73
  slow-start algorithm 73, 74
Transport Layer Security (TLS)

  about 72
Trust on First Use (TOFU) 103
two-tier architecture 64
TypeScript 9

U

Unicast
  about 190
Unity 262
Universally Unique Identifiers (UUIDs) 134
User Datagram Protocol (UDP)
  about 72
user interface (UI)
  about 49

V

Varnish 65
Varnish Configuration Language (VCL) 183
Varnish
  about 183, 184
  URL 183
view models 53
virtual file systems
  about 108
Virtual Machine (VM) 35
Virtual Machines (VMs)
  about 16
Virtual Reality (VR) 262
Visual Studio (VS)
  about 33
  used, for application profiling 33, 34, 35

W

waterfall method 10
Web API 141
Web API 2 21
web caching
  about 171
  background 172, 173
  cache busting 175
  considerations 185
  content delivery network (CDN) 184
  HTTP headers 173, 174
  proxy servers 183